ADRIAN HASTINGS was born in Malaya in 1929. He received a master's degree (Honors in History) from Oxford and a Doctorate in Theology from the Propaganda Fide in Rome. A priest of the diocese of Masaka, Uganda, Father Hastings is a teacher at Bukalasa Minor Seminary. In 1959 he edited *The Church and the Nations,* a study of minority Catholicism in fourteen countries from England to Brazil. Father Hastings is also on the editorial staff of the *African Ecclesiastical Review.*

ONE AND APOSTOLIC

ONE AND APOSTOLIC

ADRIAN HASTINGS

SHEED AND WARD — NEW YORK

Library of Congress Catalog Card Number 64-13568

NIHIL OBSTAT: EDMUND HILL, O.P., S.T.L. CENSOR DEPUTATUS.
IMPRIMATUR: ✠ ADRIANUS K. DDUNGU, EPUS. MASAKENSIS,
DIE 4A AUGUSTI, 1963.

Published in the British Commonwealth by
Darton, Longman & Todd, Ltd., London.

The extracts from C. H. Turner's *Essays on the Early
History of the Church and the Ministry*, edited by
H. B. Swete, are included by permission of Macmillan
& Co. Ltd., London, W.C.2, and those from H. W.
Turner's *Pattern of Christian Truth*, by permission
of A. R. Mowbray & Co. Ltd., London, W.1.

Manufactured in the United States of America

For My Mother

Prayer for the Unity of Christians

Deus, qui errata corrigis, et dispersa congregas, et congregata conservas; quaesumus, super populum christianum tuae unionis gratiam clementer infunde; ut, divisione rejecta, vero pastori Ecclesiae tuae se uniens, tibi digne valeat famulari. Per Dominum nostrum Jesum Christum, filium tuum, qui tecum vivit et regnat in unitate Spiritus Sancti, Deus; per omnia saecula saeculorum. Amen.

(from the Mass for ending schism)

CONTENTS

PREFACE

This book is intended as a work of dialogue, even of controversy; yet it is also, I hope, in some sense a work of vision. It is controversial; firstly, because it puts forward a point of view about the Church which may not be acceptable to all even among my unseparated brethren; secondly, because its central part is both an examination and a criticism of the views of many of my separated brethren. I think that in both ways controversial writing is very necessary, and that in the irenic atmosphere of the present there may even be a danger of the second type being neglected. The goodwill associated with the Ecumenical Movement and the 2nd Vatican Council should certainly not be a reason for fear of precise discussion and disagreement. Good will is no substitute for dialogue, and dialogue involves argument; equally, argument is no alternative to good will. The prerequisites for a fruitful argument are a certain seriousness in the subject at issue, courtesy, respect for the sincerity and intelligence of those with whom you disagree, some measure of common ground, and a willingness to listen to your opponent before you disagree with him. I have tried to fulfil these conditions and if, by chance, some phrase or another should give needless offence, I can only say that such is as far as possible from my intention. In some stages of my argument I have inserted a great many brief quotations from Anglican writers to illustrate a general attitude or line of approach. I have deliberately made them brief because there is nothing more wearisome to the reader than a sequence of long quotations much of whose matter would inevitably be irrelevant to the immediate theme; nevertheless there is a real danger here of doing some injustice to the complete thought of an individual writer, and I may at times have succumbed to it. In argument, especially with a number of people, some simplification is necessary; I can only hope that if on occasion I may have simplified, I have at least not distorted, the thought of those works which I consider.

Beyond such controversial aims and character this book tries to be also a work of vision—that is to say, an attempt to present a view of the Church for its own sake, in Newman's words: 'to investigate the essence of the Church'; what the Church of Christ on earth really is according to her central constitutive principle, that principle which alone can link every aspect of the Church together and which explains them all. Though I believe this to be the true Catholic and traditional view of the Church, nevertheless it may I suppose come as something of a surprise to many. To put it briefly: the Church's unity and nature is fundamentally sacramental. She is a communion. That is to say, if she is a visible society, that has to be understood not in the terms of some other kind of political or natural society but in concepts proper to herself as a fellowship of men made supernaturally one by conscious participation in the sacrament of the Eucharist in accordance with the meaning of that sacrament. Moreover, if the Church is also in the strictest possible sense the mystical body of Jesus Christ, it is for exactly the same formal reason as makes her a visible society. Those who eat Christ's body become it. Eucharistic participation makes men into Christ's body; it also makes them into a single visible society, the communion of the Catholic Church. The formal cause of the Church being a visible society, of her being one, and of her being the mystical body of Christ, is one and the same: the sacrament of Christ's body.

The Church and her unity are not, in a narrow sense, purely sacramental. The unity of her sacramental fellowship has to be guarded, and has always been guarded, by the unity of her pastoral government, the apostolic ministry. The one communion requires an organ of unity, and that is to be found in the corporate episcopate necessarily centred upon the Apostolic Petrine See. In that see is the indefectible focus of the corporate apostolic authority ensuring Catholic unity. The common communion of all Catholics among themselves is necessarily communion with the see of unity, with Peter. And this organ cannot be explained in purely sacramental terms. Authority and authorisation are secondary in importance in the Church to sacramental life, but their presence cannot be simply deduced from or reduced to the latter. It is as perilous for a sound ecclesiology to neglect—as some non-Catholics tend to do—the side of Church authority, as it is to neglect—as some Catholics may have done—the sacramental quality of her unity.

A sacramental eucharistic communion guarded by episcopal and Petrine authority—that is the vision of the Church which I have seen ever more clearly in the course of writing this book. Anglican theologians have really helped me to see it, and I thank them for it even though, as I believe, their theology is a logical denial of its central principle. Certainly there is a wealth of ecclesiological thought in modern non-Catholic writing, and we hurt ourselves to disregard it. The theology of the Church of the future will draw water from many different streams.

The great Catholic theologians of modern times, such as Fathers Congar and De Lubac, have helped me even more and the perennial tradition which stretches back behind one and all: the *nova* of contemporary theology must always remain faithful to the *vetera* of that tradition. To the writings of Dom Christopher Butler, Abbot of Downside, I owe a very special debt, which I feel bound to acknowledge here. So many of the ideas with which I started out on this study I owed to articles of his in the *Downside Review*. He has recently published the mature synthesis of all those articles in *The Idea of the Church,* whose general theme has, I think, much in common with that of the present work. In particular, the scriptural and patristic foundation for the view of the Church as a single visible communion is there treated at length. Much of this study takes that foundation for granted, and I warmly refer readers to *The Idea of the Church* to fill what might well be regarded as a gap in my argument here.

The core of this book was written and approved as a thesis for the Doctorate in Theology of the university of Propaganda Fide, Rome. It has been much changed and added to since then but that does not lessen what I owe to the authorities at Propaganda and especially Monsignor Vodopivec, my supervisor, for much help and encouragement. There are many others too for whose helpful suggestions on one point or another I have been most grateful, among them the late Edward Rich, Father De Menasce, O.P., Dom Polycarp Sherwood, O.S.B., Fathers Michael Winter, Walton Hannah and James Douglas. Naturally, they are in no way responsible for what I have finally written.

It is pleasant also to remember the libraries out of which a book grows: there was that of the Beda, where the first work was done assisted by many kind and knowledgeable students, personal converts to Catholic truth and unity. Then there was the Vatican library, so calm and elegant, and that little room of Protestant theology at the Gregorianum whose key it was always a battle to obtain. In England, Pusey, with its cold monastic air and wealth of theological literature, was a constant standby, as also—in the other place—the Cambridge University Library, alone in allowing one to carry off the books from within its walls. Finally, there is my own useful little set of books, which have followed me round so faithfully from place to place and now line my walls here at Bukalasa. Such books are friends indeed.

Writing these lines within a few hours of the burial of Pope John XXIII, I cannot refrain from expressing also one's overwhelming gratitude to him for the achievements of this, the shortest of modern pontificates; for the new ecumenical atmosphere he has brought about between Catholics and non-Catholics in which contact and discussion have so much more chance of bearing fruit, and for the new spirit within the Church, especially the reinvigoration of the sense of the corporate episcopate and of the Pope as being eminently a bishop, which he has given us. May he rest in peace.

I could not close this preface without speaking of my sister Cecily, who so often worked to elucidate my ideas, and of my mother who has read the book through time after time at various stages of its growth, entirely retyped it a year or two ago, and has enormously helped to ensure both its accuracy and its clarity. To her, to whom under God I chiefly owe my membership of the Catholic communion, this book is gratefully dedicated.

Bukalasa   ADRIAN HASTINGS
6 *June* 1963

ONE AND APOSTOLIC

Chapter 1

OUR CHRISTIAN DIVISIONS

Ecumenical Christendom is something new. For centuries Christendom was one, in principle at least; and then for centuries more Christendom was divided. It was the time of schism. East and West, Protestant and Catholic, and many another division—they were taken too long for granted. Unity seemed the last of items on the ecclesiastical shopping list. But today, though schism remains, our approach to it is new. We are, at last, ashamed of it. Diagnoses inevitably differ, but not the sadness springing from our apartness, from the consciousness that we have been collectively unfaithful to the Master whom we all profess to follow and yet who prayed on the night before he died 'that they may all be one'.

This division of Christians into countless sects is now seen as a continuous and crying scandal, the negation of that mark which our Lord said was to be the characteristic of his disciples—that they love one another. Hence the loving desire for reunion and, among Protestants, the movements, conferences, schemes for intercommunion and the like.

But all action, and especially all Christian action, must spring from belief. Faith must precede Order. Now the chief reason why the Catholic Church, while fully sharing in the spirit of the Ecumenical Movement, finds it difficult to co-operate in its activities, is that its beliefs about unity are deeply different. Though Protestants are divided among themselves over many things, they share a basic feeling about the Church and about the nature of schism. Active supporters of the Ecumenical Movement tend inevitably to be concerned with a Church Unity not at present existing but to be established. It is seen chiefly as something which *ought* to be a mark of Christians, something which will follow if only they are faithful to their vocation, which all hope to see again in the future, but which for the present has unhappily ceased to exist.

The Catholic idea of the Church's unity is not the same. Conversion to the Church at the present day from any ecumenically-minded milieu, it has been remarked, 'means that one has turned away from trying to build a united Church to accepting one that has always existed'.[1] For a Catholic, in fact, the essential unity of the Church is wholly unbreakable, and in face of the divisions of Christendom the crying need is not for Christians to remake the Church's unity but to enter into it. As we shall see, this is also (in spite of some waverings) the view of the Orthodox East, and some Anglicans would wish to think that it was their view too. The mere mention of it brings us up face to face with the one absolutely central question which divides Catholics from Protestants: what is the Church? This question alone is really worth discussing in ecumenical conferences,[2] and, though such discussions have certainly been held, I feel that the precise issues on the strictly ecclesiological level dividing non-Catholics from Rome are still none too clear, and that both to Catholics and non-Catholics.

Do schisms cut Christians off from the Church, or do they cut Christians off from one another within the Church? That is a key question, and one's practical attitude to reunion problems must depend on the theological answer one gives to it. It is in part the aim of this book to explain and justify the Catholic answer to it, while at the same time examining the theological coherence of some non-Catholic ones, especially such as admit that the Church, despite its divisions, remains of its nature primarily a visible body.

Besides unity there is another characteristic of the Church which is certainly of the most vital importance: authority. The Church and her ministers teach and govern. From where is the

---

[1] Michael Richards, 'The Convert's work for Christian Unity', *Life of the Spirit*, January 1957, p. 315.

[2] In the famous *Times* correspondence of 1949 Dom Columba Cary-Elwes called for friendly discussions between Roman Catholic and other theologians on this issue: 'The fundamental point should always be kept in view: the nature and functions of Christ's Church.' Doctor Selwyn, the Dean of Winchester, in replying, quite agreed with this. 'Catholicism today', *The Times*, pp. 34 and 40.

authority obtained? How is it passed on? At its most intense, how great is it? In fact, what degree of teaching authority has Christ placed within the body which stands in his place in the world?

Discussion is generally most fruitful where there is already some considerable measure of common ground. That is why it is at present more practical for Catholics within the ecumenical field to discuss theology with Episcopalians than with Presbyterians, and with Presbyterians more than with, say, Baptists, and so on. It is always by limiting a field of discussion that one can hope to obtain results or at least some real mental contact. A limited field derives from the existence of common ground and, as we shall see in a moment, the common ecclesiological ground between Catholics and Episcopalians is quite considerable. Dialogue here is particularly easy because Anglican theologians have written a great deal in recent years about the nature of the Church, and though they, and especially their Anglo-Catholic wing which has produced the greater proportion of this ecclesiological literature, doubtless do not represent the mass of non-Catholic Christians, they do nevertheless stand in a very special position within Christendom as leaders of a group midway in the spectrum of Christian divisions. In the words of Father Henry St John, 'The Church of England is a microcosm of ecumenical differences. It contains within its boundaries types of belief which put it in sympathy with every element, both Catholic and Protestant, in divided Christendom. At the same time its doctrine concerning the nature and constitution of the Church, though markedly Catholic and sacramental in type, of necessity stands for the Protestant concept of divisibility of external structure.'[3] That is to say that the tensions of the Reformation and Counter-Reformation have never been worked out within the Anglican communion. They are still there together, different approaches and contradictory beliefs jostling one another in a medley which at times makes for a genuine richness, but at others simply for a comprehensiveness which, by

[3] The Authority of Doctrinal Development, *Blackfriars*, November 1955, p. 415.

accepting incompatibles in the most sacred domain of faith and morals, seems to us to be alien to true Christianity. This state of affairs makes a fair and objective study of Anglican theology particularly difficult; it also explains the Anglican fondness for a *via media* in almost every field, and especially our own: a *via media* between the Protestant idea of an 'invisible Church' and what they take to be the Roman view of a highly centralised visible organisational Church. Their idea of the Church, which it is a prime purpose of this study to examine, is held to be 'Catholic' but not 'Roman', 'visible' but not 'organisational'.

Anglicans claim that this tenable middle way in ecclesiology between Rome and Protestantism is based on scripture and the early Church, and can be defended by the appeal to antiquity. In the words of the late E. C. Rich, 'the alternative to Protestant ecclesiology is not the ultramontane Roman but the Scriptural and Catholic, and that is the doctrine which the Church of England has tried to follow out'.[4]

Having spoken of common ground, it will be useful here to set out briefly what may be held as common in ecclesiology to Catholic and Anglican. The following words provide an interesting opening:

> It was during my training in an Anglican Theological College that my eyes were first opened to the relevance and the centrality of the Church in the Christian scheme of things. I learnt that the Church is integral to the Gospel, that it is the Body of Christ without which he is incomplete. The Church is the mystery hidden from the foundation of the world. The Church is the new Israel and its wholeness should manifest itself in its outward order. The Church is commissioned with authority to teach true doctrine and to reject the false. I discovered with some surprise that these statements about the Church, which I had considered Roman Catholic, were entirely biblical and had patristic authority behind them.[5]

This was written by an Indian Jacobite priest, Father Abraham, who has recently been received into the Church. I quote it because it may surprise some Catholics that Anglicans have so

---

[4] *Spiritual Authority in the Church of England*, p. 101. It should be noted that the author of this book later became a Catholic.
[5] 'Father Abraham's Apologia', *Eastern Churches Quarterly*, autumn, 1957, pp. 85-86.

much sound Catholic Church doctrine to teach to others. They, like us, believe that there is One Church, a fellowship of Christians, in which by the redemptive work of our Lord Jesus Christ they share in the very life of God. Therefore the Church comes from above and precedes its members; it is the body of Christ, not limited to this earth but existing also eternally in Heaven, but on earth it is a visible (not only an invisible) society, with a common faith, common sacraments, common ministry.

There is a Church. *Credo in* . . . *sanctam Ecclesiam catholicam*, in the words of the Apostles' Creed, or in *unam, sanctam, catholicam et apostolicam Ecclesiam*, in the words of the Nicene Creed, which is accepted in the Lambeth Quadrilateral as 'the sufficient statement of the Christian Faith'.

Moreover the Church is central and essential in Christianity; without it, Christ himself cannot be understood. 'The doctrine of the Church is no mere appendix or corollary of the Christian Faith. It belongs to the substance. Everything which concerns the Church is integral to the central dogmas of the Christian faith'.[6]

The nineteenth of the 39 Articles declares that 'the visible Church is a congregation of faithful men, in which the pure word of God is preached, and the Sacraments be duly administered according to Christ's ordinance in all those things that of necessity are requisite to the same'. The Church on earth then, is a visible congregation; a society of faith and sacraments. These latter are of the essence of the Church. Its faith is shown at least by the Scriptures and Creeds; its sacraments include at least baptism and the Eucharist; its communal life is ruled at least by a ministry possessing 'the commission of Christ and the authority of the whole body',[7] which for an Anglican means the episcopate.

The Church is the Body of Christ. He is its head; it is dependent on him, conformed to his life, being in some way identical with him. All this is very greatly stressed by recent Anglican

---

[6] L. S. Thornton, *Christ and the Church*, p. 9.
[7] Lambeth 1920.

writers.[8] Though, of course, this doctrine has never been forgotten, yet it was for long rather overlooked, and it can be called one of the great rediscoveries of our time; it is a discovery common to Catholics and Anglicans.

The Church is, then, the sacramental community of the faithful, sharing in the life of God through Jesus Christ by membership of his body. But it is not limited to this world, for it is the body of all those who are united with Christ, in heaven, earth and purgatory. Only on earth, and through baptism, can one enter the Church, but membership in no way ceases with death. This is important, but it is sometimes forgotten. The Church in the fullest sense is the fellowship of all the redeemed, the new Jerusalem, the Bride of the Lamb, and it has only one head—our Lord Jesus Christ. So A. G. Hebert writes that 'there is the spiritual unity of the whole body of Christ. God has knit together his elect in one communion and fellowship, and only a small portion of his Church is militant here and now on earth'.[9] And Dr Mascall stresses that 'the Catholic Church, of which the local church is the manifestation, is not just the Church militant but the whole Church on earth and beyond the grave, militant, expectant and triumphant'.[10]

The Church as a society is not just an association of Christians, or the creation of its members. It comes from above, and therefore precedes its members, who do not form its unity but enter into this unity. That is to say that the divine side of Christian life is not just the individual aspect of that life, but also its social aspect; and these two cannot be divorced. One cannot be united with Christ except through and in the Church. This point is of the greatest importance, and it is useful to see exactly what some recent Anglicans of the Catholic tradition have to say about it.

Dr Ramsey holds that 'Christianity is never solitary. It is never true to say that separate persons are united to Christ, and then combine to form the Church; for to believe in Christ is to believe

[8] I may refer especially to two books of L. S. Thornton, *The Common Life in the Body of Christ* and *Christ and the Church*.
[9] *The Form of the Church*, p. 63.
[10] *Corpus Christi*, p. 20, repeated in *The Recovery of Unity*, p. 98. For a fine Catholic treatment of this same theme, one may refer to Father De Lubac's *The Splendour of the Church*, chap. II, The Dimensions of the Mystery.

in One whose Body is a part of himself and whose people are his own humanity, and to be joined to Christ is to be joined to Christ-in-his-Body; for "so is Christ" and Christ is not otherwise'.[11] Dr Mascall states that 'The New Testament knows nothing of an isolated Christian, a Christian outside the Church. Becoming a Christian and becoming a member of the Church are synonymous.'[12] The Anglo-Catholic report entitled *Catholicity* says that 'It is a distortion of the apostolic doctrine to say that men are *first* united to Christ, through faith, within an invisible society of the truly faithful, and *then* find admission to the visible Church. The right order is not: Christ—faithful individuals—the Church; but: Christ—the Church—faithful individuals.'[13]

One more text is worth quoting, because of the special influence which it seems to have had. It is a passage in a sermon preached at Truro towards the close of the last century by Dr Frederick Temple, later Archbishop of Canterbury:

We are sometimes asked to think that the Church only exists in the union of believers, and has no reality of its own. Now, it is perfectly clear that in the New Testament the idea of the Church is not that. Men speak as if Christians came first, and the Church after; as if the origin of the Church was in the wills of the individual Christians who composed it. But, on the contrary, throughout the teaching of the Apostles, we see it is the Church that comes first, and the members of it afterwards. Men were not brought to Christ and then determined that they would live in a community. . . . In the New Testament, on the contrary, the Kingdom of Heaven is already in existence, and men are invited into it. The Church takes its origin, not in the will of man, but in the will of the Lord Jesus Christ. . . . Everywhere men are called in: they do not come in and make the Church by coming. They are called into that which already exists; they are recognised as members when they are within; but their membership depends on their admission and not upon their constituting themselves into a body in the sight of the Lord.[14]

[11] *The Gospel and the Catholic Church*, p. 36.
[12] *Christ, the Christian and the Church*, p. 109.
[13] p. 13. Cf. also Lacey, *Unity and Schism*, p. 29.
[14] Quoted in the report entitled 'Catholicity', pp. 11-12, and by Mascall, *Christ, the Christian and the Church*, p. 119.

It is possible and important, then, to discuss what the Church *is* by her unchanging nature, and not merely what she should be like as a result of the activity of her members. Christianity being a fundamentally social thing, the visible Church can be said to precede its members, and is not the mere association of those who are united first with Christ: it is the very bond which binds them to him.

All this common ground is great indeed and encouraging, and it makes serious ecumenical discussion on the themes of Church unity and authority really possible and capable of bearing fruit. It is through such immediate discussion with theologians of the 'bridge Church' that Catholics can come into the most effective theological contact with other non-Catholic Christians, many of whom indeed share most of this common ground.

One last point: I will say little about the supreme function of the Roman See as infallible teacher of truth and seat of unity. It seems to me that it is of little use to argue about whether the pope is infallible when there is no agreement as to whether there is any infallible authority in the Church at all, or whether the papacy is the divinely appointed guardian of the rights of ecclesiastical communion when it is not agreed that the Church is one communion at all. These more general issues have to be settled first. As Dom Columba Cary-Elwes has not unreasonably remarked, 'We can exaggerate the significance of Peter and his successors by forgetting the whole Church which is also guided by the Spirit which is Truth. The gates of hell shall not prevail against it. The early Fathers had not worked out the uniqueness of the Papacy; they had, however, seen the uniqueness of the Church'.[15] Anglicans, and many other Protestants too, do realise the uniqueness of the Church, and it should be through a drawing out of the implications of the Church's nature itself that we lead them on to an understanding of the papacy. One reason of the modern Catholic attitude may be found in the sudden interruption of the first Vatican Council which prevented the completion of the work scheduled, and so left the definition of Papal

[15] 'Catholicism Today', *The Times*, p. 34.

Infallibility somewhat isolated.[16] If this is so, we should be able to understand better, though we cannot as such agree with, views like those of Dr Jalland who holds that 'the crucial defect of the Constitution *Pastor Aeternus* lies in the fact that it attempted to define that the Pope was the infallible organ of the Church's infallibility without first re-examining the question of the precise sense in which such a characteristic could rightly be ascribed to the Church',[17] It should help our non-Catholic brethren then and also enrich Catholic theology itself if, without of course 'toning down' the doctrine of Papal Infallibility in any way, we can work out more clearly and profoundly its organic connection with the doctrine of the Church as a whole, and show how the Catholic position is not just a defence of Papal Infallibility *in vacuo*, but of a whole organic conception of the Church and its unity, which requires the papacy as the central 'seat of unity' and ultimate organ of authority.[18]

That is to say that what we need is a more complete theology, not only of authority in the body of Christ, but of the very body itself: for the body cannot simply be identified with its head, or rather with the vicar of its head on earth. Yet when explaining to friends that I was writing about the crucial difference between Catholic and non-Catholic ecclesiology, I have sometimes been faced with a look of quasi-incredulity. The difference, they have said, is perfectly obvious: non-Catholics do not accept Papal supremacy. But it has been my conviction all along that this was far too *simpliste* a view. Quite apart from the fact that there are papalists and perhaps some other Anglo-Catholics who do accept, or very nearly accept, the entire gamut of papal claims, and yet remain where they are, I think that the division goes deeper than acceptance or rejection of the pope; or, if not deeper—for what really can be deeper in the Church of Christ than the rock

---

[16] Mgr Carton de Wiart has written that 'the definition of Papal Infallibility has sometimes distracted the attention of theologians and led them to overlook the teaching functions of apostles and bishops. If the Vatican Council could have continued its work and undertaken an examination of the *schemata* devoted to the powers of the bishops, this inequality would have disappeared.' (Quote by P. Congar, *Divided Christendom*, p. 33, n. 1.)

[17] *The Church and the Papacy*, p. 537.

[18] So, 'Papal infallibility is intelligible only as an organ of the Church's *magisterium*, and that *magisterium* is intelligible only as the channel whereby God's historic self-revelation is conveyed to us'. Victor White, O.P. in *God the Unknown*, p. 190.

upon which it is built?—at least wider. After all, in every society authority is a means not an end, it is ordained and subordinated to the nature and end of the whole. This is so too, most certainly, in the Church. Papal authority is for the sake of the whole body, which means that the theology of the whole Church is a bigger thing than the theology of the supreme pontiff. It is because of the whole nature of the Church that we have a pope and the pope has his authority, the nature of the Church clearly demanding such an authority. If non-Catholics do not see this, it is because their idea of the nature of the Church differs from ours. We have to show them what sort of a body the whole Church really is that it should need such a centre of unity and authority as is provided by the papacy. The one society is an even bigger thing than the authority which rules it. The kind of authority and the kind of unity which the nature of the Church requires need to be understood before the organ, in which that authority and unity are located, can itself be seen to be necessary.

Chapter 2

THE DEVELOPMENT OF ORTHODOXY

Authority and Unity are closely inter-related but they are not indistinguishable aspects of the nature of the Church, and it is regrettable that some Catholics seem to give the impression that the unity of the Church is *only* the unity of common sub- mission to the authority of the Roman See. As has already been said, the nature of the Church and of her unity is something far larger than this. In the words of Father Congar: 'Those Catholic controversialists who would make submission to the same visible head, the Bishop of Rome, successor of St Peter and the vicar of Christ, practically the one and only principle of the Church's unity, give an incomplete idea of that Church and its unity.'[1] The nature of Church authority and the nature of Church unity can each be better appreciated if considered on its own, and that will be my aim—the nature of and need for doctrinal authority being treated in this chapter, while the less well-known subject of the nature of Church unity will fill most of the rest of the book.

What authority is there in the Church? To whom does the Christian owe obedience, and how much? How can he know what is revealed truth, and what is perversion? These are ques- tions which no thinking Christian can possibly shelve. Moreover the presence of a visible authority in the Church is, as almost all would now agree, not some late deviation but an essential part of the Church's character from the most primitive times. As Dr Ramsey has remarked, 'There is no Christian community in the New Testament which has not behind it some authority respons- ible to a larger whole and there is no letter in the New Testament (except the epistle to Philemon) which does not show that the local society owes obedience to someone who addresses it in the

[1] *Divided Christendom*, p. 192.

name of the larger whole.'[2] Obedience to God in Christ in the Church is the deepest principle of common Christian life. We accept the gift of God, and do not fashion it for ourselves. Christ was obedient to the Father, and just as obedience was the law of the Incarnation—'In the head of the book it is written of me that I shall do thy will, O God' (Heb. 10:7)—so it is the law of the Church, the extension of the Incarnation. It is a common obedience which underlies the society of Christians, a common acceptance of the Word of Life.

But how exactly is Christ's authority mediated to the individual Christian? Is it through the decisive voice of the living Church herself, or is the sole, ultimate norm some 'objective', fixed standard? Here lies an essential division between Catholic and Protestant. The Catholic appeals to the Living Church as having the ultimate word, whether that word be expressed through pope or general council. The Protestant appeals back to scripture or the early Church, or to some other static objective norm.

The crucial division here is over Church infallibility in itself. No one who believes in any sort of a visible Church will deny *some* guiding and interpreting authority to the Church. The real question is: the Church of today, of the changing present, has she on occasion and within certain spheres the God-given capacity to speak with *absolute* authority, so that her word will bind the future as well as the present and be accepted as possessing the same certain truthfulness as the word of the apostles or the word of the Incarnate Word himself? Defenders of infallibility do not claim for the Church the power to receive or express any new revelation, only that she is the pillar of truth in interpreting the one abiding revelation.[3] The organ of this authority is a secondary

---

[2] *The Gospel and the Catholic Church*, p. 46.

[3] We certainly cannot admit charges like those of Dr Hanson that, according to the Catholic position, 'what is multiplied is not merely ecclesiastical doctrine, but constituent elements of the Christian revelation' (*Theology*, 1954, p. 382). Yet it must be admitted that Newman himself might sometimes seem to suggest such an idea, as, for example, when he remarks that 'Supposing the order of nature once broken by the introduction of a revelation, the continuance of that revelation is but a question of degree' (*Essay on Development*, p. 85); and certainly Dr Chadwick holds Newman to have believed in a 'development in revelation' (*From Bossuet to Newman*, p. 93). If Newman did believe in any

matter: its existence at all is absolutely primary. Here certainly Catholic and Orthodox stand upon one side, Protestant and Anglican upon the other.

The universal Protestant position may be presented in the words of the Remonstrant Confession of Faith of the Dutch Arminians:

> And now because such Divine-like Authority as this belongeth unto, and agreeth with these very Books only: it is therefore even withall necessary, that by them alone, as by Touchstones and firm and unmovable Rules, we examine and try all controversies and Debates in Religion, and by them only to reason discourse and judge of them: and so to leave them to God alone and to Jesus Christ, as the only supream and infallible Judg, peremptorily to be decided; for we are not to think, that they should be decided by any judicial or authoritative right, by any visible Judg, and one ordinarily speaking in the Church sith it hath pleased him to leave us in his Word, a rule only directive, or to judge only directively by, and not withal coactively or by way of constraint: but that there ought to be an infallible Judg always speaking in the Church, he hath nowhere signified.[4]

This is also the Anglican view. There have of course been Anglicans like J. A. Douglas,[5] who have believed in the Church's infallibility, but they are quite unrepresentative. Bishop Gore expressed the normative Anglican position when he declared; 'There is no such thing as an absolute authority in the Church.'[6] Professor Clement Webb has stated the same thing at greater length:

> I believe that what is at issue is in fact the question of the presence in the Church (whether as represented by the Roman Pontiff speaking *ex cathedra* or otherwise) of an infallible *magisterium* expressing itself in irreformable definitions of dogma. I am convinced that only if the reality of such a *magisterium* be denied can we defend either the continuity of the reformed with the

---

such thing, quite certainly we do not follow him in such a belief; but in fact it is rather that the expression of his thought is not altogether clear, than that he held any real idea of a developing revelation. We have to consider his teaching as a whole and not an odd ambiguous phrase.

[4] Quoted by Rich, *Spiritual Authority*, pp. 44-45 in note.
[5] *The Relations of the Anglican Churches with the Eastern Orthodox*, pp 80-88.
[6] *Roman Catholic Claims*, pp. 48-49.

medieval Church of England . . . or the new stress laid by the 'catholic minded' theologians in the later Church of England upon doctrines which the reformers in the sixteenth century had deliberately (at the least) refused to emphasise. Not papal infallibility alone, but all infallibility described, appears to me irreconcilable with the method which God, as a matter of fact, has been pleased to follow in his revelation of himself to mankind.[7]

The classical description of the Anglican attitude to authority remains that of Bishop Creighton: 'The formula which most explains the position of the Church of England is that it rests on an appeal to sound learning.'[8] By its very nature such an appeal is from the present to the past. E. C. Rich, while still an Anglican, commented as follows:

> Here we face the real and abiding crux of the controversy between Anglicanism and Roman Catholicism. It concerns their respective attitudes towards the place and function of the *magisterium* or teaching office of the Church. All else is secondary to that. There can be no agreement between the Churches so long as Rome insists on submission to the Apostolic See and Anglicanism claims the right to the exercise of reason and historical criticism in an appeal to history.[9]

The Catholic accepts the 'appeal to history' as theologically and controversially important but not as itself providing a doctrinal norm. For him, that is to be found not in the past but in the Church's present voice: 'the *magisterium*' always living in the Church by the twofold principle of the apostolic succession and the assistance of the Holy Spirit, simply declares what *is* the belief of the universal Church.[10]

Anglican and Protestant may differ somewhat as to how they conceive the norm of doctrine, but basically they agree in locating absolute doctrinal authority in something of the past,

[7] In a letter to *Theology*, January 1937.
[8] *The Church and the Nation*, p. 251.
[9] *Spiritual Authority in the Church of England*, p. 205. Having decided that this was indeed the crux of the controversy Canon Rich was converted to Catholicism on this precise issue: 'The great cleavage separating Catholic Christianity from all forms of Protestantism is in its attitude to Divine Truth. . . . It has recently been borne in upon me with a devastating conviction that . . . the Anglican doctrine of the Church's authority . . . follows a Protestant and not a Catholic line', 'Authority and Catholic Truth', *The Tablet*, May 26, 1956.
[10] Father Congar, *Divided Christendom*, pp. 182-3.

an objective norm identical for all ages, in 'firm and unmovable Rules' to be discovered by an 'appeal to history'. Similarly, Catholic and Orthodox may differ somewhat as to where exactly they locate the organ of a living infallible voice, but basically they agree as to its existence.

In our view, the difficulty of the Protestant solution derives from three things: first, it is not in accordance with Christian antiquity; secondly, the nature of scripture itself is opposed to its being used in this way; thirdly, it is incompatible with the phenomenon of the development of doctrine.

First, in spite of claims to the contrary on this issue of the existence of a continuing infallible authority in the Church, the primitive and 'undivided' Church stands squarely with the Catholic and not the Protestant. Canon Rich was misleading when he wrote that 'the controversies that rent the early Church and which imperilled the inner citadel of Christian belief in God and in the Incarnate Lord were not settled by an appeal to a living voice speaking *ex cathedra*'.[11] Then as now, belief had to be grounded in scripture, confrontation with which was the Church's own test for sound doctrine; but equally it was then, as it still is, the living teaching Church alone which could authoritatively apply that test and define belief: she interprets the scripture which she alone has authenticated by her own continuous tradition. Strictly speaking it is true that the Church herself never appealed 'to a living voice speaking *ex cathedra*' because she is herself that living voice. The controversies that rent the early Church were not settled by an appeal *to* a living voice speaking *ex cathedra*, but they were settled (at Nicaea, Constantinople, Ephesus, Chalcedon) *by* the living voice speaking *ex cathedra*.

The appeal to scripture was a net which brought in lots of fishes, but, for instance, no *ousia*; nevertheless the Church, cognisant of that appeal, defined the *homoousion* as part of her orthodoxy and the condition of her membership. The ultimate test of belief was not the scriptural appeal but the teaching of the contemporary Church. This was so from the very start: the

[11] *Spiritual Authority*, p. 23.

New Testament writings have a clearly occasional character, and simply shared in the authority of their writers, the living teachers of the Church. Ruling and teaching belonged to those in the Church, who, as apostles or successors to the apostles, possessed authority and stood, as St Ignatius of Antioch said, 'in the place of Christ'. True in the first century, this was equally true in the second. Dr Jalland has pointed out how 'the scriptural appeal' was missing from the Church of the second century, 'the primary authority' being not 'the apostolic writings' but 'the oral *paradosis* or body of teaching, believed to have been delivered to their immediate successors by the Apostles'.[12] Again, in Father Bévenot's words, the criterion in the second century 'for judging the validity of the claim to apostolicity made by the many traditions in circulation' was not scripture but 'the concordant teaching of the apostolic churches', that is to say the *regula fidei*, the contemporary standard of orthodoxy.[13]

Secondly, of its very nature the Scriptural Canon points to the authority of the Church; in the words of Dr Dodd, 'The very idea of an authoritative Canon of Scripture is bound up with the idea of the Church.'[14] The time gap between the beginning of the Church and the writing of scripture, and even more the time gap between the beginning of the Church and the elucidation of the Canon of Scripture, point to the structural relationship existing between the Scriptures and the Church; the Church existed and taught with authority before scripture, she enshrined her own doctrine within scripture, established its Canon and has, ever since, authoritatively determined its sense. It is of the nature of the written divine word to share fully in the authority of the living voice of the Church but not to substitute for it. This is, of course, not to deny in the least the importance of the scriptural appeal, and of the value of sound learning as a help in making that appeal, but the point is that it is only the Living Church which can do it decisively and interpret scripture definitively; and such has always been the case. The mistake of

---

[12] *The Church and the Papacy*, p. 107.
[13] M. Bévenot, 'Tradition, Church and Dogma', *Heythrop Journal*, January 1960, pp. 42-43.
[14] *The Bible Today*, p. 6.

the sixteenth-century reformers, in upholding their 'naked' appeal to scripture, was to understand its authority as being apart from the authority of the Church.

Furthermore, as a matter of experiment, scripture has failed and still fails to be independently authoritative and self-authenticating. Chillingworth wrote that 'The Scriptures . . . in things necessary, is plain and perfect. Such a law, therefore, cannot but be very fit to end all controversies necessary to be ended.'[15] Yet appeal to the scriptural principle brought more disagreement and division among Christians and even within the Protestant ranks, than had ever been known before. And now in the age of form criticism and demythologising, few can still feel sure about the evident adequacy of scripture as a self-explanatory doctrinal norm. Nineteenth- and twentieth-century biblical scholarship has hit no one harder than those who would agree with Chillingworth.

But the third, and perhaps the clearest argument is that from development. In the sixteenth and seventeenth centuries Catholics were, in practice, about as convinced as Protestants of the efficacy of a fixed norm, of the clarity of scriptural evidence, that is to say of the unchanging character of the Church's doctrinal norm, and so they thought—just as Protestants thought—that they could prove their current orthodoxy to be identical with that of primitive times. As Dr Chadwick has pointed out, this was the position of someone like Bossuet, whose words are worth quoting:

> The Church's doctrine is always the same. . . . The Gospel is never different from what it was before. Hence, if at any time someone says that the faith includes something which yesterday was not said to be of the faith, it is always *heterodoxy*, which is any doctrine different from *orthodoxy*. There is no difficulty about recognising false doctrine: there is no argument about it: it is recognised at once, whenever it appears, merely because it is new. . . .[16]

Catholic and Protestant alike believed that the Church's orthodoxy was, or ought to be, unchanging. It was the contention of

---

[15] Quoted by Rich, *Spiritual Authority*, p. 49.
[16] Quoted in Owen Chadwick, *From Bossuet to Newman*, p. 17.

Protestants that the Church's current teaching differed from that
of primitive times, therefore it was wrong. It was the contention
of Catholics that the two were identical, and therefore the former
was proved right. For Catholics, however, a certain gap seemed
to remain between the scriptural evidence and the Church's
sixteenth-century orthodoxy, and as they did not question the
unalterable character of Christian teaching, they were forced to
put some stress on a 'source of revelation' other than scripture—
that is to say, the 'unwritten verities' of oral tradition. As Father
Tavard has recently shown in a very valuable book, the notion
of oral tradition as a source of doctrine entirely distinct from
scripture is not a traditionally Catholic idea, but something
making its first clear appearance in the fourteenth century with
Peter D'Ailly and Thomas Netter, and later enormously developed by the needs of Counter-Reformation apologetic.[17] At
desperate moments the gap between current teaching and verifiable primitive doctrine was filled not only by unwritten traditions
but even by the extremely dubious expedient of post-apostolic
revelations. All this was necessary because of the presupposition
that the Church's doctrine was stable, unprogressing, and always
taught in exactly the same form as that in which it was first
received.

While such ideas were normal it is not so surprising that Protestants could hold that scripture alone was sufficient authority
for a Christian's belief. The assurance of Chillingworth is
understandable, but it was surely mistaken, as mistaken as the
assurance of Bossuet. Neither scripture nor antiquity have ever
presented a clear norm sufficient to decide subsequent controversies, and to settle which views in after centuries are heresy,
which orthodoxy.

The inadequacy of a fixed norm to provide us with doctrinal
certainty is not due to the possibility that we are trying to extend
the field of certainty beyond some original limit. The fact is that
there never was a fixed norm or unchanging orthodoxy, for development in the Church's authoritative teaching began long
before the end of the apostolic age and has continued steadily

[17] George Tavard, *Holy Writ or Holy Church.*

ever afterwards. It is not just that in the course of time new doctrines, of perhaps secondary importance, have developed beside the Church's basic teaching, but that the single *ensemble* of the Church's essential teaching has developed homogeneously. This *ensemble* is what we mean by *orthodoxy*: it is that complex of dogmas which are presented at any particular time by the Church as constituting her *regula fidei*, and whose acceptance is a condition for entering and remaining in the one Church. Orthodoxy is the Church's official teaching here and now, and its denial is heresy. Now orthodoxy has constantly developed, which means that the credal condition for entering the body of Christ has developed. If the Church, in her development of orthodoxy, has not an absolute and infallible authority, then her exclusion of men from the fold for its rejection is intolerable. And yet this is what she has always consistently done.

The point is that there is no alternative. There is an inevitability in development, and there is historically no time to which we may point before the evolution of orthodoxy began. In support of this it is useful to refer to the conclusions of Professor H. E. W. Turner in his Bampton Lectures, entitled 'The Pattern of Christian Truth.' In this work Professor Turner set out to examine the pattern of Christian orthodoxy as it appeared in the Church of the first five centuries. Now the first thing which was clear about this pattern was the fact of development, 'indeed without its help' he wrote, 'the pattern of Christian Truth can hardly be traced'.[18] To be a Catholic Christian in any age means to accept the orthodox doctrine of the Church of that age, yet, owing to continuous doctrinal development, orthodoxy in one age is not coterminous with orthodoxy in another:

> Orthodoxy in the second century must be differently interpreted from orthodoxy in the fourth or fifth. If orthodoxy itself certainly antedated the achievement of fixed doctrinal norms, it begins to wear a different aspect after the process of doctrinal formulation had got properly under way. Even at the same period standards of orthodoxy might differ in different fields. In the fourth century, for example, it is not the same thing to be orthodox with

[18] H. W. E. Turner, *The Pattern of Christian Truth*, p. x.

regard to the Trinity and the Person of Christ. In the former case orthodoxy, already enshrined in formulas, was rapidly approaching maturity, while in Christology, at least before the condemnation of Apollinarius and probably for some time afterwards, it had scarcely passed beyond the stage of a tentative exploration of the theological implications of the *lex orandi*.[19]

We have then a definite historical fact: 'the development of orthodoxy'.[20]

The development of orthodoxy, being historically inevitable, would seem to be a necessary part of the Christian dispensation, but it involves as its corollary—if it is not to cut off all post-apostolic Christians from the authoritativeness of the gospel—ecclesiastical infallibility. The very nature of orthodoxy makes its development entirely intolerable if not controlled by an unerring authority: it is otherwise interposing between the infallibility of Christ and his apostles on the one side and all subsequent generations of Christians on the other, a blanket of ideas which has to be accepted but cannot be relied upon. The Church has nothing to teach but her orthodoxy, and if her authority is not unerring that orthodoxy is a worse than valueless thing. But if, on the contrary, the Church is still apostolic; if, that is to say, her teaching of every age is as true as that of the apostles was, then her orthodoxy must be guaranteed by her infallibility.

Here is the crucial issue. Is it impossible for the Christian disciples of today to hear the gospel preached with the same absolute certainty with which it was preached in the first century by Jesus to the men of Galilee, and by the apostles to the men of the Roman Empire? Was it not good for us that our Lord should go? Certainly not, if with his departure, and that of his apostles, we have lost the certainty of being taught God's truth within the Church that he founded. If we have that certainty it is because, in formulating the Church's current orthodoxy, the successors of the apostles can teach us with the same absolute authority as the apostles themselves. In Newman's words: 'We have no reason to suppose that there is so great a distinction

[19] H. W. E. Turner, *The Pattern of Christian Truth*, p. 16.
[20] Ibid, pp. 483, 497, etc.

between ourselves and the first generation of Christians, as that they had a living infallible guidance, and we have not.'[21]

One may arrive at the same conclusion through a consideration of proposed criteria for true development. How do developments in theology come to be judged so that false ones may be weeded out and true ones pass beyond the stage of theologising into that of Church doctrine? In an important page Professor Turner considers these questions:

> The doctrine of a closely knit unity between Scripture and Tradition has been widely maintained on the principle of the development of Christian doctrine which has been widely canvassed since the publication of Cardinal Newman's famous essay. There is nothing strange in the application of the law of entropy to Christian theology; indeed, it has been assumed and illustrated in the previous lectures of this course. The mere fact of development naturally tells us nothing of the value or the truth of the results of the process; it is rather a principle of genetics than a criterion of value. It is clear that many instances of development would commend themselves universally to orthodox Christians. The final formation of the doctrine of the Trinity, which was the result of a gradual process of development, represents a legitimate attempt to think together as a systematic whole the predominantly Triadic structure of New Testament religion. Nothwithstanding the criticisms to which it has been subjected in many quarters, the Chalcedonian Definition can be successfully defended as a valid attempt to set out the implications for thought of the Person of our Lord portrayed in the Gospels. But if the mere fact of development cannot by itself guarantee the theological truth of the results of the process, the necessity remains of framing adequate criteria to enable us to distinguish between legitimate and illicit developments. Those who press most strongly for the full results of the process, and raise the charge of arrested development against those who cannot accept its whole content as true, must themselves recognise and guard against the opposite danger of accretion, the accumulation of elements in greater or less degree extrinsic to the original data in the interests of a fuller or more rounded system. There is therefore need for the application of some further principle to discriminate between developments which resemble the doctrine of the Trinity and those which cannot commend themselves as equally valid reflections of the biblical data. It may be

[21] *Essay on Development*, chap. II, sect. II, no. 10.

suggested that some such distinction as that between 'explicative' and 'additive' developments, or between developments which represent the mature thought of the Church about the implications of the biblical stock of her religion and those which go beyond this, outrunning and even distorting the premises upon which her continuing life rests, will be of service here. The results of development need to be tested not only by the principle of coherence, the logical articulation of the Christian Faith into a systematic whole, but also by the further principle of correspondence with the biblical facts themselves. (pp. 487-8).

Development certainly has, and requires, criteria; and we must fully recognise the danger of accretions of one kind or another, of mixing the gold of the gospel with the dross of theories of human origin. There is no reason why we should entirely accept Newman's own criteria of true development, and I presume that every Catholic would accept as fundamental 'the further principle of correspondence with the biblical facts themselves'. But the great difficulty is to know what developments do so correspond; Professor Turner believes that the Mariological developments do not do so; I disagree. And what is one to expect but disagreement of that sort; at least, if in treating of doctrinal development, one has not a word to say of the function of authority in judging of that development? It seems genuinely naïve to me to say that 'many instances of development would commend themselves universally to orthodox Christians', because it is precisely the development of orthodoxy which is in question and it is not surprising that 'orthodox Christians' should accept the acquired positions of a previous age. But the formulations of the doctrine of the Trinity did not commend themselves by any means universally at the time that they were proclaimed to be orthodoxy, on the contrary they split Christendom into two; and the same was true of the Chalcedonian Definition.

With Professor Turner's criteria one may compare those of Archbishop Ramsey, 'The tests of a true development are whether it bears witness to the gospel, whether it expresses the general consciousness of the Christians, and whether it serves the organic unity of the Body in all its parts.'[22]

[22] *The Gospel and the Catholic Church*, p. 64.

This again is all very well, but as tests they are. too vague to be applicable in particular disputed cases with any hope of agreement. Moreover they themselves do not stand up well if tested against the measure of historical developments. For example, if we take such a 'development' as the Leonine *in duabus naturis* of Chalcedon, what shall we get? Nowadays we may agree that it bears witness to the gospel though at the time many denied it, and as for Archbishop Ramsey's other two tests, an affirmative answer could not be given: far from expressing the general consciousness of the Christians or serving the organic unity of the Body in all its parts, it caused one of the most disastrous schisms in the whole of Church history. Yet I hope that Dr Ramsey would not condemn it as a false development?

It may be evident today that the fourth- and fifth-century developments correspond with the biblical facts, but it was not so then to those who would not accept the orthodoxy defined by the great councils. The truth is that it is impossible to speak intelligibly of the development of doctrine in purely theoretical terms, the decisive element being the factual decision of Church authority. I feel that Professor Turner and Dr Ramsey have not sufficiently pondered the very great difference between the development of theology (the work of theologians) and the development of orthodoxy, which cannot be the same thing.[23] If only a development of theologising is at question, then it is sufficient to lay down some general criteria for true development and leave it at that. But if we are speaking of the development of the orthodoxy of the *Una Sancta* herself, then the essential part must inevitably be played, and has as a matter of fact in ecclesiastical history been played, not by a theologian but by the Church's *magisterium*. In the first centuries the two are both clearly present and distinct. It is a great lack in Professor Turner's work that he has so little to say of the work of the great councils. It is only via ecclesiastical authority that theological development

---

[23] As Dr Chadwick has noted (*From Bossuet to Newman*, p. 90) here lies the difference between the theory of development as held by Bishop Butler and that held by Newman. Only the latter's is 'binding upon the belief of Christians'. Now as a historian, Professor Turner has demonstrated the existence of development in Newman's sense, but when he comes to theories about it, he considers it mainly in Butler's sense.

can be transformed into that 'development of orthodoxy' with which he is concerned.[24]

The real significance of the fact of a continuous and orthodox development in Christian doctrine is, then, to multiply a thousand-fold the strength of the reasons for an authoritative continuous 'Living Voice' which alone can direct and judge that development. In Newman's own words:

> In proportion to the probability of true developments of doctrine and practice in the Divine Scheme, so is the probability also of the appointment in that scheme of an external authority to decide upon them, thereby separating them from the mass of mere human speculation, extravagance, corruption and error, in and out of which they grow. This is the doctrine of the infallibility of the Church; for by infallibility I suppose is meant the power of deciding whether this, that, and a third and any number of theological or ethical statements are true.[25]

It is interesting to observe how a phenomenon admitted for the early centuries is fiercely rejected for modern times. Yet it would be strange if the possible developments in Christian doctrine were really exhausted in the first five centuries, and anyway the phenomenon of the essential contemporaneity of orthodoxy is not one limitable to any particular period. But Dr Hanson, for example, has denounced the nineteenth- and twentieth-century papal definitions *simply* because they add to the Creed, develop orthodoxy. What after all is the Catholic conception of the 'living mind of the Church' but contemporary orthodoxy? For Dr Hanson, however, it is a 'theological will-o'-the-wisp' while developments in the living mind are ruled out *a priori* as having 'the vitality of the jungle', 'a bizarre fecundity paralleled only in Hinduism'[26]; but is it very different to say that 'the "living mind" of 1954 is not the "living mind" of 2004, and will in its turn be superseded by the "living mind" of 2054, and so on, until the Last Judgment',[27] and to say that 'Orthodoxy in the second century must be differently interpreted from orthodoxy in the

---

[24] Let me refer here to the excellent articles of Father Henry St John, O.P. on 'The Authority of Doctrinal Development', *Blackfriars*, October, November and December 1955.
[25] *Essay on Development*, chap. II, sect. II, no. 4.
[26] *Theology*, 1954, p. 383.   [27] Ibid.

fourth or fifth'? [28] The orthodoxy of any age is simply the 'living mind' of the Church in that age. The mistake is to apply quite a different kind of norm to the past from that used in the present; to reject, on principle, later Marian developments requires, as Newman discovered, the rejection of early Trinitarian and Christological ones.

Development has of course its own inner laws, and orthodoxy must always—and always will—remain in the fullest and deepest sense faithful to the original revelation. But it has been the argument of this chapter that doctrinal development is absolutely inherent in the nature of Christian teaching and that both the original character of scripture and that of this necessary development require a living and unerring voice in the Church to interpret scripture, prevent false accretions from entering into the development of orthodoxy, and so insure the truthfulness and truly apostolic character of the doctrine of the apostolic Church. That voice must have an organ if it is to live at all, but it is the aim of the argument here to establish the necessity of such a voice rather than to locate its functional organism.

[28] Turner, op. cit. p. 16.

Chapter 3

AUTHORITY AND UNITY

The conclusion of the preceding chapter was that to deny the legitimacy of development in Christian orthodoxy is to deny twenty centuries of the Church's doctrinal history, but that to admit it involves also the recognition of the existence in the Church of a living and authoritative voice fully capable of insuring that no doctrine alien to Christian revelation is being imposed as a condition for Church membership.

There are non-Catholics, especially some Anglo-Catholics, who would, I think, agree with the argument up to this point. The Church *should* indeed possess an authoritative, even infallible, voice with which to settle matters of doctrine. Moreover she *did* possess such a voice in former times. That explains the High Church emphasis on antiquity, the early Church, the first five centuries: the authority of the Church herself deciding doctrine. But why should such an authority have ceased to exist, why limit the living voice to the first centuries? The answer to this they find in the theory of the abnormality of a divided Church. The Church was indeed endowed with an authoritative living voice, but only a united Church can exercise such a faculty. The Church could speak decisively in the fourth century, she cannot today; her condition has changed in the meantime. Doctrinal authority has disappeared with the failure of unity, and though orthodoxy is not completely lost, it is 'dispersed'.[1] This would seem to be the view of Professor Turner; it was the view of Newman in his *Lectures on the Prophetical Office of the Church viewed relatively to Romanism and Protestantism,* and it is the view of all Anglo-Catholics who uphold the authority of the primitive Church but will not admit the present existence of a living voice.

[1] Turner, op. cit. p. 478.

Authority is lost, because unity is lost; hence the field of enquiry is shifted from the issue of authority itself to that of unity.

In *The Prophetical Office*, written in 1837, Newman was searching for a consistent theory of doctrinal authority which could justify the Tractarians in their position vis-à-vis both Rome and Protestantism. Unlike Rome, he wrote, Anglicans and Protestants agree 'in considering the Bible as the only standard of appeal in doctrinal inquiries' (Lecture I, sect. 1). But the Anglican differs from the Protestant in accepting the reliable interpretation of antiquity. Why only antiquity? Because, Newman replied, only the undivided Church has adequate authority. The Church's infidelity to the command of unity has curtailed her powers; since at least the great schism she has not been as she was intended to be; 'Anyone who maintains that the Church is all that Christ intended her to be, has the analogy of Judaism full against him' (Lecture VIII, sect. 10). This incompleteness of the Church is shown especially in her authority: 'it is not extravagant to suppose that she was also destined to an authoritative ministry of the word which has never been realised' (ibid.), at least never since antiquity. 'Since the Church is not now one, it is not infallible; since the *one* has become in one sense the *many*, the full prophetical idea is not now fulfilled; and with the idea also is lost the full endowment and the attribute of Infallibility in particular, supposing that were ever included in it' (Lecture VIII, sect. 12). Newman was too much of an Anglican to admit easily that the Church was ever clearly infallible, yet it is difficult to interpret in any lesser sense his notion of the undivided Catholic Church of antiquity, 'the true prophet of God'.

When Canon Rich set about writing his book *Spiritual Authority in the Church of England*, he was in much the same mood as that of Newman when composing *The Prophetical Office*. Rich himself criticised Newman in the following words:

> The whole argument suffers from one fatal flaw. It presupposes that the Church's visible unity is the condition of her infallibility, and because this unity has now been lost, so has her infallibility been destroyed. Therefore Newman justifies an appeal to a sup-

posedly united and undivided Church as our only guarantee of
an infallibility in matters of faith, a Church that is to be found
in antiquity alone. Here there are two bold and unproven assump-
tions, one that that Primitive Church was in fact truly united
visibly, and the other that she did in fact possess an *infallible*
judgment. But was there ever such a Golden Age? And if so, what
possible guarantee does it offer us that the Church was any more
infallible then than she is now? For if she were infallible at a
period in her history when she was deemed to be united visibly
as she was invisibly, her supposed infallibility nevertheless did not
prevent her committing that deadliest of all sins against the Body
of Christ, namely, the sin of schism![2]

The last argument seems irrelevant, or at least implies a certain
particular conception of what schism is; moreover Newman's
attribution of an infallible judgment to the Church was not just
an unproven assumption as Rich himself came to see in the very
course of writing his book,[3] but it was something implied by the
whole Catholic conception of the Church as he saw it. Newman's
real 'unproven assumption'—and Rich's too—was that the
Church's visible unity is something which can be lost, that the
Church is visibly divisible.

In both *The Prophetical Office* and in *Spiritual Authority* we
find an explanation of authority which is very Catholic. From
a Catholic point of view its weakness, as that of most Anglo-
Catholic ecclesiology, comes not from itself but from a mistaken notion of the Church as a divisible society. If such a
notion were acceptable, the curtailment of doctrinal authority on
account of division would not seem unreasonable, for authority
lies in the hierarchical part of the Church, and it is just that part
which is the most divided by schism. Authority *does* presuppose
unity. 'Christian faith means unity with the whole body' writes
Father Bernard Leeming,[4] and if the unity were to be broken
the expression of faith would be imperilled. 'Unless', writes
Father Henry St John, 'the unity of the Church is—and it must
be—analogous to that of a living organism, unless its inner life
is maintained, consistent with itself at every stage, by a visible

---

[2] *Spiritual Authority*, p. 71.
[3] See especially pp. 210-11.
[4] 'The Assumption and the Christian Pattern', *The Month*, March 1951, p. 145.

organic structure, undivided and indivisible, it can possess no
ultimate and absolute criterion of truth. Apart from this organic
unity the Church can have no single mind and voice to judge and
proclaim as genuine its developing insights into the revelation
committed to its care.'[5]

Authority and unity go together then, and both Catholics and
non-Catholics agree at least that a divided Church could not
speak with authority, but behind this agreement is the more
fundamental disagreement as to whether or not the Church can
be divided. Here lies the vital issue which has really divided
Christians in their thinking about the Church since the days of
the Reformation; it is an issue even more fundamental than that
of authority because it controls, as we have seen, the practical
conclusion to the argument about authority itself. And yet it is
an issue which has not been much considered. Even the thought
of Newman and Rich was hindered, right up to the time of
conversion, by non-Catholic presuppositions about Church unity
which they took for granted, apparently without examination.
Yet if they had concerned themselves as much with the Church's
unity as with her authority, they would, I believe, have found in
it the clearest of all reasons for their journey home. It is at least
the fundamental issue dividing Catholics and non-Catholics: it
is so fundamental that, though often hardly considered explicitly,
it in fact controls their thinking on almost all other theological
issues.

[5] 'Old Priest and New Presbyter', *Blackfriars*, January 1957, p. 6.

Chapter 4

THE REFORMATION AND THE UNITY
OF THE CHURCH

The question of the Church's unity is the very question of
her nature, for the Church is the administration of the fruits
of the Redemption, the reuniting of men with God, the at-one-
ment; and so to ask 'what is the Church?' is to ask 'how does the
Church make men at one with God and with one another?' If
our Lord has founded a Church, it is the obligation of all men to
be in it, within its unity, and therefore the question at once
arises—who is in this unity, and how? Is the principle by which
the unity of the Church is secured faith, or baptism, or obedience
to the pope, or charity, or what? And it is not enough to con-
centrate attention in the ecumenical dialogue on the Church in
general, we must go further, and grapple with the central question of Church unity, which is the key to the nature of the
Church itself and even of her doctrinal authority.[1]

This essential issue dividing Catholics and non-Catholics has
been summed up most precisely by the Abbot of Downside in
the following passage:

> How much trouble would be saved in all our discussions with
> our non-Catholic friends if it were agreed that the basic question
> is: What is the Church? Although Newman's submission was the
> result of his discovery of the true Church, I am not sure that even
> he saw quite clearly or ever expressed quite adequately that this
> was the vital question to ask and answer. Is the Church a race of
> the redeemed, or a proliferation of episcopal sees essentially united
> only in their derivation from a common historical source? Or is
> she a *Historical Society*, whose survival is guaranteed by her
> Founder till the day of judgement? If she is a historical society,

---

[1] 'Divisibility or unicity is the fundamental question at issue in a disunited
Christianity, and is the real crux of the ecumenical dialogue', H. St John
'Authority of Doctrinal Development', *Blackfriars*, November 1955, p. 415.

then it is obvious that the severance of unity, leading as it does to the existence thereafter of *more than one* historical society, cannot be division *within* the Church, but must entail the separation of all but one of the societies henceforward existing *from* the Church. The problem of the Church's nature is the *same* problem as that of her unity.[2]

With this identification of the nature of Church unity with the nature of the Church many non-Catholics too are fully agreed. Father Hebert wrote that 'Unity is not a mere attribute of the Church, or a quality which the Church at its best ought to exhibit, but is the very substance and essence of the Church'.[3] Again, the joint report entitled 'Relations between Anglican and Presbyterian Churches' has this to say: 'Unity is not a contingent feature of the Church's life, but is of the very essence of it.'[4]

Unity existed in the beginning, was lost with the Fall, and it was Jesus' work to give it back to us. Hence unity is so much the nature and end of the Church that one might speak of it even before speaking of the Church at all (as P. de Lubac does in *Catholicism*; chap. 1 'Dogma' is devoted especially to unity, and then follows chap. 2 'The Church'). The unity which Christ came to remake is achieved in and through his Body the Church, and in no other way. Therefore to enter into union with God and our fellow men, we must enter into the unity of the Church. But just what kind of unity is it?

The traditional Catholic view of both East and West was that it was a visible unity, the corollary of the visible Church. If there was complete schism between two groups of Christians, then only one of them could be within the unity of the Church. For the Eastern Orthodox the Western Latins were as much cut off from the unity of the Church, as were the Greeks in the eyes of the Western Church. Prior to the Reformation this belief was not called in question; I will go into a more detailed study of it later on, here I have only to register it as a fact; with it is to be compared the normal Protestant view, of which a typical statement is to be found in the Westminster Confession of 1647:

---

[2] 'The Lost Leader', *Downside Review*, 1951, p. 72.
[3] *The Form of the Church*, p. 62.
[4] Ibid, p. 3.

The catholick or universal church, which is invisible, consists of the whole number of the elect that have been, or are, or shall be gathered into one, under Christ the head thereof; and is the spouse, the body, the fulness of him that filleth all in all.

The visible church, which is also catholick or universal under the gospel (not confined to one nation, as before under the law) consists of all those throughout the world that profess the true religion together with their children. . . .

This catholick church hath been sometimes more, sometimes less visible. And particular churches, which are members thereof, are more or less pure, according as the doctrine of the gospel is taught and embraced, ordinances administered, and publick worship performed more or less purely in them.

The purest churches under heaven are subject both to mixture and error; and some have so degenerated as to become no churches of Christ but synagogues of Satan.

This sort of ecclesiology could fully justify a schism. What is primary and most important is the invisible Church, which is only partly and partially represented by the visible Church; the latter is simply the community of those who profess the true religion in any one place, and such communities can degenerate into synagogues of satan. Behind the divisions caused by the continental reformers lay a theology, and the theory at least kept up with the facts.

In England it was quite different. Neither in the time of Henry VIII nor in that of Elizabeth was there present a new theology to justify the breaking off of relations with the rest of Catholic Christendom. Doubtless many of those working for those two monarchs were Protestants believing as did the Protestants of the continent; but the decisive legislative acts of Henry and Elizabeth were not based on any such new theology, but simply on pragmatic erastianism. At the origin of the Church of England as a separate body lies no theology but an act of State, an act of Parliament.[5] All subsequent Anglican ecclesiology has been an attempt to justify theologically the state of affairs produced by that statute. Their quandary is that they believe in a visible

[5] Cf. Sir Maurice Powicke, *The Reformation in England*, p. 1. The report entitled 'Catholicity' truthfully recognises this: 'The post-Reformation Church of England was not the result of a theology' (p. 49).

Church, but are tied to a situation, created by civil law, which is justifiable only with a Protestant theology of the invisible Church. Out of this situation has developed the most characteristic and crucial of all Anglican doctrines, that is to say the divisibility of the visible Church. Abbot Chapman was quite right to say that 'the divisibility of the Church is the cardinal doctrine of Anglicanism, and its most fundamental heresy',[6] and Father Henry St John has summed up the position very exactly in writing:

> The cardinal heresy of the Reformation was the divisibility of the Church; the idea that there could be permanent schism within its boundaries. On this fundamental doctrine of the nature of the Church the pre-Reformation Church and the post-Reformation Church of England were and are at variance. Here is the decisive point at which the Church of England has separated itself from traditional Catholicism in East and West, and has ranged itself on the side of Reformation Protestantism. This was the issue that led Fisher and More to the scaffold, and moved the Elizabethan martyrs to the acceptance of a terrible death.[7]

Of course Anglicans do not accept such a reading of sixteenth-century history. They maintain that a very different thing happened. Bishop Gore declared

> there is no catholic principle which can justify us in supposing that either the Roman, the Eastern, or the Anglican Church has been guilty of the sin of schism, in that sense in which schism is the act of self-withdrawal from the Church catholic. The English Church at the Reformation claimed to reform herself, and there is no catholic principle which forbade her to do it. She did not withdraw herself in so doing from the Catholic faith of the catholic Church; indeed she professed her intention to remain as fully in submission to the Church as before.[8]

This is indeed a remarkable statement. The crucial date in the English Reformation is 1559, and who was 'she' in that year? Who could speak for the English Church? The Archbishop of Canterbury was dead, consequently the Archbishop of York, Dr Heath, was the senior bishop. Did he think that there was no question of 'self-withdrawal from the Church catholic?' On the

---

[6] *Bishop Gore and the Catholic Claims*, p. 20.
[7] 'Fallible Infelicities', *Blackfriars*, December 1953, p. 525.
[8] *Roman Catholic Claims*, p. 137.

contrary. In the House of Lords in March 1559 in the debate on the Royal Supremacy Bill he said that to forsake and flee the see of Rome would be 'to forsake and fly from the unity of Christ's Church'. In the same debate Scot, bishop of Chester, said that 'a particular or provincial council can make no determination against the universal Church of Christ'. Every bishop in the House voted against the bill, and the whole hierarchy was imprisoned.[9]

The bishops knew exactly what Catholic principles on the subject were; they knew that this was schism, and they refused to take part in it. If they had participated in it, it would have been schism none the less, but at least the subsequent Anglican theory of the Church as ruled over by the bishops would have a better basis. As it is, the Elizabethan Reformation remains an entirely lay work without any continuity of episcopal jurisdiction.[10]

But the crucial question is not the lack of that continuity; the most fundamental issue is the Church's unity, as Heath saw, and as St Thomas More had already seen a generation before. In his final speech after condemnation, the latter appealed to 'Christ's universal Catholic Church', to 'the general Council of Christendom', to the whole of the Church from which one part can have no right or power to sever itself.[11] In this St Thomas More and Archbishop Heath stood with the whole of the Catholic tradition.

Nothing is clearer than that, if the bishops of 1559 were right, if Catholic tradition of both East and West was right, the Elizabethan Church was schismatic, that is to say it was cut off from the unity of the Catholic Church. To escape this conclusion, Anglican theologians have sought to work out what is in fact quite a new theology of the Church and its unity, something broad enough to include other Christian groups besides themselves.

Which other groups these are, Anglicans have not always agreed about. In the sixteenth, seventeenth and eighteenth

[9] Philip Hughes, *The Reformation in England*, III, pp. 23-25.
[10] Figgis understood this quite clearly: 'It is the lay power which is ultimately supreme in the Reformation theory. . . . This fact must be faced, for it affords the only serviceable theory of continuity' (quoted by Sykes, *Old Priest and New Presbyter*, p. 249). But how many High Churchmen have faced up to it?
[11] See R. W. Chambers, *Thomas More*, p. 341.

centuries most included the great Protestant communions on the continent within the Church, though they excluded English dissenters on grounds of schism, and some also excluded Rome on account of doctrinal corruption. Others, however, like Archbishop Laud, freely acknowledged that Rome was 'a true church', though not 'the only true church'. In the nineteenth century, following the Tractarian movement, the tendency was to exclude all non-episcopal communions but to include Rome and Constantinople: that is to say, to uphold the classical 'branch theory'. In the present century, under general ecumenical influence, the common view is to include all more or less orthodox Christian groups within the visible Church, though Anglo-Catholics of the strict Tractarian tradition will still not recognise the Church status of non-episcopal Protestant communions.

Details of recognition of this or that body in different ages do not matter to us here. The point is that Anglicans, and Episcopalians in general, have never identified their own Communion with the visible Church and have hence been forced by this basic position to try and reconcile two very different beliefs: one is that the Church has a real visible unity—this follows from their traditional stress on Church order and adherence to the Catholic approach; the other is that the visible Church is not confined to any one visible unit. A key principle of this theology became at once the distinction between Church and communion; the visible Church, it must be maintained, consists of several communions.

That Anglicans themselves are well aware of the difficulty of defending the unity of the visible Church in these circumstances is shown by some initial remarks of two of their most distinguished theologians.

Bishop Gore began a consideration of the unity of the Church with the words:

It is a question often asked of English churchmen 'In what sense do you believe in *one* Holy Catholic Church? You do not claim that the English Church is of itself and alone the whole Church; you admit the Roman and Eastern branches to be, equally with your own, parts of the Church; that is to say, you admit permanent and apparently radical divisions in the Church in matters of doctrine no less than of Government, and yet you say the Church is one. Surely you are here giving words an unreal meaning.[12]

More recently Dr Mascall has commenced a study of the same topic in a similar way: ' "I believe . . . in one . . . Church." This is a provocative statement and, on the lips of an Anglican, it would not appear at first sight to be a particularly sensible one.'[13]

With the attempts of Anglicans, and especially of their finest group of Anglo-Catholic theologians, to solve this difficulty and to give the words 'one Church' a real meaning, the next chapter is concerned. Through this consideration of their views, I hope to bring into a clearer light what does constitute the essential bond of unity of the visible Church.

[12] *Roman Catholic Claims*, p. 25.   [13] *Corpus Christi*, p. 1.

Chapter 5

SOME ANGLICAN PROBLEMS

How is the Church one? How did the divisions of the Reformation not entail separation of all but one party from the visible
Church? How indeed has the Church always been divided and
yet one, ever since the great schism of East and West? Many
Anglican theologians have posed themselves such questions and
set to work to answer them, and this chapter is concerned with an
evaluation of their answers. Naturally Anglo-Catholics, holding
particularly strongly to a Catholic and visible view of the Church,
have felt the difficulty more strongly than others; furthermore
they have also produced a particularly large number of able
theologians seriously concerned to justify the Anglican situation
theologically. Hence it is especially with their ecclesiology that
this chapter is concerned, though certainly no clear distinction
between Anglo-Catholic ecclesiology and that of other Anglicans
can possibly be made. An ecclesiology must be based on the facts
of one's Church, and all Anglicans have the same fact—that of
the Anglican communion—which they have to explain and
justify theologically. Moreover at the present day the Archbishop
of Canterbury, Dr Ramsey, is himself both a very distinguished
theologian and a member of the Anglo-Catholic tradition. His
position gives his views a very special importance, not only within
the Anglican communion, but also within the whole of Christendom, and a careful Catholic consideration of them would seem
to have particular point at the present time. But his views can
best be appreciated when linked with those of a fairly well-defined
group of very able modern theologians of the same tradition and
with whom he has worked in the past. It is the group which
produced the symposium entitled *The Apostolic Ministry*, edited
by the late Kenneth Kirk, Bishop of Oxford, and published in
1947. Again, it is the group which presented the report entitled

Catholicity to the former Archbishop of Canterbury in 1947. That group had Dr Ramsey for its chairman and Dom Gregory Dix and Father A. G. Hebert for its secretaries. A. M. Farrer, now Warden of Keble College, Oxford, L. S. Thornton, and T. S. Eliot were among its other members; Dix, Hebert, Thornton and Farrer had all been contributors to *The Apostolic Ministry*. To these names we must join that of Dr Mascall, Professor of Theology at London University, the best known professional theologian in Britain today. Behind these figures of our own generation stands Bishop Gore, who more than anyone else was the link between the Anglo-Catholics of the twentieth century and the fathers—the Tractarians and F. D. Maurice—of the nineteenth.

This chapter is not, however, intended by any means as a mere study of some Anglican opinions, its aim is rather to demonstrate the impossibility of producing *any* other adequate ecclesiology of the visible Church than the Roman one; beyond this, it is also hoped to clarify Catholic ecclesiology itself through the study of views in many ways not far from our own; it seems to me that the position of the Church of England and the ideas of Anglo-Catholics especially, can be peculiarly useful for the elucidation of the nature of Church unity. In the same way the existence of the Donatists helped St Optatus and St Augustine in a similar work.

The following analysis is divided into ten parts which do however to some extent overlap. The first section considers the basic pattern of Anglican ecclesiology, while the second is chiefly concerned with the old bugbear of governmental unity. The following seven sections treat progressively of various ways in which the Church's unity is explained or defended by Anglicans; these ways may for some be alternative theories, but more often they should be understood rather as clarifying and supplementing one another. A final section provides a summary of the whole, together with my own personal judgment.

1. *Faith, Baptism and the Episcopate*

'We acknowledge all those who believe in our Lord Jesus Christ, and have been baptised into the name of the Holy Trinity, as sharing with us membership in the universal Church of Christ which is His Body.'[1] This would seem to establish faith and baptism as the necessary and sufficient conditions of continuing Church membership. More and more this is tending to become the accepted Anglican view. 'All who are baptised into Christ are members of his Church' says Dr Ramsey,[2] following a central Catholic tradition, and he goes on to say that one can only leave the Church by a 'renunciation of the Spirit'[3] which means, I suppose, complete loss of faith.

In this combination of faith and baptism, the former represents the invisible element of Church membership, the latter the essential visible element; in some way or other every ecclesiology worthy of the name has to do justice to both the visible and the invisible, and it may be noted in passing that the Lambeth formula of faith and baptism already corresponds, at least in part, to a traditional formula: *Ecclesia fundatur in fide et sacramentis.*[4]

Many Anglo-Catholics felt more than uneasy about the Lambeth formula because it seems to accept non-episcopal bodies as parts of the visible Church. They take their stand on a more rigid application of the 'Lambeth Quadrilateral' not only as a condition for intercommunion, but of any recognition of full ecclesiastical status. Intercommunion ought to exist between the branches of the Church and if it cannot be allowed with non-episcopal bodies, it must be because the latter cannot as such be admitted as branches of the Church.

The Quadrilateral was first drawn up by the Anglican bishops of the United States in 1886, and published in the following form.

> We do affirm that the Christian unity now so earnestly desired . . . can be restored only by the return of all Christian communions to the principles of unity exemplified by the undivided Catholic Church during the first ages of its existence; . . .

---

[1] From the 'Appeal to all Christian People' of the Lambeth Conference 1920, to be found in Bell, *Documents on Church Unity*, 1920-4, p. 1.
[2] *The Gospel and the Catholic Church*, p. 84.
[3] Ibid. p. 139.
[4] St Thomas, Com. in IV Sent. d. 17, q. 3, a. 1, sol. 5.

As inherent parts of this sacred deposit, and therefore as essential to the restoration of unity among the divided branches of Christendom, we account the following; to wit:

1. The Holy Scriptures of the Old and New Testament as the revealed word of God.

2. The Nicene Creed as the sufficient statement of the Christian Faith.

3. The two Sacraments—Baptism and the Supper of the Lord—ministered with unfailing use of Christ's words of institution and of the elements ordained by him.

4. The Historic Episcopate, locally adapted in the methods of its administration to the varying needs of the nations and peoples called of God into the unity of His Church.[5]

Two years later, in 1888, the same four points were adopted by the third Lambeth Conference as 'a basis on which approach may be, by God's blessing, made towards Home Reunion'.[6]

It is because these are held to be 'the principles of unity exemplified by the undivided Catholic Church' that many Anglicans believe them to be a *sine qua non* of the Church. 'Bible, Sacraments, Creed and Ministry are essential forms of the Church, such that without them it would not be the Church.'[7]

As all Protestants accept the two 'Dominical' sacraments of baptism and eucharist, though vastly differing as to their interpretation, and as scriptures and creeds are not entirely believed even by all Anglicans, the chief point at issue in all discussions of Church recognition and intercommunion is that of the ministry. Does it, or does it not, require an episcopate claiming lineal descent from the apostles? It should be noted at once that when the four points of 1886 and 1888 were republished by the Lambeth Conference of 1920, the phrase 'historic episcopate' was abandoned; it spoke instead of 'a ministry acknowledged by every part of the Church as possessing not only the inward call of the Spirit but also the commission of Christ and the authority of the whole body'.[8] To this, however, was added the question, 'May we not reasonably claim that the episcopate is the one means of providing such a ministry?'

[5] Text in Lacey, *Unity and Schism*, Appendix VI, pp. 216-17.
[6] Quoted in Sykes, *Old Priest and New Presbyter*, p. 219.
[7] Hebert, *The Form of the Church*, p. 41.   [8] Bell, op. cit. p. 2.

In practice there is no question of the Anglican Church entering into official intercommunion with entirely non-episcopal bodies, although some Anglicans desire it. Dr Greenslade, for instance, writes 'it is only if, given the divisions of the Church, episcopacy in apostolic succession is a *sine qua non* of the existence of real ministries and sacraments in those divisions (that is, if Christ cannot or will not give them ministries and sacraments), that it can rightly be made a condition of intercommunion; and that I do not believe'; and again, 'as regards many of the major denominations of Christendom I cannot but record my conviction that not to recognise each other as sister churches, with whatever faults, is spiritual blindness. We ought to be in communion with one another.'[9] But the normal Anglican view may be found expressed in the report on the recent Anglican Presbyterian theological discussions: 'From the Anglican side it was clear that full intercommunion and unity could not be realised apart from episcopacy.'[10]

If the Church of England is not in direct communion with any non-episcopal church, it should nevertheless be noted that she is already in 'mediate communion' with some, through her direct communion with the Church of Sweden and the Church of South India, which are themselves in communion with non-episcopal churches.

Behind the practical issue of intercommunion is the theological question of what intercommunion signifies. If for some it might seem to be little more than a mutual recognition of Christian sincerity, at bottom it is difficult to see how it can imply less than mutual recognition of Church membership and a valid ministry. Certainly for other Christians it has seldom as strict a sense as for a Roman Catholic or a Greek Orthodox, but for Anglicans it does still imply a recognition of ecclesiastical status. The crisis over communion with the Church of South India showed that they were unprepared to grant that to a not clearly episcopal body. The real issue, in fact, facing Anglicans in that crisis was not whether CSI ordinations were valid, but what was to be thought of the CSI *qua* church? Did its acceptance of

[9] *Schism in the Early Church*, p. 221.
[10] *Relations between Anglican and Presbyterian Churches*, 1957, p. 11.

episcopacy justify its inclusion within the recognised ecclesiastical world, and hence allow intercommunion? Or did the intercommunion which it maintains with non-episcopal communities such as the English Methodists place it outside the visible Church? Though the immediate scope of the decisions of the convocations of Canterbury and York was very limited, nevertheless the first view was really accepted, and basically on the grounds that the Lambeth Quadrilateral was outwardly preserved in the CSI. The following words of Donald Rea may summarise the view which has come to be accepted: 'Contrary to what many have said, CSI does not think of itself as a new church built by human efforts, but as a reunion of Christians who have found, in their historic heritage, the Church given by God to the Apostles, have regrouped themselves round the Anglican episcopate, and, moreover, claim to be nothing else but members of the Universal Church.'[11]

Episcopacy is officially put forward by the Anglican Church less as a theological than as a practical condition for reunion. It is here that the normal Anglo-Catholic view divides from the official Anglican one. For the former a theological issue is certainly at stake, for the latter that is not so; the sense of the episcopate in fact remains quite undecided, and the Church of England is willing to discuss reunion with a body which is willing to 'take episcopacy into its system' as a form of government, even though no particular doctrine is attached to it. Bishop Headlam, though he included the historic episcopate within the basis for Christian reunion as he expounded it in *The Doctrine of the Church and Christian Reunion*, recognised all non-episcopally transmitted orders as valid, if imparted with prayer and the laying on of hands, and he thought episcopacy 'the creation of the Church'. Certainly Anglo-Catholics had little reason for horror that the Church of South India accepted episcopacy but not 'any particular interpretation of episcopacy',[12] because many of their fellow Anglicans hold that this has been the traditional

[11] *CSI and the Church*, p. 32.
[12] *Constitution of the Church of South India*, p. 9. It should be noted that the CSI does not seem to have succeeded in maintaining this 'uncommitted' attitude, for in September 1957 its Theological Commission stated that 'The CSI does not

position of their own Church as well: the conclusion of Professor Sykes's study on the history of Anglican Church theory was that 'the Church of England has never set forth any theological or doctrinal theory of episcopacy'.[13]

How anomalous is the present position of Anglo-Catholics within the Church of England may be shown by a comparison of the above citations with the following words of Dr Gregg, Archbishop of Armagh:

> I am not sure if a good deal of this laxity of conviction is not to be traced to the very dangerous suggestion which has been current for some twenty years past, to the effect that, while the acceptance of episcopacy as a practice is indispensable for those who would enter into communion with the Anglican Church, no particular theory of episcopacy need be insisted on. I regard this view as both unsound and unprincipled. It seems to me nothing less than the rankest ritualism. To urge the acceptance of an institution without insisting on any reasoned meaning of it reduces it, in my opinion, to something like mumbo-jumbo.[14]

This has been quoted as an 'admirably lucid statement' by Dr Mascall.[15] It means that the official position of the Church of South India, and also a widely-held view within the Church of England itself, reduce episcopacy, in the eyes of Dr Gregg and Dr Mascall, to 'something like mumbo-jumbo'.

Yet, more and more, under the influence of the ecumenical movement and of historical scholarship, even Anglo-Catholics are being forced to attempt a conciliation of belief in the episcopate as of the divinely constituted *esse* of the Church with a recognition of the ecclesiastical status of non-episcopal bodies, that is of the enduring sufficiency for Church membership of faith and baptism. The apparent contradiction is overcome by stress on the inevitable abnormality of conditions prevailing in 'a divided church'.

consider episcopal ordination essential for a valid ministry'. This statement implies a particular interpretation of episcopacy and goes far to justify the Anglo-Catholic view of the matter. By this statement the CSI has gone far beyond official refusal to commit itself to 'any particular interpretation of episcopacy', and has in fact committed itself to a non-Catholic interpretation.

[13] *Old Priest and New Presbyter*, p. 244. But Sykes did not prove his case in spite of all his learning. His book should be read in conjunction with the mordant criticism of it in Dr Peck's *Anglicanism and Episcopacy*.

[14] *Reunion*, p. 8, Pax House, Westminster.   [15] *Corpus Christi*, pp. 15-16.

This is, of course, to abandon the principles of Tractarianism.
The Tractarians and their successors maintained that the essential note of the Church was 'the possession of the Apostolic
succession'.[16] *Ubi episcopus ibi Ecclesia.* 'The unity of the
Church', said Archdeacon Manning, 'inheres in the one origin,
the one succession, and the one college of Catholic Bishops.'[17]
In more recent times the same view has been defended by Bishop
Kirk, Dr Mascall and Dr Peck, to name only a few. The episcopate is of the Church's *esse,* and therefore those who have not
the episcopate are outside the visible Church. 'Where there is
no Apostolic Ministry there can be no Church.'[18]

In contrast with this view, the Protestant or Evangelical wing
of the Church of England believes the episcopate to be no more
than of the Church's *bene esse*: it is a useful and traditional
method of Church ministry, which Anglicans would be very
ill-advised to give up, but it is not a condition of Church membership. All the baptised are within the visible Church.

Between these two views is a third, perhaps the nearest to the
traditional position of the Church of England, which has, on the
whole, upheld divine authority for episcopacy while refusing to
'unchurch' non-episcopalians. According to a recent formula,
the episcopate is of the Church's *plene esse*.[19] Non-episcopal communions are indeed within the visible church, whose unity sub-
sists in baptism, nevertheless they lack something of the fullness
of Church life. The episcopate does not *effect* the Church's unity,
and yet it is the only institution through which that unity can
and should be maintained. 'The historic episcopate embodies the
unity of the Church vertically as well as horizontally through
space. It does not guarantee unity any more than it guarantees a
splinter-proof orthodoxy: but it is the God-given focus of unity.'[20]
Archbishop Ramsey comes very near to this view, for, though he

---

[16] Newman, 'The Catholicity of the Anglican Church', in *Essays Critical and Historical*, II, p. 39.

[17] *The Unity of the Church*, p. 156.

[18] A. L. Peck *Anglicanism and Episcopacy*, p. 96, cf. also p. 99.

[19] This formula is defended in the recent volume of essays by Westcott House men, entitled *The Historic Episcopate*, ed. K. M. Carey. This book should be read in conjunction with A. L. Peck's *This Church of Christ*, which criticises its thesis and arguments very effectively.

[20] H. W. Montefiore in *The Historic Episcopate*, p. 118.

speaks of the episcopate as of the Church's *esse*, he refuses to 'unchurch' the non-episcopalians.

We are led, therefore, to affirm that the episcopate is of the *esse* of the universal Church; but we must beware of mis-stating the issue. All who are baptised into Christ are members of his Church, and baptism is the first mark of churchmanship. Yet the growth of all Christians into the measure of the stature of the fulness of Christ means their growth with all the saints in the unity of the one Body, and of this unity the episcopate is the expression. It speaks of the incompleteness of every section of a divided Church, whether of those who possess the episcopate or of those who do not.[21]

To sum up: the first and third opinions are agreed on the *divine* authorisation of the episcopate: it is not merely a useful and ancient form of government linking the modern Church with primitive times. But the second and third opinions agree against the first in not regarding possession of the episcopate by a Christian body as a necessary condition for membership of the visible Church, and that is the question which interests us in this book. Adherents of the second and third views, such as Archbishop Ramsey, Professor Sykes, Dr Greenslade, R. F. Hettlinger, and the Westcott House contributors to *The Historic Episcopate*, are consequently forced to place the visible principle of Church unity in baptism. Adherents of the first view, such as E. L. Mascall and A. L. Peck, find this visible principle not in baptism but in the episcopate. Whereas Archbishop Ramsey, in the passage just quoted, holds that 'all who are baptised into Christ are members of his Church'. Dr Peck maintains

that the notion that anyone who has been baptised is once and for all a 'member of the Church' is mistaken. Baptism does not make a person once and for all a member of the Church. . . . The Church is not a society which is constituted by a large number of baptised persons: millions of such persons might exist and yet fail to constitute the Church. The Church is constituted by God through the threefold apostolic ministry, and those who wish to live in that society, sharing its life and learning salvation, will conform to its manners, which are also the divinely appointed means whereby God acts upon each soul. The notion that 'membership

[21] *The Gospel and the Catholic Church*, pp. 84-85.

of the Church' is a status once and for all acquired through baptism is responsible for much confused thinking on the subject of the unification of Christendom.[22]

But whether an Anglican holds baptism or whether he holds the episcopate to be the sacrament of unity, the fact and the problem of Christian disunity still remains. How can the Church be at once one and divided?

2. *One, but Divided*

For if all Anglicans do believe in 'One, Catholic Church' it is clear that all equally admit that the Church's unity is at present in some way broken; they can speak with Dr Ramsey of 'a divided Church',[23] even if all would not go so far as to appeal with Dr Greenslade for 'a theology of disunity'.[24] Some like Dr Greenslade believe that 'the one holy catholic and apostolic Church exists, on earth, in its divisions, comprising a number of communions which unequally manifest and live by various elements in full Christianity',[25] while others consider that only those communions which may be thought to possess all the elements of full Christianity can be truly called parts of the One Church. The essential for us remains the same: there is in the Church a sphere of unbreakable unity and a sphere of division.

The first point is to distinguish within the latter between legitimate divisions and those which are not. As Lacey says: 'there are divisions, articulations, which do not destroy unity, but are rather needed for its perfection.'[26] Of such kind are divisions due to rite, language, religious order and such like; without damaging the true unity of the Church, they help to express and manifest her catholicity. They are not the divisions responsible for the 'divided Church' of the present. These are schisms—the separation of Church life, communion and ecclesiastical government—which have been an almost continuous feature of Christian history but have been particularly numerous in the last centuries. The Church is divided because

[22] *Anglicanism and Episcopacy*, pp. 100-1.
[23] *The Gospel and the Catholic Church*, p. 85.
[24] *Schism in the Early Church*, p. 11.
[25] Ibid.   [26] *Unity and Schism*, p. 5.

of the break between East and West, and then because of the numerous breaks of the Reformation period and subsequent centuries. To the exact idea of schism I shall return, here it is sufficient to say that it is held by Anglicans to divide the Church rather than to divide from the Church, and so the resultant fragments all remain within the one body. Hence the possibility of the modern situation and equally of an appeal back to the earlier 'undivided church'.

It is clear that all Anglicans do not view this present state of division in quite the same way. For some, it was fully justified by reason of the corrupt state of the Roman Church; for others, it is an almost natural consequence of the autonomous character of local churches, which at the best of times should only be linked together in some sort of loose federal unity; for others it is a great tragedy. But, for all, the division is normally to be explained as one of government. 'Only from a governmental point of view can we be said to believe in a church which may be divided', wrote Mr Warner of Campbell College, Belfast, in *The Tablet*, June 2nd 1956. Its origin, indeed, is understood to be deeper than that, because it is rooted in the sins of men. There is truly a 'scandal of outward division',[27] which, Archbishop Ramsey feels, has affected the significance of the whole of Christian sacramental life: 'When historic Christendom is divided, the meaning of its orders and its Eucharist is maimed; no longer are they performed with the authority and the outward commission of the *whole* visible Church.'[28] He can even go so far as to say 'this sense that a divided Church is a monstrous impossibility, is indeed the needful basis of all Christian thinking about the Church'.[29] Yet this monstrous impossibility is a fact! And it may be noted that deep as is Dr Ramsey's sense of the division of Christians, he still expresses it in governmental terms—'authority' and 'outward commission'.

The 1920 Lambeth 'Appeal to all Christian People' went deeper than government when it declared that 'this united fellowship (the Catholic Church) is not visible in the world today. . . . We

---

[27] A. M. Ramsey, *The Gospel and the Catholic Church*, p. 223.
[28] Ibid. [29] p. 151.

acknowledge this condition of broken fellowship to be contrary to God's will'.[30] Unfortunately Anglicans have considered too little the significance of the state of divided fellowship, and too easily limit themselves to a picture of governmental division, seen as a serious yet ultimately superficial effect of human sin.

> Nor is there any difference in kind between a quarrel of two Christian neighbours and a schism between two churches. Both are in different degrees painful and scandalous; and yet neither of the two can affect either the victory which Christ has won, or the unity which he has established for men in his Body. The quarrels and the schisms, like all the sins of Christians, are anomalous, and utterly contrary to the nature of the Church. Here is a paradox indeed: the Church is indivisible, and yet divided, and it is holy and yet defiled with sin.[31]

'Indivisible, and yet divided.' However strongly Anglicans may stress the present division of the Church, they will continue to maintain that beneath these divisions the Church remains one and undivided. There is a unity which no schism can effect, an unbreakable unity, unbreakable because it is the unity which God has made, not man. Hence they can appeal to the Church's 'underlying theory of unity',[32] to 'the real unity of the Church',[33] to 'our fundamental unity'[34] which in spite of all Christian divisions remains 'a fact, not an aspiration'.[35] This unity continues, Dr Ramsey insists, 'despite the scandal of outward division' (p. 223). The Church remains one. How? Answers vary, and it is of them that I must treat in the following sections. I have only to note here that for Anglicans this paradox is almost a commonplace: the Church is one (with spiritual unity, or racial unity, sacramental unity or doctrinal unity) and yet at the same time she is divided (in government).

It may be noted in passing that this paradox is so stressed as to present at times a sort of logical absurdity which does not really assist the understanding of a Christian mystery. If the

[30] Bell, *Documents on Christian Unity*, vol. i, pp. 1-2.
[31] Hebert, *The Form of the Church*, p. 63.
[32] E. Milner-White and W. Knox, *One God and Father of All*, p. 152.
[33] Lacey, op. cit. p. 156.
[34] *Relations between Anglican and Presbyterian Churches*, p. 4, quoting from the Report of the Lund Conference on Faith and Order.
[35] Lacey, op. cit. p. 158.

essential unity of the Church continues to exist in spite of schisms and 'it is not inherently impossible that there should be schisms',[36] it is not strictly meaningful to go on to say that 'we ought indeed to think of schism as a denial of the Church's essential nature'.[37] If it is to be admitted that we live within 'a divided Church',[38] it is to overstate one's case to say that we need the 'sense that a divided Church is a monstrous impossibility'.[39]

Apart from this sort of loose statement, the Anglican position is fairly clear: essentially, fundamentally, the Church remains one; governmentally, she is divided.

Before examining the answers to the question as to how she remains one, it will be useful to add some remarks about Anglo-Catholic criticism of the Catholic view of the Church's essential unity. The chief criticism is just this: Roman Catholics identify the Church's essential unity with her governmental unity, and consequently refuse to admit that the visible Church is larger than their own governmental *bloc*. So E. Milner-White and Wilfred Knox spoke of the Roman Catholic idea of unity as 'a Unity of Government and Discipline',[40] Father Hebert speaks of 'a totalitarian system',[41] while Dr Mascall thinks that the Roman Church has gone wrong 'in treating the Church's visibility as an organisational rather than as a sacramental one',[42] and Dr Ramsey sums up the later developments of Catholicism with the words 'The Papacy grew in such a way that the idea of unity in terms of government took the place of the idea of unity in terms of race'.[43]

Without doubt, this is the stock accusation levelled by Anglicans against Catholics in the field of ecclesiology; it must be admitted that they can find passages by some Catholics which seem to prove them right. For instance, in the *Theologia Fundamentalis* of Mons. Parente one reads 'Unitas: evidentissime patet in regimine'.[44] Some Catholic authors seem to have little sense

---

[36] Hebert, op. cit. p. 63.
[37] Ibid.
[38] Ramsey, op. cit. p. 85.
[39] Ibid. p. 151.
[40] *One God and Father of All*, p. 149.
[41] *The Form of the Church*, p. 103.
[42] *Corpus Christi*, p. 18.
[43] *The Gospel and the Catholic Church*, p. 163. Cf. also Gore, *The Church and the Ministry*, p. 51; Lacey, *Unity and Schism*, p. 56, etc.
[44] p. 176; cf also p. 182.

of any unity except that of a common submission to authority,[45] while occasionally one can find such strange examples of the reduction of the whole of ecclesiology to its governmental aspect as the following:

'There are two intrinsic notes of the Church, viz. that *unity* of government which excludes all schismatical divisions within the body of the Church; and one regarding its life, viz. holiness of government.'[46]

It is of course true that every Roman Catholic believes unity of government to be an essential element in the Church's life, and I shall return later to the exact relationship between government and unity. Nevertheless, Anglicans are mistaken in thinking that the Catholic idea of Church unity is purely, or even primarily, governmental. They have, as we shall see, failed to perceive the central idea of the Catholic idea of Church unity, and this failure results not only in an unjust criticism of Roman Catholic theology, but also in a fatal weakness in their own views. For the present it is sufficient to quote once more the balanced words of Father Congar:

'Those Catholic controversialists who would make submission to the same visible head, the bishop of Rome, successor of St Peter and vicar of Christ, practically the one and only principle of the Church's unity, give an incomplete idea of the Church and its unity.'[47]

3. *Visible and Invisible*

The unity of the Church is an 'extension' of the unity of life of the most Holy Trinity. The latter is the foundation of the former, and the ultimate reason why the Church's unity is not breakable; it is also, clearly, an invisible unity. 'The Church . . . cannot but be one, its existence being grounded in that Divine realm where disunity is unthinkable . . . this fundamental

---

[45] For instance Mgr Vernon Johnson in *One Lord—One Faith*, while rightly insisting that 'Authority and unity were inseparable' (p. 171), seems to think of the latter only in terms of obedience to the former.

[46] Bishop Meurin, S. J., *The True Basis of Christian Fellowship*, p. 32, quoted by Dr Gore in *Roman Catholic Claims*, p. 34.

[47] *Divided Christendom*, p. 192.

unity.'[48] 'The unity with which the Church is one is nothing other than the unity with which the Persons of the Holy Trinity are one.'[49] This undoubted fact is often appealed to by non-Catholics as the ultimate proof that separated Christians remain still within a single Church unity: human divisions cannot break a divine unity. But that, of course, is to beg the whole question. The divine unity has been brought to earth in the Church, and is certainly unbreakable; but it is not *forced* upon individual men. The question remains—not, is there a divine, unbreakable, Church unity?— but, how does an individual man enter that unity and remain there? Unless the Church be merely the aggregate of men separately taken into the unity of God, one has to ask what, within the economy of the Redemption, is the principle of ecclesiastical unity through which man may enter the divine unity.

Undoubtedly the essence of the life bestowed, the unity shared in, is the spiritual reality of supernatural life: faith and hope culminating in vision, and charity. These are invisible realities, and the meaning of Church unity lies in the invisible sphere. '*Primarily,* the unity of the Church is in Scripture a unity of inward life, an invisible fact: it is in this that her essential unity primarily consists.'[50] The first meaning of 'the Unity of the Church', Father Hebert says, is 'the spiritual unity of the whole Body of Christ'.[51] I think that 'primarily' and 'first' can be misleading words. Certainly the spiritual unity of faith and love is primary in importance, and it is the reason why the visible aspects of the Church exist at all. But here on earth visible and invisible are inextricably mixed, and though visible baptism itself presupposes a right invisible disposition, nevertheless it is that visible sacrament which is the gate of entry into the Church, and that is to say into a visible unity. Moreover, the word 'Church' traditionally refers first to the visible society of Christians, the word primarily refers to that, and hence the

[48] Joint Report entitled *Relations between Anglican and Presbyterian Churches,* p. 3.
[49] E. L. Mascall, *Corpus Christi,* p. 6.
[50] Bishop Gore, *Roman Catholic Claims,* p. 30.
[51] *The Form of the Church,* p. 63.

'primary' unity of the Church would rather seem to be the visible than the invisible aspect of the one reality.

The important question here, however, is not exactly that. The question is whether the essential and quite unbreakable unity of the Church can possibly be *limited* to the invisible sphere. Some Anglican, and even Anglo-Catholic, writings would seem to imply this. An example can be found in E. C. Rich's valuable chapter on 'The Nature of the Church' in *Spiritual Authority in the Church of England* (pp. 98-112).

> 'Faith in Jesus is the act by which a believer passes into the Church.'[52] We here reach the ultimate basis of the Church's unity. For Jesus Christ is he in whom 'all things consist. And he is the Head of the Body, the Church . . . that in all things he might have pre-eminence' (Col. 2:19). For if a man does not 'hold fast the Head' (Col. 2:19) he is none of His. So it must follow that anyone who loves the Lord Jesus Christ in sincerity or uncorrupt-ness must belong to the Body (cf. Eph. 6:24). For 'no man can say Jesus is Lord, but in the Holy Spirit' (I Cor. 12:3). Therefore every-one who confesses Jesus as Lord is already a member of Christ's Body. We must recognise therefore all who profess the name of Christ as our brethren in Christ Jesus.[53]

I do not wish to deny all truth to these words by any means; nevertheless—if they be considered as in the last resort an adequate account of the Church's nature and unity—it is difficult to see how they differ essentially from pure Protestantism. The unity of the Church is seen as a unity of faith, an invisible unity; there is here no necessary unity of earthly society at all, but only the spiritual unity of those who share faith in Jesus. I feel myself that this paragraph, though given as a final conclusion to the author's study of the nature of the Church, did not fairly re-present the wholeness of his thought. The desire to express the 'ultimate basis' has driven him to a view which is clear but one-sided, with no adequate conclusion to his discussion. I do not deny at all that the hidden brotherhood of the faith is the inner mean-ing of the Church's unity; but the question is whether the essential unity of the Church can be so restricted to its invisible aspect.

[52] Quotation from H. S. Holland, *God's City*, p. 20.
[53] *Spiritual Authority in the Church of England*, pp. 110-11.

In another place Canon Rich, after summing up a sectarian view of the Church, spoke of the Roman Catholic doctrine—both are instances, for him, of failure to do justice to 'the Church's twofold nature'.

> There is also another extreme doctrine of the Church, which in effect (though not in reality) would tend to regard the two natures of the Church 'without distinction'. It applies with strict logic to the earthly representation all the characteristics that are attributable only to the Church triumphant. Because the mystical Body of Christ cannot be divided, so it is argued, the Church visible cannot be divided. Schism is then looked upon as schism *from* and not *within* the Church militant. It follows that the Church on earth remains and must always remain visibly one (pp. 99-100).

Canon Rich's solution to our problem was, then, to place the *essential* unity of the Church wholly in the invisible mystical body as contrasted with the Church visible. But does this show fidelity to the Christological counterpart? Christ's unity is not just a matter of his divine nature; it is an essential character of the whole Christ, and nothing else would make any sense at all. So it is with the Church; if unity is not a quality of the Church as such, visible or invisible, militant or triumphant, but instead 'a characteristic attributable only to the Church triumphant', what right have we to speak of both as *the* Church? Her identity is based on her unity.

The statement that 'the Church is primarily not a juridical but a spiritual or mystical reality' (p. 101), is misleading for the reasons suggested above, but the real question here is not so much one of 'primacy' between spiritual and visible, as whether the Church's essential characteristics can possibly be attributed to only one or the other.

If one places the essential unity of the *Una Sancta* entirely in the invisible nature, contrasted with a visible Church divisible into numerous different and uncommunicating societies, how can one escape a Nestorian view of the Church, an ecclesiology which has divided instead of distinguishing?

Elsewhere the same author again wrote 'we have lost our outward unity',[54] that is to say the visible unity of the Church: only

---

[51] *Spiritual Authority in the Church of England*, p. 106.

an invisible unity remains. But does not such a view fall subject
to the criticism that Anglo-Catholics themselves have made of
Protestant theology: 'Again and again the attempts of Protestants to work out a doctrine of the visible Church are hampered
by an inevitable recourse to "invisibilist" ideas'?[55] Nor was E. C.
Rich the only Anglo-Catholic to render himself liable to such a
stricture. The *Catholicity* report would seem to do the same itself.
On the one hand it tells one that the Church is a 'visible society'
(p. 12) with, therefore, a visible unity, 'the primitive unity created
by Our Lord' (p. 11); this unity the Report generally speaks of as
a 'wholeness' which it describes as 'the "wholeness" not of an
ideal but of something that *is*' (p. 17); that is to say, the unity
and visibility of the Church are not of its *bene esse* but of its
esse, required not just for its good working but for its very existence: 'the "is-ness" of the visible Church has too widely become
the missing element in the belief of Christians about their common salvation' (p. 17). 'And yet', the Report goes on to say, 'the
present state of Christendom is precisely characterised by the
loss of this "wholeness" ' (p. 17). But what is lost, *is not,* and
hence can be not a fact but only an ideal, and the whole tenor
of the Report shows it as just that—an ideal to be striven for.
To be told that the same thing is and is not, comes, I suspect,
from fear of a few scholastic distinctions. But it does illustrate
the Anglo-Catholic dilemma: forced by their Catholic theology
to maintain an existing visible unity, equally forced by their
Protestant status to deny one. The logical conclusion of their
position is surely to assert the non-existence of the Catholic
Church at the present day. In the words of the 1920 Lambeth
Appeal to all Christian People, by the Catholic Church we mean
'an outward, visible, and united society', but 'this united fellowship is not visible in the world today'.[56] This means that what we

[55] *Catholicity,* p. 43. Cf. the words of P. de Lubac: 'When we recite the Credo
we profess our belief in the Church; and if we believe that that Church is both
a universal and a visible community, then we cannot—without betrayal of our
faith—be content to grant that the universal Church is made visible and concrete
to the individual by that particular community which is his, regardless of the
separation of these communities one from another. This would only be another
way of resolving the problem of unity by appeal to an "invisible Church" ', *The
Splendour of the Church,* p. 56.
[56] Bell, *Documents on Christian Unity,* I, p. 1.

mean by the Catholic Church is not to be found in the world today.

That is a radical view, incompatible with the elementals of Catholic Christian faith, but it is the logical conclusion of the view that it is wrong to argue 'because the mystical Body of Christ cannot be divided, so the Church visible cannot be divided',[57] and of any attempt to make too radical a division between 'the empirically manifested Church now militant on earth' and 'the archetypal Church'[58] of Heaven or the Spirit.

No, the essential, unbreakable unity of the Church must be located not only in the spiritual, invisible sphere, but also in the visible, for there is not only one Spirit, but also one body.[59] The Church is visible, and her unity must be visible too. Anglicans do realise this, even if they are at times driven back to 'invisibilist' ideas. It is why E. Milner-White and W. Knox agree that 'a merely spiritual invisible unity' is not enough; they offer instead 'a visible fact' with 'adequate outward expression'[60]; T. A. Lacey maintains that 'the visible unity of the Church exists',[61] and Dr Mascall admits 'I think the Roman Church is right in insisting that the Church is a visible and not an invisible body'.[62]

Both the visible and the invisible, both the present Church and the Church triumphant must have the characteristics of unity, catholicity, holiness. There is only one Church and it is in it, as actually existing, that we express our faith. The *Una Sancta* is the vessel in which we pass through life, not just the final kingdom of the saints. The latter's unity, catholicity and holiness will be without doubt far greater and more manifest than anything to be found on earth. Certainly there is real progress to be made in these characteristics, but there is also—and it is the essential foundation for that progress—a basic element which is absolutely immutable. Christ is with the Church not only at 'the consummation of the world' but also 'all days even to the consummation

---

[57] Rich, op. cit. p. 100.
[58] Mascall, *Christ, the Christian and the Church*, p. 123, n.1.
[59] As Dean Armitage Robinson wrote 'the notion that there could be several "bodies" with a "unity of Spirit" is entirely alien to the thought of St Paul', *St Paul's Epistle to the Ephesians, An Exposition*, p. 129.
[60] *One God and Father of All*, p. 153.
[61] *Unity and Schism*, p. 136. [62] *Corpus Christi*, p. 18.

of the world'. The word *Church* has always meant primarily the visible community of the faithful, and it is of that visible community that we must first predicate unity.

For Anglicans of the Catholic Tradition, then, the problem of Church unity is indeed a difficult one: spiritual unity is not enough, while governmental unity (at least) is not to be had. They have to search for a unity which is visible but not governmental.

4. *A Unity of Race*

A word very frequently used when Anglicans of recent times have attempted to explain the ultimate, visible unity of the Church is that of 'race'. The unity of the Church is a racial, or family unity, they explain, and so it is now necessary to see just what is meant by this, and how much of truth there is in it. Let me say first that this exact idea does not seem to be a very old one, nor part of the traditional theology of the Church of England. I have the impression that it is a development of this century, and that the influence of T. A. Lacey (and also, curiously, of Harnack), is largely responsible for it. I should also note that it seems to have little importance for some Anglo-Catholic writers, for instance Bishop Gore, Father Hebert, Dr Mascall.

The Church is the New Israel, the continuation of the Old. Now the Old Israel was a chosen people, a consecrated race or family, and so the New Israel of God will be so too. Doubtless its principle of cohesion is more intimately spiritual: entry is through baptism, not by claims of blood; but still, the Church remains a family, and it is characteristic of a family that its unity survives quarrels and separations; regrettable as these are, the family continues to exist, and to be one. Brothers never cease to be brothers, kinsmen to be kinsmen: and this is a unity of the visible order. The Church is the same: she possesses a family unity of the visible order, which can survive even schism among her members.

This view of Church unity has never been more clearly stated than by T. A. Lacey in his lectures entitled 'Unity and Schism'.

The Church began as the Remnant, the true Israel. This nation, the ideal family of Abraham, had its proper unity, marked by natural birth and by the covenant of circumcision. Into this stock, says St Paul . . . are engrafted the wild olive-branches of the Gentiles. The result is an organic whole, a living unity, a work of God. As such it is in the visible order of nature. A family, a nation, is in this sense visible. It is visibly one. The nation of Israel was visibly one, the more so when the unfaithful fell away and the Remnant alone was left. There is nothing to indicate any variation of this character when the Remnant expands into the Catholic Church of Christ. It is an organic unit in the visible order of nature.

The unity of the Church appears in various metaphors, . . . but without metaphor it is the People of God. And since the nation is both historically and ideally a development of the family, so the Church is spoken of in terms of family. Its members are brothers. It seems to have been one of the earliest names by which they were known—'the Brethren'.

What is implied in Brotherhood? It is an indestructible relation. Brothers do not cease to be brothers when they are divided by a family quarrel. Nor does the family cease to be one because it is divided. An errant brother who breaks away from family ties does not cease to be a brother.[63]

In the preface of *One God and Father of All*, E. Milner-White and Wilfred Knox recommend the reading of Dr Lacey's book, and their own explanation of the unity of the Church has clearly been greatly influenced by his. 'The Church took over, just as we might expect, its view of its own unity from Judaism. The unity of the Jewish faith was founded on *race*. The Jews were an elect, a chosen *people*. . . . The new Church, born by the purpose of God in the womb of his older Church, regarded itself at once as a New Israel, a new elect *race* in the world. Its unity indeed was of a higher type than the old: the bond of blood gave way to the bond of the Holy Spirit. It is the central thought of St Paul everywhere that the unity of the Church is visible because Christians are manifestly a new race. 'Ye are an elect race,' wrote St Peter, 'a royal priesthood, a holy nation, a people for God's own possession.' Harnack in his vivid and learned *Mission and Expansion of Christianity* shows in detail that the gospel of the New Race was one of the great and pivotal preachings, along with

[63] *Unity and Schism*, pp. 139-40.

the gospel of the Resurrection and the gospel of love, of the early Christians'.[64]

These same authors consequently define the Church's 'underlying theory of unity' as *a racial consciousness*.[65] Others come back to the same basic point. Thus E. C. Rich appealed to Dr Lacey and to his idea of unity at the end of his own chapter on *The Nature of the Church*: only 'Brotherhood in Christ' can provide the ultimate basis of Church unity; 'if this is lacking, there can be no family. Brothers may and do quarrel; they may live in separation. But they still remain brothers.'[66] The important report entitled *Doctrine in the Church of England* makes the same point when it says 'This fellowship between Man and God can be otherwise described by saying that the Church is the whole company of those who share in the regenerate life. When the Church is so conceived, its unity is comparable to that of a race or people, which, while it may be divided as regards the outward organisations which condition its life, yet has a real and concrete unity underlying these divisions.'[67]

But probably the best-known statement of Church unity in terms of race is to be found in Dr Ramsey's own *The Gospel and the Catholic Church*. The present Archbishop of Canterbury is intensely preoccupied with the oneness of the Church, and on almost every page of his book speaks of 'the one, universal Church', or 'the one Body', 'the one, historical society', 'the one people of God', 'the one family' or 'the one race'. But I do not think it can be said that he analyses very exactly in what this unity finally consists. He seems to sense the difficulty of calling the Church one, visible society, though he does it at times: after all, one, visible society is just what does not exist between Catholic and Orthodox, Anglican and Protestant; the common society of these people has been broken and not mended, and it is not surprising that Dr Ramsey turns willingly to that less definite notion of a unity of race. At the conclusion of his book he writes that the Church 'is the people of God, whose unity of race con-

[64] *One God and Father of All*, pp. 150-1.
[65] Ibid. p. 152.
[66] *Spiritual Authority in the Church of England*, p. 111.
[67] *Doctrine in the Church of England*, p. 106.

tinues despite the scandal of outward division'.[68] Birth into this common race is through baptism, henceforth nothing can exclude a member provided he does not 'renounce the Spirit'.[69] Baptism is the sacrament of the Church's unity, and the type of unity baptism provides is a racial one.

The usefulness of the notion of a unity of race is evident; it seems to provide just what an Anglican theologian is looking for: something more than invisible unity, less than one of government. But is it really a satisfactory way of explaining Church unity?

It is perfectly true that the Church is 'a chosen race, a holy people', the new 'Israel of God'[70]; the question is what the unity of a people means in Christian terms. How much does it involve? By what norms is it to be interpreted? The writers whom we have considered in this chapter, and especially Dr Lacey, explain it chiefly in terms of the unity of a natural family. 'Brothers do not cease to be brothers when they are divided by a family quarrel. Nor does the family cease to be one because it is divided. . . . The Christian Church is one family, and Christians are brothers. It is a fact not an aspiration.'[71] All well and good, but if this analogy really applies and explains the nature of Church unity, then literally nothing can separate someone from the unity of the Christian Church once he has entered it, for absolutely no division can break natural brotherhood. But it is just this which is admittedly not true. Dr Lacey accepts the possibility of apostasy, of, that is to say, 'a real cleavage separating from the brotherhood those who were really brothers',[72] a 'separation from the Church'.[73] Bishop Gore also admitted 'that there is such a sin as schism which in and by itself is sufficient to unchurch a community',[74] and Archbishop Ramsey too sees that churchmen may be excluded from the family if 'they renounce the Spirit'.[75]

---

[68] *The Gospel and the Catholic Church*, p. 223. Cf. the similar statement on p. 139: 'Its unity is a unity of race, which can persist beneath all the scandals of outward division.'
[69] Op. cit. p. 139.
[70] For this I may simply refer to L. Cerfaux's most valuable study *La Théologie de l'Eglise suivant S. Paul*, especially book I, *La Théologie du Peuple de Dieu*.
[71] *Unity and Schism*, pp. 157-8.   [72] Ibid. p. 146.
[73] Ibid. p. 149.   [74] *Roman Catholic Claims*, p. 132.
[75] *The Gospel and the Catholic Church*, p. 139.

Once this is admitted, and even so tolerant a theologian as Dr Greenslade appears to see the possibility of it,[76] the strict explanation of Church unity in terms of race falls to the ground. No one can exclude himself from the unity of his natural race, but a man can exclude himself from the unity of the Church-race. What, then, is the ultimate principle of Church unity?

If the Church is to be understood as one race, the meaning of the latter must be sought in scripture and traditional Church teaching, not by comparison with some recent political 'parallel'. An example of this latter method may be found in the Report of the First Anglo-Catholic Congress (1920), which explained Church unity by comparison with the racial unity of the Polish people which survived political division between the Russian, Austrian and German empires.[77] Similarly the report entitled *Doctrine in the Church of England* says that 'even if there is division in political organisation, the unity of a race or people may find external expression in a common outlook and common practices'.[78] It surely is not necessary to point out how far removed such a conception is from the Old Testament idea of one people centred on a single temple, ruled by a single law, and led by a single priesthood?

In fact the Old and New Testament idea of a chosen people was far more than that of a race or people in the modern sense. It was that of a religious society, into which one entered not just by right of blood, but through a visible rite; a society possessing a common worship, common doctrine, a common priesthood, above all a common life. This is even clearer in the New Testament than it is in the Old. Holy nation, yes, but a holy nation forming a 'Church', 'assembly', or 'fellowship'. If we want to understand what the New Testament idea of the Church was, it is no use to take one term for it, that of 'race', and then interpret it in accordance with modern notions; we must interpret it according to the whole body of New Testament teaching about the Christian community.

Bishop Newbigin of the Church of South India summarises that teaching in the following words: 'The Church is portrayed

[76] *Schism in the Early Church*, p. 214.   [77] p. 87.   [78] p. 106.

in the New Testament as a spiritual and corporeal unity. It is both one in the sense that it is not divided, and one in the sense that it is unique. There is but one Christ and therefore there is but one Church. Outward division of the Church can only mean that Christ is divided, which is absurd.'[79]

Dr Ramsey has himself told us the same thing. 'There is no Christian community mentioned in the New Testament which has not behind it some authority responsible to a larger whole, and there is no letter in the New Testament (except the epistle to Philemon) which does not show that the local society owes obedience to someone who addresses it in the name of the larger whole.'[80] Again, 'the one universal Church is primary, the local society expresses the life and unity of the whole.'[81] Authority and obedience therefore express, and are required by, the unity of the first Christians in the Church. The unity of the New Testament Church was a unity of sacramental life lived in common under visible authority, it was not just the sort of family unity which survives 'all the scandals of outward division'. It could, of course, stand a lot of bickering, whether at Corinth or elsewhere, but not the solemn division of the fellowship.

It is clear, then, that a bare notion of racial unity is both inadequate to express recognised facts about Church unity, and unfaithful to the New Testament writers. The latter show us not just a race but a society, a fellowship actually possessing and sharing sacraments, doctrine, authority.

Anglo-Catholics themselves recognise at times the inadequacy of this view of Church unity. The latter still needs to be expressed in more positive terms—of doctrine, episcopate or sacraments: at least there must be a community of visible possessions. 'Unity of race', in fact, is not by itself a sufficient formulation of the character of Church unity; it must be expressed, explained, justified, in other terms. So E. Milner-White and W. Knox, ardent upholders of the race theory, admit that 'unity of race must be a visible fact and find adequate outward expression'.[82] That

[79] L. Newbigin in *The Reunion of the Church*, opening of chapter entitled 'The Extension of the Incarnation'.
[80] *The Gospel and the Catholic Church* p. 46.   [81] Ibid. p. 48.
[82] *One God and Father of All*, p. 153.

outward expression they find realised in the following way: 'Constantinople, Rome, and Canterbury are one in faith, one in worship, one in Holy Order, one in fruits, one in outlook and atmosphere.'[83] Whether this statement is by any means true does not matter here, the point is what it is intended to prove. If the common race meant for E. C. Rich an invisible, spiritual brotherhood, here it requires a whole multitude of common possessions, which exclude the non-episcopal churches. In what, then, does the unity of the one race subsist? In one baptism? In the common possession of the Lambeth Quadrilateral? In a common valid Eucharist? Further, is common possession, even of all the recognised elements of Catholicism, a sufficient bond for the unity of the Church?

Such questions show that we are back where we were before, and the introduction of the word 'race' has not greatly helped us. To say 'unity of the one race' is to say 'unity of the one Church', for it is agreed that the one Church is the chosen people of God. But the problem is in what precisely its unity consists, and who is consequently within it; hitherto that problem has not been greatly clarified.

5. The Organ of Unity

We have already seen in section 1 how even Anglo-Catholics are divided on the problem of the ecclesiastical status of non-episcopal bodies. Is possession of episcopacy required or not for recognition of a Christian community as a true part of the visible, Universal Church? Evidently W. Knox and E. Milner-White, when writing One God and Father of All, thought that it was, as appears from the outward expression they consider necessary for unity of race; but many Anglicans hold that this is not so, and that the ecclesiastical status of the definitely Protestant bodies resulting from the Reformation movement cannot be denied. This difference of opinion is bound to affect Anglican ideas about the real function of episcopacy. For all Anglo-Catholics it is of the esse, and other Anglicans too are agreed that it has a special function to perform in regard to unity. It is this function which

[83] One God and Father of All, p. 154.

I will now examine, and if this investigation may seem the slightest bit out of the direct line of my argument, I think nevertheless that it will throw important light upon the whole subject, and it also prepares the way for the next section on the essential elements of Catholicism.

In the very official Report on *Doctrine in the Church of England*,[84] one may read the following statement: 'We are convinced that the Anglican Communion has been right to regard the historic Episcopate as in a special sense the organ of unity and continuity' (p. 122), and again, 'the Bishop is the proper organ of unity and universality' (p. 123). Already in the seventeenth century it was held that 'the bishop is the band and ligature of the Church's unity',[85] and this notion of the bishop as the Church's organ of unity, as also of universality and continuity, is very frequently to be found in modern Anglican, and especially Anglo-Catholic, theology,[86] and the soundness of the feeling that visible unity requires some sort of an organ is surely not to be called in question. If the Church has a visible unity, it requires to be focused or centred in something, a visible landmark or institution with which the individual member may be connected. Anglican theologians have realised this need, if they are not always clear as to how it is to be met. 'It would be surprising', writes Dr Mascall,[87] 'if there were no visible organ by which the Church's unity is expressed and maintained, although that unity is not a merely moral, political or organisational unity but an inner and sacramental one.' Again, 'the Church, as a visible and tangible society, living in the historic process, needs a visible and tangible organ of its unity, though that union is, as I have emphasised, an interior and mystical unity and not a moral or political one. The Church is a visible and tangible society, but it

---

[84] One must note that this is an official report of doctrine held at the time (1938), *in* the Church of England. It does not aim to state officially the doctrine *of* the Church of England.

[85] Jeremy Taylor.

[86] One may refer, for the older generation, to Gore's description of the Episcopate as 'a bond of union' (*The Church and the Ministry*, p. 64) or to A. Robinson who held of the Episcopate that 'the very *raison d'être* of which is the preservation and the restoration of unity' (*The Vision of Unity*, p. 14). More recent writers are considered in the course of the chapter.

[87] *Corpus Christi*, p. 13.

is a sacramental one, and the organ of its unity will be a sacramental organ.'[88] Finally, 'As a visible reality in the historic order, the Church's unity is established in our Lord's institution of the Apostolate, which is continued in the universal episcopate'.[89]

Dr Mascall's position is clear. The episcopate is the adequate and effective organ of Church unity; if one asks how it can be effective in a 'divided Church', he will reply that the Church is only divided between bodies possessing the episcopal succession, and further that it is only divided from the governmental viewpoint, not sacramentally. The episcopate is a sacramental organ of unity, effective of sacramental unity. To this position I shall return in a subsequent section; here I wish to treat of those authors who agree with Dr Mascall that episcopacy is to be regarded as the organ of unity, but are not equally confident that it has proved an *effective* organ. For them it is rather a signpost towards unity, a *signum*, but not a *signum efficax*. They are driven to this by the position of the non-episcopal communions. If the episcopate is an effective organ of unity, then those who lack this organ must be outside that unity. Dr Mascall, I think, would agree that they are, but those who are not thus willing to 'un-church' the Free Churches are driven to an idea of the episcopate as an organ of Church unity, which it is not easy to clarify.

The Presbyterian theologian Dr Torrance has suggested that episcopacy is an *essential* sign of the Church's unity, but not an *effectual* one;[90] this may seem a strange view for a Presbyterian theologian, but it is not far removed from a very common Anglican one. Dr Torrance's sympathy for episcopacy is easier to understand if we remember that he has recently been a member of the Church of Scotland delegation in conversations held with the Church of England; these resulted in a joint report entitled *Relations between Anglican and Presbyterian Churches*, which proposed the establishment in the Presbyterian Church of 'Bishops-in-Presbytery' who would evidently fulfil the function

---

[88] *Corpus Christi*, p. 17.   [89] Ibid. pp. 18-19.
[90] Dr Torrance *Royal Priesthood* (Oliver & Boyd, Edinburgh, 1956); see Abbot Butler's comments in the *Downside Review*, no. 237, pp. 265-6.

of a Church unity organ. In the eyes of all Presbyterians, and at least many Anglicans, this step would not, of course, be required to bring Presbyterians within the unity of the Church (which they already are by baptism), but for Anglicans it would guarantee the value of their Holy Communion. If the last phrase sounds very vague, I can only say that I do not know how to make it more precise: 'validity' in the Catholic sense does not seem to be considered in the question. The Report states that

> Anglicans emphasise the view that the celebration of the Holy Communion is an activity of the whole Church of God in its worshipping approach to the Father, in thanksgiving and praise for the redemptive acts of the Son, in the fellowship of the Holy Spirit. It is for this reason that they think it important that the liturgical celebrant should possess (so far as is possible in a divided Christendom) the authorisation of the whole Church. Episcopal ordination is stressed because of the representative character of the bishop who is chief pastor of the local Church in the diocese and is linked, in virtue of his consecration by bishops of other sees, with the wider ministry of the Church Universal through the ages. The Holy Communion is thus regarded as essentially integrated with the ordering and continuity of the Church and of its ministry. Accordingly, on the Anglican side, full intercommunion would be impossible without raising the question of episcopacy as a thing deemed requisite for its fulfilment between the Churches, even if otherwise agreement had been reached as to doctrine and practice.[91]

The point intended here is that only episcopacy can guarantee 'the authorisation of the whole Church'; that is to say that it is the only recognised organ of the one Church. Nevertheless, in qualifying the statement with the clause 'so far as is possible in a divided Christendom', the Report admits that the existence of episcopacy is not in fact sufficient to effect this authorisation: instead of *effecting* a united Church, it is being *affected* by the condition of a divided Church.

There is great danger here of giving to episcopacy with one hand what is taken away with the other. The practice is very clearly illustrated by the report entitled *Church Relations in England*, published in 1951 as a follow-up to the Archbishop of

[91] *Relations between Anglican and Presbyterian Churches*, p. 14.

Canterbury's suggestion at Cambridge in 1946 that the Free Churches should 'take episcopacy into their system'. On the one hand episcopacy has to be demonstrated to be something of value, or why should the Free Churches bother to fit it in at all? On the other, it must be shown to have no necessary meaning, or the Free Churches will reject it as an intrusion into their quite different church system. It must be an organ of unity, or why should its acceptance be a condition for reunion? Yet its possession is not required for status within the unity of the Church, or the Free Churches would be unchurched. On the other hand, it is 'a link with the ministry of the ancient Church and an expression and safeguard of the unity of the universality of the faith', on the other it 'has not always secured or guaranteed the unity, continuity or apostolic faith of the Church, though it has borne witness to them'. Episcopacy safeguards the unity of the faith but does not guarantee this unity; it bears witness to something which it has failed to secure. Here surely is obscurity, but it is at least meant that episcopacy, if an organ of unity, is not a necessarily effective one: it does not, consequently, fulfil the real function required of the Church's organ of unity.[92]

The difficulty of fitting an organ of Church unity into a divisible and actually divided Church can be sensed most clearly if one turns to Dr Ramsey's work *The Gospel and the Catholic Church*. The unity of the one Christian society, he says, is ensured by the apostles and their successors, the bishops, who are 'the organs of the Church's unity'.[93] The latter, in apostolic as in subsequent times, was not something purely of the invisible or sacramental order; it was ensured by a whole Church structure. It is a point which Dr Ramsey, with Protestants, not Roman Catholics in view, insists on. St Ignatius's letters, he tells us, 'show an intense sense of the unity of the whole Church, in prayer and in suffering and in outward structure'.[94] 'The bishop does not have a greatness of his own, he is the organ of the one Body who represents to the Christians their dependence within the Body,

[92] See Father Maurice Bévenot's comments on the 1951 report in the notes entitled 'Church Relations in England', *The Month*, March, 1951, pp. 175-8.
[93] *The Gospel and the Catholic Church*, p. 77.
[94] Ibid. p. 78.

and to the local Church its dependence within the historic family, whose worship is one act.'[95] The episcopate is therefore of the Church's very *esse*, 'the organ of the one people of God'.[96]

It is indeed difficult to see how it can be true on the one hand that the Church is one, and this central fact about her be expressed by her outward structure, which is of her *esse* and an utterance of the gospel itself, and then on the other hand that the unity of the Church and her structure are now so divorced that the first endures while the structure is divided. How can it be admitted that the episcopate is the visible 'organ of the Church's unity' if on precisely the structural level of the episcopate the Church is divided? It is so much more tenable to see the unity of the Church as a unity of race embracing all baptised Christians, if one holds with Congregationalists and others that the Catholic structure is irrelevant to the nature of the Church. But to make the episcopate the organ of unity, and at the same time to admit a multitude of Church members unconnected with the organ seems too much. 'All who are baptised into Christ are members of his Church, and Baptism is the first mark of churchmanship. Yet the growth of all Christians into the measure of the stature of the fullness of Christ means their growth with all the saints in the unity of the one Body, and of this unity the Episcopate is the expression. It speaks of the incompleteness of every section of a divided Church, whether of those who possess the Episcopate or of those who do not.'[97] How the episcopate can express the unity of episcopal and non-episcopal Christians when division is precisely due to the latter's refusal of episcopal authorisation for their sacramental life, it is impossible to see. Either Church life requires this authorisation, and the authorisation consequently bestows a unity upon this life, in which case the episcopate may be described as the organ of Church unity; or Church life does not require this authorisation (i.e. it can exist without it), in which case what will the episcopate add? No more than an organisational unity covering up two conflicting theologies. It seems to be towards

---

[95] *The Gospel and the Catholic Church*, p. 80.
[96] Ibid. p. 84.   [97] Ibid. pp. 84-85.

this that recent Anglican efforts at reunion with Presbyterians and Methodists really tend.

The insuperable problem which Dr Ramsey tries in vain to solve is to reconcile early Christian doctrine and practice of episcopacy with the Church status of those who have rejected bishops. We have seen what he has to say about the apostolic doctrine on the unity and authority of the Church in the previous section, and we have heard speak of the views of St Ignatius, the leading writer of the sub-apostolic age. The next period brings us to St Cyprian, whose central ideas about Church order are not different from those of his predecessors. But the direction of the development seems too clear, and I can understand that Dr Ramsey is a little alarmed by it. He feels, in part rightly, that too much is being asked of the episcopate:

> While the Episcopate is essential, along with the scriptures and sacraments, to the Church's one and complete life, it may be asked whether it is legitimate to treat the episcopate as *in itself* the ground and the test of Church unity. There is in Cyprian an attempt to base unity upon episcopacy as the one and outstanding bond. But episcopacy cannot bear alone the whole weight of the tensions of controversy; and the pure Cyprianic theory seems to break when St Cyprian himself is found in an *impasse* with his brother Bishop Stephen of Rome.[98]

The answer to the *impasse* was surely to be found—and who can doubt that most Christians of the second and third centuries would find it?—in the 'greater authority' of the apostolic see.[99] The situation showed, as did the later Donatist troubles, that a simple appeal to episcopacy as such was not a *sufficient* test of Church unity. This is quite different from saying that communion with the Catholic episcopate was proved not to be a *necessary* test. Cyprian's real point is not that the episcopate *alone* bears the burden of Church unity, but that the Church's indivisibility is necessarily manifest in the episcopate. Rejection

[98] *The Gospel and the Catholic Church*, p. 151.
[99] As T. A. Lacey wrote 'Cyprian might protest, but it was none the less true that the Church of Rome had a weightier authority than any Church in Africa; The Carthaginian schismatics who appealed *ad ecclesiam principalem* were keeping fairly close to the line of Christian tradition', *Unity and Schism*, p. 40. For St Cyprian's idea of Church unity see especially Father Bévenot S.J.'s edition of *The Lapsed; The Unity of the Catholic Church*, Longmans, pp. 74-75.

of episcopal authority must mean schism from the Church, for there cannot be division on one level and unity on the other. Can we imagine St Ignatius or St Paul thinking any differently?

Church structure represents an essential part of Church life, and a breaking away from that visible structure means a breaking away from that life. But a bishop can himself break away from the Church, and bishop may be in schism from bishop. This suggests that if the episcopate can indeed be a valuable organ and expression of the visible Church's unity and communion, it cannot of itself be a fully effective one. It requires further specification. And as a matter of fact it would be difficult to find much evidence in the Fathers to suggest that episcopacy as such was ever thought to be so.

I may now sum up the perhaps rambling argument of this section by formulating a question and giving the three possible answers to it; they represent the three positions around which the discussion of this section has revolved.

If the episcopate is the organ of the Church's unity, how are the present divisions of Christendom possible?

1. The episcopate is not the effective organ of Church unity. The latter is to be found only in Baptism. Episcopacy only points towards unity in some not easily defined way.

2. The episcopate is the effective organ of Church unity. But this unity is to be found on the sacramental level, not the jurisdictional. Sacramentally the Church is one, and this unity is guaranteed for all episcopal bodies by their sacramental episcopate.

3. Not the episcopate as such but the central chair of the episcopate is the only wholly effective organ of the Church's visible unity. This unity is guaranteed by the communion of the see of St Peter which St Optatus once described as 'the chair of unity'.

6. *The Essentials of Catholicism*

Behind the disagreement as to whether or not the episcopate is an essential element of Catholicism, there is substantial agreement among Anglicans over a certain way of looking at the

nature of the Church and the requirements of Church unity.
This way may be summed up in the statement that the Church
is constituted and can be recognised by a certain number of
essential elements, which together give one Catholicism and the
Catholic Church. It they are present, the Church is present; if
they are absent so is the Church. Anglicans may disagree as to
what exactly should be included within the list of these elements,
but they do not disagree on the significance of those judged
essential. P. Congar has very well expressed this Anglican presupposition, as also the form which it normally takes, in the
following remarks: 'There is, for them, a set of realities such
as the canonical books of Holy Scripture, the ancient Creeds,
especially the Apostles' and Nicene Creeds and the Creed of St
Athanasius, the sacraments and the doctrines taught by the undivided Church, which constitute the concrete substance of the
Church.' Again, 'wherever the fundamental realities of the undivided and apostolic Church are held, there is the Church'.[100]
Where the essentials of Catholicism are to be found, there the
Church exists; further, these essentials are normally understood
as equivalent to the 'Lambeth Quadrilateral', which is held to
represent the decisive characteristics of the ancient, undivided
Church. As we already know, the Lambeth Quadrilateral remains
deliberately vague on the subject of the ministry.

Recently Dr Greenslade has called for 'a reconsideration of the
whole problem of schism', of which the 'starting-point is not in
the question: has this body left the Church? But rather in the
question: has it sufficiently the marks and essentials of the
Church to be recognised as part of it?'[101] Dr Greenslade is theologically far removed from Dom Gregory Dix or Dr Mascall, but
on this way of viewing the problem of Church unity they are
agreed. Dom Gregory asked of the Church of England, 'The
question really is: were the essentials there in the system which
Parker and Guest and the others felt obliged to accept? That is
a much wider question than Anglican orders, and I am not going
into it now. But I cannot see that they were not. And if they

[100] Congar, *Divided Christendom*, pp. 169-70, 173.
[101] *Schism in the Early Church*, p. 201.

were, then for three centuries the Church of England taught the essentials of the Catholic Faith and ministered the essential Catholic Sacraments.'[102] Dr Mascall has expressed himself in the following way with the Church of South India in mind: 'It needs to be emphatically asserted that a body which possesses all the essentials of Catholicism, whether it is vigorous or weak, whether it is fervent or corrupt, is a branch of the Holy Catholic Church, and its members are members of the Holy Catholic Church in the full and unqualified sense.'[103] How obviously true this sounds! Yet I believe it to be deeply misleading, being based on a confusion between what *characterises* and what *constitutes* the Church.

High Church ecclesiology differs from Low Church views and from Protestant doctrine in general by the number of necessary characteristics which it attaches to the Church—Anglo-Catholics having the fullest idea of the structure of the Church and of what is required for her unity. When Anglicans criticise one another in these matters, it is often for neglecting one or other of the necessary constituents of Catholicism—or, alternatively, for adding to them without justification, but both sides are agreed that Catholic unity can be guaranteed by the possession of a number of things. It is the Anglican Papalist who has gone furthest on this road of thought. I have seen it asked by one how it is possible not to be a Catholic when one believes absolutely everything that the Roman Church believes, including Papal Infallibility and Indulgences, and when one even receives communion in only one kind! Catholicism is thus understood as a vast collection of beliefs and practices, whereas in fact it is the living membership of a visible society.

I am of the opinion that with this idea we have reached the deepest common idea to be found in Anglican ecclesiology: the unity of the Church consists in the unity of common possessions. It is the justification of every form of the branch theory: 'Constantinople, Rome, and Canterbury are one in faith, one in worship, one in Holy Order, one in fruits, one in outlook and

---

[102] *The Question of Anglican Orders*, p. 91.
[103] E. L. Mascall, *The Convocations and South India*, p. 12.

atmosphere.'[104] The clearest statement of it which I have come across is to be found in the following words of the late A. S. Duncan Jones, Dean of Chichester. He wrote of 'the Anglican Churches' that 'their unity is not the result of subjection to an authority, but the fact that they are identical in kind'.[105] In this remark the Dean of Chichester, after rightly maintaining that a purely authoritarian idea of Church unity is inadequate, put forward this other, still more inadequate: a conception which is material rather than formal, one of common, identical possessions, heedless of the community which must possess them. Inevitably, as we shall subsequently see, such a conception makes the traditional Catholic conception of schism entirely meaningless. The 'essentials of Catholicism'—Creeds, orders, sacraments, scriptures—can be found equally well on both sides of a schism, as for instance in the case of Donatism. On the principle of Church unity as identity in kind the Donatist community ought certainly to be recognised as 'a branch of the Holy Catholic Church' in the full and unqualified sense.

In 1867 The Theological Commission of Canterbury Convocation stated: 'Intercommunion must be interpreted as mutual acknowledgement that all Churches which are one in the possession of a true episcopate, one in sacraments, and one in creed, are by this union in their common Lord, bound to receive one another to full communion in prayers and sacraments as members of the same household of Faith.' Here again we find the view that Christian communities fulfilling certain objective requirements have simply to be *acknowledged* as integral parts of the One Church. The intercommunion, which ought to follow, is not understood as essential to unity, but as the due consequence of a unity already existing through the common possession of creed, sacraments, episcopate.

The weakness of this view of the Church's unity is that it does not agree with the traditional Catholic and Christian doctrine of the Church as a visible fellowship with a traceable continuity

[104] W. Knox and E. Milner-White, *One God and Father of All*, p. 154.
[105] *Ecumenica*, March 1934, p. 33-34, quoted by Fr Congar, *Divided Christendom*, p. 194.

of life and authority. Certainly holders of this view do still stress the importance of a visible continuity: [106] a continuity in structure resulting in what Manning, as an Anglican, called 'objective unity'. It is strange that Anglo-Catholics who so much criticise 'institutionalism' really arrive at a highly institutional view of Church unity: a unity maintained by the possession of certain objective realities, and chiefly the institution of the episcopate.

It was, perhaps, to balance this weight laid on the purely 'objective', almost non-human, side of Church unity that the notion of continuity of race was developed, and the two ideas can best be seen together. 'The unity of a race or people may find external expression in a common outlook and common practices' says the report on *Doctrine in the Church of England*:[107] a race may be divided politically, but it continues to be one race because of its common possession of certain race characteristics, culture, language. The race is the body of which the common possessions are the structural bones. Each provides a type of continuity and a certain degree of unity. What they fail to provide is either a note of continuity or one of unity compatible with Catholic tradition: a continuity of Catholic authorisation, a unity of fellowship. Only within that unity of fellowship can there be a full unity of alikeness or common possessions; but some, even a very large measure of, similarity can either survive rupture from the one society, or come to be shared by a group which has never (as a group) belonged to it at all. Such similarity, though it will always follow from the true unity of the one *koinonia* of the Christian Church, can never of itself constitute it, and a theory identifying the two must always fall down when faced with the traditional idea of schism.

The fundamental fallacy here is very clear. It derives from a certain sleight of hand between the contrasting 'Cyprianic' and 'Augustinian' views of the relationship of Church and sacraments. On the latter view valid sacraments (including the objective institution of the episcopate and an ordinational continuity of apostolic succession) can exist in more than one visible

[106] Cf. H. Burn-Murdoch, *Church, Continuity and Unity*, Cambridge, 1945.
[107] p. 106.

communion, that is to say outside the visible Church. Accepting this view, Anglo-Catholics maintain the validity of their orders as well as those of Roman Catholics. But then, in asserting ecclesiological significance for the Church of England because of the objective possession of episcopacy, they are quietly returning to a Cyprianic view of things. The fallacy is evident. Either (in Augustinian fashion) the possession of episcopacy does not guarantee Church status, or (in Cyprianic fashion) the possession of episcopacy can be claimed only after proof of Church status has been made. This very important point will be treated more fully in the next chapter.

We cannot build the Church by joining together various elements which do in fact belong to her, even though we obtain them in good faith and authentically. The Church is not the sum of her characteristics but the unique historical visible society which possesses them and has always possessed them. If another society comes to possess some of them, it does not thereby become the Church, or part of the Church; it can arrive at a state when it should indeed be received into the Church, but not recognised or acknowledged as being already within. The crucial difference here is between recognition and admission.

The point is that the Church, having been founded in a certain way by Christ, has of course a nature, an intelligible character, of which one can obtain an exact idea. But the acceptance of this idea by a community as its own ideal of life is not the same thing as entering the One Church. 'There is a world of difference between the *idea* of a Church and the *fact* of *the* Church' writes Abbot Butler,[108] and one might add that there is still a world of difference between the *idea* of *the* Church and the *fact* of *the* Church. But ideas are always more easy to accept than facts.

7. *The Nature of Schism*

'Schisma autem est contra ecclesiasticam unitatem.'[109] Schism is opposed to the unity of the Church. Consequently any study of Church unity must also be concerned with the exact nature

---

[108] In *The Spirit of Unity*, Blackfriars Publications, p. 11.
[109] St Thomas, *Summa Theologica*, II-II, Q. 39, a. 2.

of schism. What is a schism? What effect does it have? What historical divisions among Christians can truly be called schisms? We shall find that, roughly speaking, two answers are given as to the nature and effects of schism, one Catholic and Orthodox, one Protestant and Anglican. Nevertheless all Anglicans are not precisely agreed among themselves as to the meaning and applicability of the term. A Joint Committee of Convocations in 1955 spoke of the 'theological ambiguities attaching to the word "schism" ',[110] and these ambiguities are certainly to be found within Anglican writing.

Even Anglo-Catholics, for example, are not agreed as to whether the act of the four Anglican dioceses which entered the Church of South India, thereby at the time leaving the communion of the Church of England, did or did not constitute a schism. Dr Mascall has written that 'a method which involves, as a preliminary to future unity the secession of four dioceses from the Anglican Communion is a method which seeks for unity at the price of schism, and falls under the condemnation which moral theology passes upon those who do evil that good may come'.[111] But it may be asked what absolute value the Anglican communion may be supposed to have theologically, that secession from it can entail schism; as Mr David Chellappa has written, not irrelevantly, 'even the Anglican Church is not a Dominical foundation or of universal necessity'.[112] Mr. Donald Rea, for his part, believes 'it would be wrong to regard the Anglican bishops now working in C.S.I. as "schismatic" or "seceding" '.[113]

In this disagreement Mr Rea, I feel fairly sure, is expressing the normal Anglican view, while Dr Mascall is trying to salvage a Catholic concept of schism in an Anglican sea. How different Anglican and Catholic concepts of schism are, we shall presently see, and I cannot find that Dr Mascall has much success in his attempt to remain a Catholic on this subject. Another instance of disagreement may be found in Father Hebert's remark that

---

[110] Quoted in E. Mascall *The Convocations and South India*, p. 13, n. 1.
[111] E. Mascall, *The Convocations and South India*, p. 5.
[112] 'I believe in the C.S.I.—Reflections of an ex-Anglican', *Theology*, 1954, p. 252. [113] *The C.S.I. and the Church*, p. 34.

'we are all in schism';[114] this again would seem to be normal Anglican theology, the report on *Doctrine in the Church of England* saying quite the same, while the Anglo-Catholic report *Catholicity* speaks of 'the healing of schism in the Church at large'.[115] Dr Mascall on the other hand condemns as 'slipshod' the 'view that, because of the divisions between Christians, we are all equally in schism'.[116]

At the beginning of a discussion on schism, it is certainly necessary to make some distinctions. If a schism is a division among Christians, it is not *any* division, and I think that the best way to start the examination of just what it is, is by listing four ways in which Christians may be divided.

1. Legitimate divisions within the Church: 'there are divisions, articulations, which do not destroy unity, but are rather needed for its perfection';[117] of this kind are divisions of rite, language, religious order, etc. No one suggests that these constitute schisms.

2. Harmful divisions within the Church, quarrels of all sorts among Christians; these divisions do not as such involve the breaking of ecclesiastical fellowship, but tend towards it.

3. The definite breaking of ecclesiastical communion between people who still claim on both sides to be Christians.

4. The total rejection of Christ and his Church by a Christian or a group of Christians: apostasy.

No one, I think, will dispute the existence of categories 1 and 2: there are rightful divisions in the Church, and there are also harmful and sinful ones, feuds, quarrels of all sorts, failures to practise charity. Again, few will question category 4. A Christian may give up his faith, reject both Christ and his Church, apostatise; this act will separate him from the unity of the Church, Christ's mystical Body.

The controversial question is the division between category 2 and category 3. Sociologically, it cannot be disputed that there is a difference. In one case Christians quarrel among themselves

---

[114] *Intercommunion*, p. 104.   [115] *Catholicity*, p. 54.
[116] *The Convocations and South India*, p. 12.
[117] Lacey, *Unity and Schism*, p. 5.

as men, but because they continue to worship in the same Church, admit the existence of the same authority, communicate from a common altar, they are not divided precisely as Christians. In the second case their separation has entered the very practice of religion. They have separate altars, separate authorities, they will not communicate one with another.

Is the difference here not only sociological but also ecclesiological? Does it not only imply a graver sin to cause so serious a division, but also result in a changed status? Catholics believe that the first type of division is one within the Church, but that the second type separates one or other group from the Church. It has become a division *from*, not a division *in*. Only this second type (category 3 above) do we call by the name of schism.

It should immediately be noted that this is not the New Testament idea of Schism. The word 'Schism' ($\sigma\chi\iota\sigma\mu\alpha$) appears only three times in the New Testament in a Church context; all three cases are to be found in I Corinthians (1:10; 11:18; 12:25). Each time there is question of a quarrel or division within the Christian community, not breaking the unity of the one communion but the harmony and charity which ought to exist between all Christian men.[118] Early Christian writers such as Clement of Rome and Ignatius of Antioch continued to use the term 'schism' in this sense. It is essential to distinguish clearly in this question between words and the realities represented by words. St Paul and the Apostolic Fathers meant by 'schism' a division within the Church,[119] modern Catholics mean by 'schism' a division separating from the Church. Are the latter, then, not faithful to the former? This difference of terminology as such implies no infidelity to scripture or tradition, because the same term has come to be used in connection with a different sort of situation, and necessarily therefore also with a different meaning. St Paul had not to consider the situation of a broken communion, but

[118] See J. Dupont, 'Le Schisme d'après Saint Paul', in *L'Eglise et les Eglises*, I, pp. 111-27.
[119] But the Early Fathers were fully aware of the possibility of a man being separated from the Church, and they knew too that a rent within the Church could quickly lead to such separation from her.

only that of quarrelling within the one communion. Hence, because the divisions which he called schism could exist within the one Church, it does not follow that the divisions which we call schisms also exist within the Church. To settle that problem we must consider more than the terminology of antiquity; we have to consider its treatment of the situation which we call by the name of schism, and that consideration will show us that the mind of antiquity is quite contrary to the idea that schisms (in the modern sense) exist within the body of the Church.

Catholic doctrine, then, distinguishes clearly between categories 2 and 3 (as listed above). It also distinguishes clearly between categories 3 and 4. That is to say that we recognise the possibility of the separation of believing Christians from the visible unity of the Church. Schism cannot be equated with apostasy.

The chief characteristic of most Anglican thought in this matter is the refusal to recognise the separateness of category 3. Either schism involves apostasy, and separates from the Church on account of a denial of Christ; or it does not involve apostasy, in which case it exists within the Church, like any other quarrel among Christians. Thus Father Hebert denies 'any difference in kind between a quarrel of two neighbours and a schism between two churches'.[120] Dr Lacey sums up the whole position quite clearly:

> It is not every heresy or schism that cuts men off from the Church, it is that only which proceeds to apostasy, to the denial of the Name of Christ. We may now see our way out of a theological difficulty. We shall no longer be puzzled to understand how some schismatics can be acting within the Church while others are said to be excluded from the Church. There is a real difference. We shall be rescued from the impossible absurdity of saying that there are some Christians who are not members of the Christian Church. What is a Christian but one who is in Christ, a member of Christ's Body? To schismatics who are apostate we must refuse the name of Christian; in act, if not in word, they themselves refuse it. Schismatics who confess Christ must, on the other hand, be included within the Church.[121]

[120] *The Form of the Church*, p. 63.
[121] Dr Lacey, *Unity and Schism*, pp. 149-50.

It is, here, well to remind ourselves that this is only the necessary and logical conclusion of explaining Church unity simply in terms of race or identity in kind. A race continues to exist even if divided into several societies and ruled by separate governments. If the Christian Church is similarly divided, say Anglicans, a state of schism does indeed exist; it is a deplorable state, but not one destructive of the Church's fundamental unity which is racial and extends beyond the divisions of schism. The same conclusion is arrived at if Church unity is considered in terms of identity in kind. Intercommunion should follow upon such unity, but if through human weakness it fails to do so, the unity of identity still remains. Schism breaks intercommunion, but it does not affect identity: consequently it can co-exist with Church unity.

The most authoritative statement of the Anglican conception of schism is probably to be found in the following passage from the report on *Doctrine in the Church of England.*

> The term 'schism' has historically been used with some fluctuation of meaning. It should, however, be recognised that 'schism' is, in fact, a division within the Christian Body. That Body is not to be thought of as consisting of a single true Church, or group of Churches, with a number of 'schismatic' bodies gathered about it, but as a whole which is in a state of division or 'schism'. The various 'denominations' may and do differ in respect of the degree in which they approximate either to orthodoxy of doctrine or to fulness of organised life; but, just in so far as their very existence as separate organisations constitutes a real division within Christendom, it becomes true to affirm that if any are in schism, all are in schism, so long as the breaches remain unhealed, and are affected by its consequences, at least in the sense that each in its own degree suffers the loss or defect involved in schisms; and this irrespective of the question on which side rests the major responsibility for the schism.[122]

This notion of schism as a lasting division between parts of the Church is an essential of Anglican theology. Without it, it is impossible to justify any form of 'branch theory'; moreover it naturally follows from the interpretations of Church unity

[122] *Doctrine in the Church of England*, p. 112.

already examined. It is also the basis for that notion of the divisibility of the Church, which, as I pointed out early in this book, is the cardinal doctrine of Anglicanism. But here, as elsewhere, a difference of opinion is to be noted. It derives from the old issue—the status of non-episcopalians in contrast with the episcopal communions. Those who place the unity of the Church firmly in baptism and (or) faith, seeing the Church as the family or race of the faithful baptised, of course accept all professing Christians as members of the Church. Basing themselves on this, some will therefore hold that if all are not in communion with one another, all are equally in schism. Others, such as Dr Ramsey, while refusing to un-church Free-Churchmen, still hold episcopacy to be of the *esse* of the Church; consequently, if all Christians suffer from the schisms existing within the Church, some will suffer more than others because their possession of the essentials of Catholic life is less complete: all do not equally 'approximate either to orthodoxy of doctrine or to fulness of organised life'.[123]

However, the stricter group of Anglo-Catholics, as we know, are not prepared to admit all Protestants as members of the visible Church. Episcopacy is an essential of Church life, and consequently those who do not possess it cannot be said to be within the visible Church. Hence they continue to recognise the possibility of a schism which can divide professing Christians from the Church. Without further specification Dr Mascall speaks of 'the slipshod view that all divisions between Christians are divisions within the Church'.[124] Dr Gore has an important chapter on this in his *Roman Catholic Claims,* in which he distinguishes between a breach of communion within the Church and schism from the Church. The first also may be called schism, and hence we have the possibility of schism both *in* the Church and *from* the Church. This view, instead of fusing category 3 above in part with category 2 and in part with 4, divides it into two independent sections of their own. As a result we have the gradation:

[123] *Doctrine in the Church of England,* p. 112.
[124] *The Convocations and South India,* p. 12.

1. Legitimate Church divisions.
2. Harmful divisions not involving a break in communion.
3. Breaches of communion within the Church.
4. Breaches of communion separating Christians from the Church.
5. Apostasy.

Dr Gore defines schism in the sense of No. 4 as 'wilful self-withdrawal from the legitimate succession of the Catholic Church on the part of an individual or party'.[125] He sums up his whole position in the following words:

> We have established hitherto two principles: that there is such a sin as schism which in and by itself is sufficient to unchurch a community; and, secondly, that short of this, there is such a thing as a breach of communion *in* the Church, which is due to the 'old leaven' working in her—the temper of schism militating against the temper of love. A little consideration and reading will show that the separation of East and West and the separation of England and Rome were not due to conduct which constitutes schism in the primary sense of the term—not, that is, to self-withdrawal from the Church Catholic; but that they *were* due to that temper of schism which is always at work and, like sin in any shape, mars the manifestation of God in the Church at large.[126]

Dr Gore and Dr Mascall presumably hold the Free Churches to be in strict schism, that is to say outside the visible Church. The reason being that they have abandoned 'the legitimate succession of the Catholic Church' (i.e. the episcopate), an essential of Church life. Not possessing one of the essentials of Catholicism, they lack that identity in kind which is the condition of Church unity. Rome, Canterbury, and Constantinople, on the contrary, possess these essentials and are therefore not in schism, but the temper of schism working within them has caused a breach of communion.

We can, then, distinguish two main groups of Anglican theologians. One group agrees with Catholics in equating schism with a breach of communion, but places this breach firmly within the Church; the other group agrees with Catholics that schism excludes from the Church, but refuses to equate it as such

---

[125] *Roman Catholic Claims*. p 126.   [126] Ibid. pp. 132-3.

with a breach of communion. What is common to all Anglican writers is the refusal to equate Church unity with communion, from which schism (breach of communion) excludes one, and the great question is: what can justify refusal to accept this perennial Christian belief? The chief argument used against it would seem to be that it is irreconcilable with the facts of Church History. R. P. C. Hanson, for instance, wrote recently in criticism of a Catholic work on the Church:

> The theory that Christ's visible Church can only be a single institution was gravely shaken by the Monophysite controversy, rendered very precarious by the rift between East and West in the eleventh century, and (we cannot help believing) proved utterly untenable even on Roman Catholic principles, over a century before the Reformation, by the great schism of 1378-1414. This was surely, even by Roman Catholic standards, the division of the indivisible.[127]

I agree that the Great Schism of the West presents a situation over which Catholic theologians must ponder. If the unity of the Church is an always existent unity, then it existed in all the crises of history, and consequently it is certainly fair to examine such crises to see what Church unity can, and what it cannot, involve. Another historical situation which, Anglicans argue, invalidates the Catholic theory of a Church unity of communion is that of the fourth century schism of Antioch, when Meletius and his successor Flavian, recognised for years by St Basil and most of the East as bishops of Antioch, were not acknowledged by Rome and the West, which recognised instead their rival Paulinus. This has always been regarded as a test case. Dr Greenslade sums up the situation as follows:

> It is of considerable importance to observe that East and West, though divided over Antioch, were not *en bloc* out of communion with each other. Mediate communion was possible. Basil seems to have been in communion with both Athanasius and Meletius, though Athanasius was in communion with Paulinus. From 382 Nectarius was in communion with Damasus and Flavian, while Damasus accepted the communion of Nectarius and Paulinus.[128]

---

[127] 'A Modern Defense of Infallibility', in *Theology*, 1954, p. 380.
[128] *Schism in the Early Church*, p. 165.

F. W. Puller, in *The Primitive Saints and the See of Rome*, made of this case the cornerstone of his criticism of the view that communion with Rome is a requisite of Church membership. Dr Gore also is agreed that it 'illustrates an important principle—that there can be schism *in* the Church, as well as schism *from* the Church—a schism in the Church leaving both separated parties within the communion of the Church Catholic'.[129] That is to say that the schism of Antioch, the Great Schism of the West and perhaps other historical divisions make it impossible to hold the view that a definite and prolonged breach of communion between two churches, even if one of them be Rome, necessarily involves separation of one or the other party from the Church.

I do not see how the mere fact of a schism can shake this view, as Dr Hanson seems to think. Only if one sets out with the principle that no considerable number of Christians can exist outside the visible Church, can one use divisions like that of the Monophysites as an argument against the Catholic view; but that is to abandon the Catholic view in advance. Historical facts can only be brought as arguments against the traditional conceptions of the Church if they do not seem reconcilable with them. Now the only facts of which such a thing might be able to be said are these two—the Meletian schism of Antioch and the Great Schism of the West. For this reason these two cases are examined in detail in chapter VIII where, I believe, it is clearly shown that neither is in any way incompatible with Catholic ecclesiology. Furthermore one is very ill-documented, and they are both exceptionally confused moments of Christian history. It is reasonable to demand that they be shown to be not incompatible with our theology of the Church; it is not reasonable to build a new ecclesiology upon their supposed interpretation, an ecclesiology moreover in contradiction to the perennial practice of Catholicism. Faced with the fact of the Tudor ecclesiastical revolution, a political action more easily justifiable in terms of a thorough-going Protestant 'invisibilist' theology out of bounds for most Anglicans, the latter have had to defend

[129] *Roman Catholic Claims*, p. 129.

the subsequent position of the Anglican Church by a rejection
of the central ecclesiological affirmation of all Christendom prior
to the sixteenth century, one still held to by both Rome and the
East, and to appeal in self-defence to the strained interpretation
of such obscure situations as that of the Church of Antioch in
Arian times.

On this fundamental issue—is the unity of the Church the
unity of a communion, or can there be a number of separate
communions within the one Church?—Anglicans have indeed
a great weight of authority against them. For if we are not to
be ruled in our conception of the Church by purely personal
preferences, and if we have ruled out the authority of the 'Living
Voice', what authority other than antiquity have we to recognise? What judge to set over us? Antiquity indeed is the court
to which Anglicans have frequently appealed as the authority
which can substantiate the justness of their position. Thus E. C.
Rich claimed that 'the alternative to Protestant ecclesiology is
not the ultramontane Roman but the Scriptural and the Catholic,
and that is the doctrine which the Church of England has tried
to follow out'.[130] In this claim that Anglican ecclesiology represents the scriptural and primitive view, Canon Rich was only
echoing many another Anglican writer. Wilfred Knox and E.
Milner-White wrote: 'It is important to explain how the unity
of the Church is viewed in Scripture, for until clearer guidance
than the writings of the Apostles is vouchsafed, the Anglican
theory of unity is based on it and follows it.'[131] Again, Bishop
Gore maintained that 'the primary sense of Church unity, as
taught in Scripture and held by the Fathers' was such that 'it
covers our position and enables us to give a rational account of
it'.[132] Such statements could doubtless be multiplied almost
indefinitely.

What, then, has antiquity to tell us about the unity of the
Church and the nature of schism? In scripture we find the seed
bed of Catholic ecclesiology: an awareness of the Church as a

[130] *Spiritual Authority in the Church of England*, p. 101.
[131] *One God and Father of All*, p. 150.
[132] *Roman Catholic Claims*, p. 26. Similarly Dr Mascall appeals to the 'primitive and Catholic doctrine of the Church', *Corpus Christi*, p. 38.

single community, at once visible and invisible, the Church at Corinth or at Rome, but primarily the Church of God, the Body of Christ. It was for later generations to work out the corollaries, but the essentials are already clear in the New Testament. 'Primitive Christianity,' wrote Dr Swete,[133] 'recognised no invisible Church on earth as distinct from the visible society of the baptised; no self-governing power in the local congregation apart from the authority of the whole Body of Christ; no assured gifts of grace outside the Catholic communion.' The most complete, scholarly, and recent study of the idea of schism in the early Church is that of Dr Greenslade, and his conclusions are the more reliable in that they are in complete agreement with those of numerous other scholars; several of these I have already mentioned, to them I should add in particular the name of C. H. Turner. These conclusions are historically indisputable.

> We must always be mindful, [writes Dr Greenslade], that the Fathers, together with most early heretics and schismatics, were substantially agreed upon certain principles regarding the unity of the Church. It was held on biblical grounds not simply that the Church ought to be one, but that it is one, and cannot but be one. This unity was predicated of the visible Church, and the visible Church was thought of organically as one structure, one communion. To their minds divisions, breaches of communion, were not embraced and overcome by a spiritual and invisible unity, nor could a number of denominations aggregate into one Church. There was but one visible Church in one communion; bodies separated from that communion were outside the Church. . . . In such controversies as the Novationist and Donatist, each side believed itself to be the true and only Church. Schism was not inside the Church, and transcended by a higher unity.[134]

Elsewhere the same author remarks that

> there is a vital difference between the surrender of one communion to another, on the ground that the latter alone is the Church of Christ, and the reunion of sundered parts of the Church. In the second case, as we know today, the thorniest problem is commonly to agree upon a mutual recognition of ministries, or, where this is impossible, to settle what remains to be done in order to achieve

[133] In the preface to *Essays on the Early History of the Church and the Ministry*, ed. H. B. Swete, 1921, pp. xii-xiii.
[134] *Schism in the Early Church*, p. 18.

a unified ministry. The early Church, like Rome and Orthodoxy now, assumed that recognisably schismatic bodies had departed from the Church and must return to it. It was therefore legitimate for the Church to impose terms.[135]

Dr Greenslade is not perturbed by his historical conclusions; he knows what Christian antiquity believed about the unity of the Church, but he does not find it satisfactory. Far from appealing to antiquity, he appeals away from it to a 'reconsideration of the whole problem of schism',[136] for he finds 'the thought of the early Church' to be 'open to much objection'.[137] But how can one dream of reuniting Christians on a theological basis of one's own construction? Such a position is at least a rejection of the traditional Anglican claim to find support in antiquity, for let us be quite clear that what is involved in such a position is not simply the rejection of Cyprian's views or Augustine's but the basic conception of the Church as it was accepted by all the ancient Fathers, and by the chief schismatic bodies as well—Donatist, Novationist, as well as Catholic, Cyprian as well as Augustine, Rome as well as Africa, East as well as West, all were agreed about this. Here indeed is a principle to which the Vincentian Canon—always so dear to Anglican hearts—could be applied: *Quod ubique, quod semper, quod ab omnibus traditum est.* Such is the constant teaching of Catholicism, a doctrine implied in the Archbishop of York's warning to the Parliament of 1559; to pass the Royal Supremacy Bill, he said, would be 'to forsake and fly *from* the unity of Christ's Church'. What Catholic principle is to be invoked to show that the effects of the Anglican schism were not of such a kind?

8. *Sacramental Unity*

Frequently in the course of this study I have had occasion to refer to the views of Dr Mascall, but in this section I propose to consider them as a consistent whole because they seem to me to represent the most thorough-going attempt to avoid the inconveniences to be found in every Anglican formulation of what the Catholic Church is. Perhaps, too, his theology represents the

---

[135] *Schism in the Early Church*, p. 147.
[136] Ibid. p. 201.   [137] Ibid. p. 213.

nearest an Anglican can genuinely come to a Catholic view of the Church, and it is therefore by contrasting it with our own that one may see most precisely the exact and necessary dividing line between Catholic and Anglican ecclesiology.[138]

Let me begin with a statement of Dr Mascall's intentions. 'I think that if we inquire how it is possible to maintain that the Church is one when we believe that it is neither purely invisible nor, on the other hand, a mere unity of organisation, we may be led to a more profound understanding of the unity of the Church than we should otherwise have had.'[139] Here we find a clear statement of that Anglican approach which I have been investigating throughout: the search for a Church unity which is visible but not one of mere organisation. Dr Mascall undertakes that search with a more Catholic outlook than most of his colleagues. He is quite clear, for instance, about the nature of the sacraments, especially the Eucharist, about the meaning of sacramental validity, the necessity of Orders. Far more than most of the other writers I have been considering, his inspiration has been found inside the Catholic theological tradition.

In the Foreword to *Corpus Christi* Dr Mascall tells us that the subsequent essays are 'dominated by one overarching conception, the conception of the Church as a reality of the sacramental order, the Mystical Body of Christ, preserved and nourished by the Sacrament of the Lord's Body and Blood'.[140] To this initial definition of the Church, for we may take it broadly as such, there may be added two others: 'As a fully operative reality in the historical order, it is the Catholic Church that is the organism in which men, by sacramental incorporation into Christ, are elevated in to the life of the Holy Trinity and, by the Sacrament of the Eucharist, are maintained therein.'[141] 'The Church has many functions *in* society, but it can never become a mere function *of* society, for it *is* a society—the Society of God, the life of

---

[138] Dr Mascall's views are not, of course, entirely peculiar to himself. A similar approach may be found in two remarkable essays, one by Dr A. Farrer entitled 'Eucharist and Church in the New Testament', the other by Dom Gregory Dix 'The Idea of "The Church" in the Primitive Liturgies', both printed in the book of essays entitled *The Parish Communion*, edited by A. G Hebert (S.P.C.K., 1937).   [139] *Corpus Christi*, p. 2.
[140] Ibid. p. ix.   [141] Ibid. p. 12.

the Holy Trinity communicated to men. Before the Church teaches, it lives; and before it teaches about society it lives as a society, as the supernatural and sacramental society that it is.'[142]

The Church is, then, 'a reality of the sacramental order', a 'sacramental society'. This is the key idea of Dr Mascall's ecclesiology, that is to say of what he believes to be the 'primitive and Catholic doctrine of the Church'.[143] The Church's nature and unity on this earth is to be explained, not in purely invisible terms of faith and love, nor in governmental or jurisdictional terms, but by means of the sacraments, and especially baptism, the Eucharist, Holy Orders. This is a noble conception and in great part a true one. Too often the sacraments have been left aside as almost irrelevant to a discussion about the Church. In fact the latter is meaningless without them; the delicate joining of visible and invisible, they represent the most characteristic element of the Christian economy.

Dr Mascall sees the Church as a sacramental society, that is to say a society which exists by the effective force of the sacraments which constitute it. The sacraments, validly and properly received, unite one to Christ, and at the same time, by the very force of their being, unite one to all other members of the Church. It is clear that men may be divided from one point of view, united according to another; thus they can be members of one family society, but divided in their political society, or contrariwise. Church unity too does not guarantee complete unity, even from the religious viewpoint; thus it does not guarantee 'a moral or political' unity,[144] but only a spiritual unity present within a sacramental one. The Eucharist, above all, is 'the sacrament of unity', and every sacrament is an efficacious sign, not just a pointer; consequently it effects what it signifies, and the Eucharist actually unifies those who possess it. Consequently Christians, possessing in sincerity a valid Eucharist, may be divided in all sorts of ways, but they nevertheless retain their strictly sacramental society. They remain joined together on this essentially religious, Christian, sacramental level by their common participation in the Eucharist of the Lord.

[142] *Corpus Christi*, p. 45-46.   [143] Ibid. p. 38.   [144] Ibid. p. 17.

Incorporation into this society is made through the sacrament of Baptism; by it one becomes a member of the visible Church. But Baptism alone is not the sufficient effective sign of membership, a baptised Christian may fall into schism, and Dr Mascall recognises that there are Christians outside the Church.[145] The effective sacrament of unity is therefore, not baptism but the Eucharist; it is this which 'maintains' Christians in the Church[146] and is consequently causative of the Church's unity: '*Because the Bread is one, we being many are one body, for we all partake of the one Bread.*'[147] The Eucharist, then, is far more than an expression of the Church's unity; it is its very cause. It is possible to be such on account of its strictly supernatural character as instituted by Christ, and as carried out by consecrated priests. The existence of the Eucharist depends on the existence of Holy Orders, and where these are lacking a valid Eucharist is also bound to be lacking; and that means the absence of the effective cause of Church unity.[148] Holy Orders themselves depend on the episcopate:

> The sacramental functions of the presbyterate are limited and partial, and nowhere in Catholic Christendom has the bishop abandoned his status as the sole minister who can sacramentally delegate, even partially, the apostolic character to others. Every presbyter has received his partial apostolate from the hands of the bishop in the sacramental rite of ordination; while the bishop himself has received his full apostolate from other bishops who together represent the apostolate of the universal Church.[149]

On the episcopate depends Holy Orders, on Holy Orders depends the Eucharist, and the Eucharist is the effective cause of the unity of the Church, maintaining the unity of this sacramental society. Consequently where the episcopate is lacking, so also is the unity of the Church. The episcopate is therefore to be regarded as 'the organ of the Church's unity'.[150] As 'a reality

---

[145] *The Convocations of South India*, p. 12.   [146] *Corpus Christi*, p. 12.
[147] *Christ, the Christian and the Church*, p. 193. Cf. I Cor. 10:17.
[148] Nevertheless bodies like the Free Churches, possessing some but not all of the essentials of Catholicism, have a 'relation to the Catholic Church', but their 'Catholic status is defective' (*The Convocations and South India*, pp. 12-13).
[149] *Corpus Christi*, p. 19, repeated in *The Recovery of Unity*, pp. 173-4.
[150] *Corpus Christi*, p. 17.

of the sacramental order', it is an adequate organ for 'the unity of a sacramental organism';[151] it is, that is to say, in the right order of things: only a strictly sacramental organ can really be the effective cause of a sacramental unity. Moreover the episcopate clearly is the condition *sine qua non* of the Eucharist, and all Catholic tradition regards the latter as the sacrament of Church unity. 'The *res* of this sacrament is the unity of the Mystical Body', says St Thomas, quoted by Dr Mascall.[152]

'Intercommunion', of the sort which does not exist between Canterbury and Rome, is a valuable expression of sacramental unity, but must not be confused with it. The latter can exist without the former, and a break in intercommunion does not necessarily involve schism in the strict sense. Schism is opposed to Church unity, and it involves not only a break in intercommunion, but a breaking away from the causative sacrament of unity (a valid Eucharist) involved in breaking away from the organ of unity (the episcopate). The papacy, on the other hand, cannot as such constitute the Church's organ of unity, and to break away from unity with it is not, therefore, a cause of schism. 'The papal character is not conferred by a sacramental act at all, but by the purely administrative and organisational process of election,'[153] consequently 'by its very constitution the papacy does not, so far as I can see, possess the nature which is required in the organ of the Church's unity.'[154] That is to say, the papacy has no special sacramental, but only a special jurisdictional, character; consequently it cannot effect a sacramental unity but only a jurisdictional unity. As the Church's essential unity is sacramental and not jurisdictional, the papacy cannot be its organ or effective cause. Rome 'has gone wrong in treating the Church's visibility as an organisational rather than as a sacramental one, and so in locating that unity in the organisational organ of the papacy rather than in the sacramental organ of the episcopate.'[155]

---

[151] *Corpus Christi*, pp. 17-18.
[152] *Summa Theologica*, III, 72, 3; *Christ, the Christian and the Church*, p. 195.
[153] *Corpus Christi*, p. 17.
[154] Ibid; see also *Christ, the Christian and the Church*, p. 153.
[155] Ibid. p. 18. Cf. *The Recovery of Unity*, p. 208.

That is Dr Mascall's view of the Church and its unity; I have done my best to give it full justice, and I confess that I am not surprised if some people find it satisfying, for it is very close indeed to Catholic truth. Having stated it I must now turn to its criticism.

We might begin by asking whether it is not all a vast over-simplification. Can one really explain the essential nature of the Church simply by repetition of the word 'sacramental'? A criticism of Dr Mascall in a pamphlet of the Anglican *Annunciation Group* may be worth quoting here.

> The unity of the Church is threefold (at least): there is sacramental unity, there is unity of faith, and there is unity of organisation. Perhaps none of these would be conceived in quite the same way by Roman Catholics and Orthodox, but both would agree that at least these three strands were essential to the unity of the Church. I do not mean to suggest that Dr Mascall would deny this; but it does seem as though he exalts the sacramental unity to the point of neglecting the necessity of unity of faith and unity of organisation.[156]

At least, if we are to explain the whole in terms of one of these strands, we must so do it as to include the substance of the other two in a synthesis which does justice to all the elements of a complex reality. It is this which Dr Mascall fails to do. Sacramental unity, as by him conceived, does not include, for instance, unity of organisation, or of visible fellowship: similar organisations, similar fellowships, yes; one organisation, one fellowship, no. The simple fact is that the constant traditional Catholic view of schism directly contradicts his idea of the Church's unity. No Catholic denied or denies that the Donatists or Novatianists had continued and carried out the external conditions for sacramental validity, no one questioned that they possessed—from an 'objective' Augustinian viewpoint—'the essentials of Catholicism' (Episcopate, Sacraments, Scriptures, Creeds), but they were none the less in schism, that is to say cut off from Church unity. Dr Mascall's notion of the Church's unity is, verifiably (as we have already seen) not the 'primitive and Catholic doctrine'.

[156] The Annunciation Group, *Dr Mascall and South India—A Reply*, dated December 31st, 1955, pp. 3-4.

In recent years there has been a strong tendency in Anglican circles to return to a 'Cyprianic' theory of the Church and sacramental validity. St Cyprian did not admit sacraments to be valid if administered outside the one communion of the visible Church. St Augustine, following another traditional view, disagreed. Bodies which had left the Church might still possess and pass on valid sacraments. But much modern 'Cyprianism' tends to put the cart before the horse: wherever there are valid sacraments, the Church is present; and sacraments are often judged as valid rather because of their apparent fruitfulness than for any other cause. However if Dr Mascall might be said to be 'Cyprianic' in his linking of Church and sacraments, he remains, I believe, firmly Augustinian in his view of the conditions for sacramental validity, and this really brings him to a basic position much like that criticised by Dr Ramsey in the following passage from *The Gospel and the Catholic Church*:

> In the face of Erastian perversions of the ministry the Anglo-Catholic revival has borne witness to the fact of 'Our Apostolic Descent'. But it has sometimes obscured its witness by expounding the ministry as if it were a channel of grace isolated from the life of the body. Whereas in the more primitive view, seen both in St Cyprian and in the Eastern Church, validity of orders depends upon the life of the Church, some of the Tractarians and their successors were led into a view which is Augustinian and 'clericalist' rather than Catholic, and which treats validity of orders as in itself the first basis of the Church's life, and even as the sole test of membership in the Church of God.[157]

I cannot entirely agree with these remarks of Dr Ramsey, but I do completely subscribe to his criticism of a view 'which treats validity of orders as in itself the first basis of the Church's life'. But I do not know how Dr Mascall can fail to fall beneath it.

'The Church's unity is established in our Lord's institution of the apostolate, which is continued in the universal episcopate; the bishop is the link between the local and the universal Church.'[158] What does Dr Mascall mean by such a link? Is it irrespective of any communion between a particular group of bishops and the rest of 'the universal Church?' Presumably so, else the break of communion between two 'branches' of the

[157] pp. 218-19.   [158] *Corpus Christi*, pp. 18-19.

Church would break their sacramental unity. But if so, every *episcopus vagans* is an organ of the Church's unity. Is Dr Mascall willing to admit that? Any irresponsible bishop can validly consecrate other bishops, who will undoubtedly have an episcopal character conferred by sacramental act, but is this sufficient 'to express and maintain' the Church's visible unity? The weakness of Dr Mascall's theory is to single out one essential element to the neglect of another. In a speech to the Convocation of Canterbury in May 1943 Archbishop William Temple spoke of the Apostolic Succession: 'I was myself admitted to the episcopate by the twofold succession—succession in office and succession of consecration.'[159] A succession of consecration by itself is not sufficient, there is also required that 'succession in office', and this requires authorisation, jurisdiction, the recognition of a minister—be he bishop or priest—by the Church as a whole.

It is this twofold character of orders and jurisdiction which characterises the position of a bishop in the Church. Dr Mascall does not like the idea. He stresses that the episcopate is 'a reality of the sacramental order' and not 'a merely governmental and organisational contrivance'.[160] His vocabulary, of course, is tendentious: the word 'contrivance' is meant to excite distaste for the governmental side of things, while 'merely' is simply an evasion of the issue. It is not *merely* governmental, but it is also not *merely* sacramental. The report on *Relations between Anglican and Presbyterian Churches* defines *Episcopé* as 'pastoral government',[161] and an adequate notion of the Catholic episcopate must be both sacramental and governmental; only thus understood could it possibly begin to qualify for the title 'the organ of the Church's unity'. In fact our Lord himself located the organ of Church unity in the realm of pastoral government when he said that 'there shall be one fold and one shepherd' (John 10:16). He himself was that shepherd, but before leaving the earth he gave Simon the office (John 21: 15-17) and so also constituted him organ of the unity of the flock.[162]

---

[159] Quoted by Dr Ramsey in *The Gospel and the Catholic Church*, p. 230.
[160] *Corpus Christi*, p. 18. [161] p. 11.
[162] Cf. B. C. Butler, 'St Peter: History and Theology', *Clergy Review*, August 1958, p. 451.

Anyway, once the essential government aspect of episcopacy is recognised, two important points follow. Firstly, Church unity can no longer be explained simply in terms of Baptism, Eucharist and Holy Orders, even joined to correct doctrine. Something more is required: the authorisation of the Church. That is to say that the Church is, in a way, prior to the sacraments. She is the community which possesses them, and alone can authorise their use. It is strange that Dr Mascall has so consistently and entirely avoided a serious discussion of the nature and sources of Church authority.

Secondly, the argument levelled against the papacy as the organ of unity falls to the ground. Just as the Catholic episcopate signifies a combination of orders and jurisdiction, so does the papacy. It is simply not true to say, as Dr Mascall does,[163] that the papacy is a purely 'juridical and administrative function' of the Church, imparted by a purely 'administrative act'. It most certainly requires also the sacramental act of consecration. An elected but as yet unconsecrated Pope does indeed at once receive in Church law—to avoid confusion—full papal jurisdiction *ad interim*. But, strictly speaking, he is not and cannot be Pope until he is a bishop, because the Pope is essentially St Peter's successor in the apostolic see of Rome, and a non-bishop cannot be that. Both the Catholic episcopate and the Catholic papacy are functions of the Church which imply the imparting of both sacrament and jurisdiction. In neither case could it be argued that consecration is a sufficient condition. The papacy, we believe, is the Church's organ of unity because it is that episcopal see which possesses in itself, because of its Petrine succession, the whole of the jurisdiction which is possessed by the Church as a whole: what was promised to the apostles as a body was equally promised to Peter alone. Their authority is focused in him, and consequently in him and in his see it is indefectible. But whether the organ of unity is located in Rome or in the universal episcopate, it is located in something which is jurisdictional as well as sacramental, and hence Dr Mascall's argument against the possibility of its location in the papacy is invalid.

[163] *The Recovery of Unity*, p. 208.

To sum up: It is true that the Church is a sacramental society, but Dr Mascall's way of interpreting that fact fails to do justice to the very notion of a visible society or association; it does not explain the traditional Catholic ideas of schism, of the Church as a visible communion, and of the necessity of authorisation in the Church and in sacramental life. The sacraments are visible signs, possessions of a visible Church. On Dr Mascall's view they would rather be visible signs belonging to an invisible Church. A sacramental society is one visibly linked by its sacramental possessions: not merely do two groups of people possess the same sacraments, but they must visibly possess them together and with a common authorisation. Not only do they both have communion, but they have intercommunion. Without intercommunion there is no sacramental society.

This indeed is the primitive and patristic Catholic doctrine: the Church is one visible sacramental society, that is to say, one communion, united by the actual participation of its members in the same sacraments. A dissident group, possessed of valid sacraments, but not in visible communion, was never understood to form part of the One Church; far from being united sacramentally, it was divided sacramentally, divided precisely—and most terribly—at the very heart of Christian life and source of Christian unity, the Holy Eucharist. No theology which distinguishes between 'Church' and 'Communion', recognising within one Church a number of un-communicating communions (and every Anglican has to maintain a theology of this type)[164] can be faithful to the Catholic and traditional conception of the sacramental unity of God's Church.[165]

9. *The Appeal to Antiquity*

Throughout this study, but especially in section 7 above, I have had occasion to refer to 'the traditional Anglican appeal to the Scriptures and the Fathers and the undivided Church';[166] in

[164] Cf. *Corpus Christi*, p. 2.
[165]. Dr Florovsky sums up 'the doctrine and practice of the "undivided Church"' with the words 'Communion and an integral unity were exact correlatives' ('Terms of Communion in the Undivided Church', in *Intercommunion* edited by D. Baillie and J. Marsh, p. 57).
[166] E. L. Mascall, *The Recovery of Unity*, p. xii.

this section I propose to consider this appeal more precisely and in connection with a recent controversy carried on within the Anglican Communion.

In *Old Priest and New Presbyter* the late Dr Sykes, formerly Dixie Professor of Ecclesiastical History at Cambridge and then Dean of Winchester, set himself to examine the normal Anglican view of the nature of episcopacy. If one considers the history of Anglican thought during the last four centuries, what will stand out as the characteristic Anglican attitude on this point? Not, he decides, the Tractarian and Anglo-Catholic position; this he considers to be unfaithful to the true Anglican tradition. 'The Anglican tradition has espoused a *via media* in regard to episcopacy, constructed by its defenders against the two extremes of Rome and Geneva. In accordance with this tenacious adherence to the mean, the Church of England has nowhere formulated any theoretical or theological doctrine of episcopacy; but has contented itself with the assertion of the historical ground of the continuance of the threefold ministry in the Church since the apostolic age.'[167] Again, 'the traditional Anglican position in regard to episcopacy commends it on the strength of its long historical continuance since the apostolic age, as being of the *bene* or *plene esse* of the Church; and consequently a condition of union of other Churches with itself'.[168]

Dr Sykes's thesis raised two questions for Anglicans, and for Anglo-Catholics especially: firstly, is his analysis of the Anglican tradition historically correct? Secondly, can an analysis of this kind produce an authoritative theological norm for Anglicans?

On the first question it is probable, as has already been said, that Dr Sykes considerably misinterprets the traditional Anglican attitude to episcopacy, although the Anglo-Catholic position is about equally untraditional. But that is a historical question, and Dr Mascall, for instance, in his reply to Sykes, admits it to be of secondary importance. Although he questions Sykes's historical conclusions, Mascall is prepared to pass over the point and examines instead their real theological significance. To what

[167] N. Sykes, *Old Priest and New Presbyter*, p. 259.
[168] Op. cit. p. 245.

extent, he asks, is a modern Anglican theologian bound by the views of his predecessors? Can an Anglican honestly repudiate the normal view that the Church of England has held on an important doctrinal question from the sixteenth to the nine-teenth century? Sykes thinks that an Anglican cannot, or at least ought not, to do so: 'The apologetic position of a church thus placed in the strait of seeking to repudiate nearly four centuries of its history as "the times of ignorance which God winked at" would be hardly reassuring or sound.'[169] In reply Dr Mascall adroitly asks:

What, I wonder, does he (Dr Sykes) think the Church of England did at the Reformation? If it was then prepared to repudiate nearly a thousand years of its history for the sake of Gospel truth (and I think Sykes would hold that this is what it did), why should it not repudiate four hundred years of its history if truth required this? Furthermore, if the norm to which Anglican theology and practice is bound to conform is the period from 1558 onwards, what was the norm to which it was bound to conform when it entered on that formative and normative period? What was the norm before the norm existed? What were the Reformers themselves trying to do? What in fact was the authority to which they appealed? Whatever it was, it could not have been Sykes's "authentic Anglican tradition".'[170]

For his part Mascall believes that a true Anglican is bound by the traditional Anglican appeal to tradition and antiquity. 'He is, I would maintain, bound to adhere to that appeal to primitive wholeness which so notably distinguishes the great post-Reformation Anglican divines, with their emphasis upon Scripture and the Fathers. But I cannot see that he is bound to hold that either the Anglican liturgy or the Anglican divines were at all points successful in making that appeal'.[171] That is to say, Dr Mascall believes in the Anglican appeal to tradition, but not in any decisive sense in the appeal to Anglican tradition. The episcopate, he holds, is of the Church's *esse*, and that is part of the Church's teaching and of the witness of antiquity, no

[169] Op. cit. pp. 260-1; for Dr Peck's cutting reply to this argument, see *Anglicanism and Episcopacy*, pp. 11-12.
[170] *The Recovery of Unity*, pp. 168-9.
[171] *Corpus Christi*, pp. x-xi.

matter how obscured it may have been in the Church of England in the first centuries after the Reformation. In spite of that obscuring, Dr Mascall holds, the episcopal succession was not lost, and the modern Anglican will remain loyal to his forefathers by his agreement with them, not materially as to doctrine, but formally in the authority claimed for doctrine—that of antiquity. To this effect he quotes Robert Wilberforce. 'If there should be any point, therefore of vital importance . . . anything affecting the foundation of her faith or practice, in which our Church has departed from the maxims of antiquity, *her own principles demand* that it should be examined and amended'.[172]

Dr Mascall's position on this matter may be summarised thus:

1. An Anglican must accept the appeal to antiquity as normative for doctrine.

2. This appeal shows episcopacy to be of the Church's *esse*.

3. This doctrine may have been misunderstood by Anglicans for centuries after the Reformation.

4. This wrong tradition need not matter to the modern Anglican.

5. Providentially the episcopate did survive.

6. A modern Anglican's duty is to follow the appeal to antiquity and the doctrine of the episcopate to be found therein.

What I must now suggest is that a very similar line of thought applies equally well in the field of the Church's unity. Let me formulate it thus:

1. An Anglican must accept the appeal to antiquity as normative for doctrine.

2. This appeal shows the unity of the Church to be one of visible intercommunion. Authority for this statement is to be found throughout the present book. Here I will simply add that of the Anglican scholar R. F. Hettlinger: 'On the strictly logical interpretation of the doctrine of the Church held from the third to the sixteenth century, the only possible position is that of the Roman and Orthodox Churches which deny the existence

[172] Quoted in *The Recovery of Unity*, p. 164; the italics are of Mascall not of Wilberforce.

of any Church which is not in communion with themselves.'[173] Nor does the pre-third century Church offer any different norm.

3. This Church unity was certainly misunderstood by Anglicans in the sixteenth and subsequent centuries.

4. This error cannot bind modern Anglicans.

5. But this unity did not and could not survive the rupture of communion.

6. A modern Anglican's duty is to follow the appeal to antiquity and the doctrine of Church unity to be found therein.

But how is that duty consistent with the Anglo-Catholic position? As Abbot Butler once asked, 'If antiquity settles the case for the Church of England against Presbyterianism in the matter of episcopacy, why does it not settle the case for Roman Catholicism against the Church of England in the matter of "visible unity"?'[174] There is quite as much authority from antiquity for the intercommunion doctrine of Church unity as there is for episcopacy. On what grounds does Dr Mascall reject the one while he defends the other?

Would he at this point substitute for the appeal to antiquity an appeal to reason? That too, after all, is part of the traditional Anglican theological authority. In the words of Dr Peck: 'How does one ascertain what is the divinely appointed order for the Church? Some hold that it is papacy; some episcopacy; some presbyterianism, and so forth. The traditional Anglican criterion is a twofold one: the appeal to antiquity, and the appeal to reason; but to neither alone.'[175] Perhaps, then, at this point in the argument Dr Mascall would shift his ground from an appeal to antiquity to an appeal to reason. In the present divided state of Christendom, he might say, it is obviously unreasonable to apply the ancient norm of a single communion to determine the extent of the Church. It would be unreasonable to unchurch any such venerable bodies as the Church of England or that of Rome. In this case the appeal to reason must prevail over that of antiquity.

[173] Fairweather and Hettlinger, *Episcopacy and Reunion*, p. 88.
[174] Letter to *The Tablet*, 14 July, 1956.
[175] *Anglicanism and Episcopacy*, p. 32.

But why only in this case? Why not also in that of the ministry? Antiquity indeed shows that only an episcopal ministry is valid or divinely authorised, but in view of the state of modern Christendom it would be as unreasonable to stick to that ancient doctrine as it would be to cling to the old communion idea of the Church. It is quite as reasonable to admit the sacramental validity of the long and fruitful ministries of the non-episcopalians as it is to recognise the Church status of bodies separated in communion.

In fact, of course, neither the one nor the other is particularly reasonable, because in theology there is only one type of reasonableness—conformity with the original revelation. Because we recognise a spiritual fruitfulness in *bona fide* non-episcopal ministries and in *bona fide* membership of schismatic Christian bodies, we do not need logically to recognise divine authorisation for either such a ministry or such a church. This has been very clearly pointed out by Dr Peck in the case of the ministry: 'It cannot be supposed that, however irregular these sacraments and ordinations are, God refuses outright to use them if men perform them in good faith, whether constrained by force, or misled by ignorance and sin.'[176] But this, he continues, does not entail admission of non-episcopalians to the *sacra* of the Church. 'It is this confusion which is at the root of much discussion during these last decades: it is the assumption that, because God's grace is given to those who follow some "careful, strict, and orderly plan" other than the episcopal order, therefore somehow this plan acquires an independent and significant standing, that somehow it becomes habilitated in its own right, and that account must henceforward be taken of it on equal terms with episcopacy.'[177]

Similarly, it is assumed that because God's grace is given to those who are gathered together in a Christian community other than the one Catholic communion, therefore somehow this community acquires an independent and significant standing, that somehow it becomes habilitated in its own right, and that account must henceforward be taken of it on equal terms with the

[176] *Anglicanism and Episcopacy*, p. 30.   [177] Ibid. p. 55.

Catholic communion. If Dr Mascall and Dr Peck reject this assumption as regards the ministry, how can they accept it for the Church?

10. *Conclusion*

It is not easy at the end of this analysis to make a fair general assessment of Anglican ecclesiology. It has presented us with many of the essential elements required of the Catholic view of the Church—some of which many a modern Catholic theologian has hardly appreciated at all—but it has failed, I believe, to order them in a way consistent with tradition, or indeed consistent with itself. Among the elements we must note especially are faith, baptism, eucharist, and episcopate. Some theologians stress one point more, some another, correspondingly extending or contracting the frontiers of the visible Church; but not one has discovered a convincing theological reason for his own point of view. Moreover, apart from the ecumenical pragmatism which urges that we draw the frontiers of the Church ever more wide, there does not seem any principle or authority, by which Anglican theologians might come to agree among themselves. The voice of the past, of antiquity, is rejected as incompatible with the experience of the present, while the authoritative living voice of the contemporary Church is denied to exist. It is indeed to the future that many Anglicans look, to a great reunited Church: but reunited on what principles? If the reunion is to be God's work but is not to follow the principles of tradition, it will need to be based on a new revelation, on some quite special guidance of the Holy Spirit. But this is to do exactly what non-Catholics always rightly denounce, but wrongly accuse Rome of doing: it is to appeal to a new revelation, instead of admitting the full adequacy of the old.

One of the best summaries of Anglican ecclesiology may be found in the following passage from Dr Lacey.

The connexion between the unity of the Christian Church and a common participation of the Lord's Table is sufficiently obvious. St Paul put it at the highest when he wrote to the Corinthians, 'Since there is one bread, we being many are one body, for we all partake of the one bread.' But we are not to infer that this common participation makes us one. That is effected rather by the one baptism, and by the bond of peace in which we labour to maintain the unity of the Spirit. The Eucharist is but one element in that endeavour, and the common participation is rather a consequence than a cause of our unity, as it is also a public manifestation thereof. The Eucharist is not happily called, as in a well-known hymn, the 'sacrament of unity', for in the language of St Cyprian, from whom the phrase was borrowed, the episcopate is the *sacramentum unitatis*, holding together in one society the members of the Church resident in a certain place, and also holding together by mutual intercourse the groups of Christians dispersed throughout the world. This episcopate has fallen away from Cyprian's ideal, and the Eucharist cannot be said to have taken its place; both indeed, have developed divisive tendencies.[178]

The Eucharist cannot be the cause of Christian unity; the episcopate ought to be but is not; only Baptism remains. Put briefly, that is not an unfair statement of the most common Anglican position.

The New Testament certainly teaches that Christians form a new race, of which one becomes a member through baptism. Nevertheless this alone cannot provide a sufficient explanation of the Church's unity. Once a member of a family or race, always a member, nothing can make brothers cease to be such. Once baptised, always baptised, nothing can take the mark away; a man once baptised is always a member of the Christian race. This holds true even of the apostate; he cannot cease to be our brother. He retains the ineffaceable seal of baptism upon his soul, and, if converted and received once more into the Church, he is not again baptised. All along he has retained his baptismal character; but he has not, as all admit, been within the unity of the Church all along. The unity of the Christian race grounded in baptism is not the same, then, as the unity of the Christian Church which is the continuing society of the baptised. All the baptised are our brethren, but some our separated brethren, separated not only from us but from the unity of the Church into which they were baptised, and whose seal they continue to bear upon their souls. Baptism alone does not explain the unity of the Christian Church.

[178] *The One Body and the One Spirit*, pp. 204-5.

Dr Lacey's firm rejection of the claims of the Eucharist is enlightening, and it is very true to the Anglican position. Certainly Dom Gregory Dix and Dr Mascall have attempted to restore the traditional Catholic view of the Eucharist as the effective sacrament of Church unity, and this attempt has brought them, in one way, very near to our point of view. But basic facts are against them, and it is in the end on the episcopate that even Dr Mascall falls back as the effective sacrament of unity. Possession of baptism or possession of the episcopate, or even possession of a valid eucharist, it is all in the end the same thing. Here is the great division. It does not lie between a sacramental view of the Church and a governmental one. The question is whether the Church is simply the sum of those communities possessing (on Augustinian principles) either a valid baptism or a valid episcopal succession, or is she a Eucharistic society? Catholic ecclesiology unhestitatingly places the unity of the Church in the effective power of the Eucharist to make one those who communicate together. The Church is one communion. No Anglican can say this, as Dr Lacey so rightly saw. St Paul's words must be explained away and Eucharistic unity becomes just a manifestation of the essential unity which already exists.

The chief value to be found in the study of Anglican ecclesiology lies, I think, in this location of its essential weakness. It has so much, yet it lacks the king-pin. A precise comparison of their view with our own helps to reveal just what is at the heart of the Catholic view of the Catholic Church. Further there are individual elements in Anglican ecclesiology of the very greatest importance which should find their true home within Catholicism, but which even Catholic theologians have neglected. Chief among these elements is the ecclesiological significance of the sacraments and the sacramental character of the Church. They have well understood the effect of baptism in creating a new race, they have sensed to some extent the need for a consecrated organ of unity, they have never forgotten the essential significance of the corporate episcopate in the government of the one apostolic Church, they have appreciated the great symbolic effect of the Eucharistic meal. Their failure is really one to take St Paul's words about the Eucharist *au pied de la lettre,* and the fact is not that Anglican ecclesiology is too sacramental, but that it is not sacramental enough!

The Eucharist is the meal, the communal religious act of a *society.* Anglicans do not deny that the Church is a visible society, but one cannot see what real meaning they give to the word. Of the fact of it there is no doubt. The Church, says Dr Mascall, is 'a visible and tangible society';[179] she is, according to Dr Ramsey, 'the one society', 'the one historic society', 'a continuous, visible, historical society'.[180] But here it is difficult to see what the words can mean. Anglicans, Roman Catholics and Orthodox may be said to belong to one religious family or race, but not to one visible religious society: the simple meaning of the words cries out against such a statement. Margaret Clitherow and her persecutors belonged to one religious family, a divided family, but not to one society or fellowship. Society implies a living together, an association of members sharing visibly a common existence; a religious society implies a praying together; a Christian also the breaking of bread together, the one bread of intercommunion. Whatever else there is or is not, there is no intercommunion and no society joining Anglicans and Roman Catholics. Whose fault it is, is not here the question: it is the bare fact which matters. The common society was deliberately broken in the sixteenth century and has never been restored. Hence, if Roman Catholics and Anglicans are both within the visible Church, the Church is not one visible society.

If Anglican theologians have not faced up to the meaning of the statement that the Church is a society, they have equally not faced up to the correlative notion of schism, to the tradition of the Church that Christian bodies possessing outwardly the apostolic succession of the episcopate and also substantial orthodoxy of doctrine can yet be outside the Church's visible unity, because out of communion. The episcopate as such cannot, consequently, be the fundamental organ of Church unity, and while we must welcome the clear Anglican recognition of the need for

---

[179] *Corpus Christi,* p. 17.
[180] *The Gospel and the Catholic Church,* pp. 73, 83, 196.

such an organ, we must ourselves locate it not there, but in the one central apostolic succession line of the church of Rome.

On this central organ is based the unity of the Church's government. Anglicans do not, in general, give a sufficient weight to the need for unity of government, yet they have to recognise that it was part of the Church from the beginning. It is in governmental terms that they explain the present division among Christians, and they too often pass over the theological significance of the deeper division of Christian fellowship and communion. Here, again, the central failure of Anglican ecclesiology is seen to be its failure to think of the Church in the terms of communion: to equate communion with integral unity.

How is it, one may ask, that Anglicans can feel secure of a position which their own scholars agree to be in contradiction with the whole of Christian tradition up to the sixteenth century? The chief reason is that few have ever really seen what the central point at issue is; they do not realise how isolated they are theologically. Aware of minor similarities between their system and that of the primitive Church, they have never been brought up face to face with the fundamental dissimilarity. Linked with this, there is the naturally great difficulty of admitting that one's own religious group, one's own national church, could possibly be excluded from the Church universal. How could the great and venerable body of Anglican Christians really have been mistaken all these centuries in holding themselves part of the Church? Yet an appeal to the subjective conviction of a multitude as proof of an objective truth is a dangerous line of argument, and there is not one of us who is not convinced that the sincere beliefs of vast groups of people on this earth are erroneous. What security can agreement with post-Reformation Christians give, when it is opposed by the consensus of all the rest of Christian tradition? H. E. Manning when still Archdeacon of Chichester, years before his Catholic conversion, wrote the following warning in the very act of defending the position of the Church of England: 'It must be perfectly obvious to every reasoning mind, that the condition of a part of Western Europe during the last three centuries cannot avail to unsettle the fixed

rule of the Catholic Church for fifteen hundred years.'[181] When
he wrote that, Manning was quite unaware that future scholarship, Anglican as well as Catholic, would demonstrate that 'the
fixed rule of the Catholic Church' in the matter of visible unity
stands clearly against the Anglican position.

In 1887, forty-five years later, Bishop Gore wrote that 'Christ
our adorable master has given us no guarantee that his Faith
will not be rejected by Englishmen, as it was once by the Jews'.[182]
There is equally no guarantee that they have not already rejected
the unity of Christ's Church, as it was once rejected by the
Donatists. If there is no such guarantee, what reason can Anglicans give to show that this is not in fact the case? No Catholic
reason, most certainly, for the whole of tradition is against them.
If they once recognise that there is no Catholic view of the
Church which can admit both the Pope and the Archbishop of
Canterbury within her visible unity, there may be few so bold
as to assert that it is the Pope who is excluded.

[181] *The Unity of the Church*, p. 370.
[182] Quoted by J. Moorman, 'Charles Gore and the Doctrine of the Church',
Church Quarterly Review, 1957, p. 138.

Chapter 6

SACRAMENTAL VALIDITY AND THE UNITY OF THE CHURCH

The last chapter has clearly shown how closely linked the sacraments are with the Church in both Anglican and Catholic theology. One cannot speak of the Church without also speaking of the sacraments, but what is the exact relation of one to the other?

The life of the Church is essentially the sacramental life; how, then, if one possesses the sacraments can one fail to be within the Church? Alternatively, how can anyone outside the Church possess the sacraments? Can a heretic or schismatic baptise validly? If he is a bishop can he ordain validly? And if so, what is the ecclesiological significance of such sacraments? Can one indeed carry on a sort of apostolic succession outside the one apostolic Church? To these questions Cyprian gave one answer, Augustine another; and the answer one accepts inevitably decides also, to a large extent, one's theology of the Church herself. For this reason we need now to consider the question of sacramental validity in so far as it bears on our general theme.

The first point is to establish, so far as is possible, the position of antiquity, to which Anglicans appeal in this as in other fields. A second section deals with later Eastern Orthodox doctrine and practice, both because it has influenced recent Anglican thought, and because it throws light upon the points at issue. In a third part I treat of the modern Anglican tendency to 'Cyprianic' doctrine and its ecclesiological significance, while in conclusion I try briefly to relate the whole subject to Catholic doctrine on Church unity. Clearly I am not concerned in this chapter with a complete discussion of the conditions of sacramental validity but only with the light they throw on Church unity or (even more) the objection they may appear to provide to the view that the unity of the Church is that of a single visible sacramental society.

In this chapter the words 'valid' and 'validity' recur frequently, and as non-Catholic theologians use these words in a variety of ways, I will briefly state here the meaning I give to them. It is, I believe, the normal Catholic sense.

Our Lord Jesus Christ instituted certain sacraments as covenanted instruments whereby grace and status are given within the Christian community. When these are deliberately carried out, with whatever essential conditions he intended them to have, they are valid. As our Lord did not lay down the details of how they are to be performed, valid sacraments differ as to their accidental rites. However, if someone keeps the name of a sacrament, but changes its intrinsic meaning or abandons one or another of its essential conditions, he is destroying it as a divinely instituted sacrament. The rite he performs will not constitute a valid sacrament, and of itself (not possessing divine authorisation) it will be an empty ceremony and spiritually fruitless. Nevertheless, if he or his successors perform this rite in good faith, God may be presumed to use it as a regular means of 'uncovenanted' grace. Hence, though invalid, it may be spiritually fruitful (efficacious).

Moreover, a valid sacrament may be inefficacious. The aim of a sacrament is (at least partly) to impart grace, but it cannot force the will of someone receiving it in bad faith (cf. I Cor. 11:29).

Hence we may list the following possibilities:

1. A valid sacrament, which is also efficacious (the normal).

2. A valid but inefficacious sacrament.

3. An invalid sacrament (i.e. no sacrament at all, though it looks like one), of itself inefficacious.

4. An invalid sacrament, efficacious *per accidens* (that is to say, made use of by God as an uncovenanted means of grace, which God will never refuse to those who ask for it).

1. *Early Doctrine*

At the beginning of the Church the whole of the Christian religion was vividly understood in its organic unity; few distinctions were made or felt to be needed. The history of subsequent theology has been very largely the history of distinctions, qualifications, precise definitions. In this way understanding of the original revelation certainly grows, but there is equally a danger of dividing up an organic unity, and of misinterpreting a part which has been separated from its whole. True development or false aberration? That is the question which the Church must ask about every growth in Christian doctrine in the post-apostolic ages.

For the first Christians, the Church was the community of the saved, of those who believed in Christ, had been baptised into his death and renewed in themselves the saving power of his passion in their eucharistic meal. Visible community, salvation, faith, sacraments: these four were linked together in the simple awareness of an organic unity. Christians did not particularly deny that one of them might be present without another, but they hardly considered the possibility. They accepted the Church without a scientific theology of its elements or a consideration of what might happen in circumstances which had not then arisen.

Baptism was the sacrament of faith, the visible rite administered by a representative of the Church whereby a non-Christian became a Church member and so a sharer in the economy of the Redemption. If one had asked an early Christian whether baptism or Holy Orders could be valid if administered by an unauthorised person cut off from the Church's visible fellowship, he might well have found the question rather puzzling. A reply to it presupposes other points, not then clarified: the distinction between sacramental rite and its ecclesiastical authorisation (or between order and jurisdiction); the distinction between the unbreakable seal which baptism sets upon a man and the divine life which it brings him, but which he is free to reject; the distinction, then, between a valid and a fruitful sacrament. The ground of such distinctions is certainly to be found in apostolic teaching, but not their precise formulation. Yet without an appreciation of these distinctions it would be difficult to justify recognition of the validity of schismatical sacraments. Consequently the primary sense and meaning of the sacraments might at that time be most safely defended by a refusal to recognise sacraments administered outside the *Catholica,* for that primary meaning is only reconcilable with such recognition when recourse is made to these distinctions not then clearly appreciated.

This seems to have been a fairly general attitude in the early Church, though positive evidence is scarce indeed. It was a practical, not a theoretical attitude; not the answer to an abstract problem but to an immediate difficulty. In the world of that time 'dissident' for the most part meant Gnostic. It was impossible to accept the intention with which such men performed the sacraments, or to trust the form which they used, and though Christians may not then have argued their conclusions with the sort of analysis which we can now make, they sensed the right practical decision: heretical sacraments are no sacraments at all.

In the third century the Church began to be faced with large groups of people outside her visible communion but still substantially orthodox in doctrine. This presented a problem which, at least in its extent and practical gravity, was new. Faced with groups of schismatics, rather than heretics, she was bound to ask herself again: are their sacraments also invalid? It is unlikely that such a situation had not already arisen in many parts of the Church on a small scale, personal quarrels must often have produced little schisms of one kind or another, and this is important as providing a foundation for subsequent practice; but there had hitherto been no need to decide the whole issue in an authoritative and universal way.[1]

The immediate issue concerned baptism, and it came to a head in 255 bringing Pope Stephen of Rome into conflict with Bishop

---

[1] For detailed discussion of the historical evidence I must refer to C. H. Turner, 'Apostolic Succession' in H. B. Swete, *Essays on the Early History of the Church and the Ministry,* pp. 93-214; and B. Leeming, S.J., *Principles of Sacramental Theology,* pp. 497-541. C. H. Turner's article is really the fountainhead for the widely held modern Anglican belief that Cyprian best represents the primitive Church. Both writers, I feel, too easily interpret doubtful evidence in favour of their own view. Furthermore Father Leeming never really seems to appreciate the very great difference between denying the validity of schismatic sacraments and denying that of those performed by an unworthy Church minister. His arguments, like those of many Catholics in this matter, are really concerned with the quite easy problem of the latter, while the much greater difficulty is that concerned with the former.

Cyprian of Carthage. St Stephen maintained the validity of schismatic baptisms, St Cyprian denied it. For the time being neither view prevailed throughout the Church, but in the fourth century the recognition of schismatic, and also some heretical, baptisms became more and more general. Furthermore, the question could not be limited to baptism; orders were of almost equal importance, though for various reasons there was a greater reluctance to recognise a schismatic ordination. The protagonists of the belief that outside the Church all sacraments must be invalid were, of course, the Donatists, relying on the authority of St Cyprian, and it was in controversy with them that St Augustine clearly formulated in an argued theological way the contrary view that sacraments imposing 'character' (baptism, confirmation, orders) are as valid outside the Church as inside, so long as the right administrative and ministerial conditions be fulfilled. This view has come to prevail in the Western Church and, as regards baptism, it is the doctrine defined by the Council of Trent.[2]

In this study of the two views, conveniently named 'Cyprianic' and 'Augustinian', I will not consider the case of the personally unworthy or even disbelieving minister because those modern theologians who tend towards a Cyprianic approach agree with the Augustinian on this point: the personal unworthiness of the minister does not invalidate a sacrament. The question at issue is the ecclesiological one: as sacraments are the visible signs and acts of the Church—as baptism means entry into the one, true, visible Church—as the Eucharist is the sacrament of the Church's unity—as orders mean the consecration of ministers for the Church's service, how can such sacraments have meaning or validity when performed outside the borders of the visible Church? Does not the 'Augustinian' view involve an unacceptable 'divorce' between 'the theology of the sacraments' and 'the theology of the Church'?[3] Furthermore, is not this latter view, though it has come to be accepted by the Western Church, really a personal creation of St Augustine, something opposed to the primitive doctrine even of the West, and never accepted in the

[2] Denzinger, 860.   [3] C. H. Turner, op. cit. p. xxxiii.

East? Does not St Cyprian truly represent the outlook of the primitive Church, and did not St Augustine, in his praiseworthy anxiety to end the Donatist schism, misunderstand the true Catholic doctrine of antiquity? In this section I consider the historical side of these questions, leaving the strictly theological issue for later examination.

St Augustine has certainly been made by some to bear a heavy responsibility in this matter. Take Dr Ramsey for example. 'In his longing for peace St Augustine abandoned the rigid and Cyprianic view that baptism and orders are invalid outside the Church. By delicately and reverently challenging the authority of the greatest African doctor then known he insisted that baptism and ordination are valid wherever carried out.'[4] He can even speak of the Augustinian as 'a new view', 'St Augustine's own contribution'.[5] Now as regards baptism, this is certainly and evidently not the case. The Western Council of Arles in 314, long before St Augustine's birth, had already re-affirmed the existing Roman rule against the baptism of those already baptised in the name of the Trinity, and applied it to Africa.[6] In 325 the First Council of Nicaea accepted the baptism of Novatianists,[7] and in the course of the fourth century that of almost all heretics who believed in the Trinity, as well as of pure schismatics, was admitted.

If St Augustine was not innovating in the field of baptism, he was at least, so it is said, in the field of orders. Dr Greenslade, following C. H. Turner,[8] holds that 'Augustine's chief innovation was the extension of this line of thought to ordination'.[9] I do not believe that even this view is defensible historically. It must certainly be admitted that, prior to Augustine's time, very little recognition had been afforded in the Church generally to orders received within a separately organised Communion (as distinct from orders imparted by Arians, who were not generally organised apart, but simply held a number of Catholic sees at various times). Possible reasons for this I will consider later. Yet

[4] *The Gospel and the Catholic Church*, p. 154.   [5] Ibid.
[6] Denzinger, 53.   [7] Denzinger, 55.   [8] Op. cit. pp. 170, 181.
[9] *Schism in the Early Church*, p. 175, also p. 178.

Augustine's own recognition of Donatist orders was no personal contribution but, at most, a theological defence of the previous consistent Catholic attitude towards the Donatists. Ever since the very beginning of the Donatist schism the validity of Donatist orders had been recognised by Catholics. It was already decided at the Roman Council of 313. Furthermore I do not see the point of Optatus's criticism of the Donatists that they have made bishops and priests into laymen ('invenistis diaconos presbyteros episcopos, fecistis laicos') unless Catholics themselves recognised ordained converts as ordained.[10] The background of Catholic-Donatist history clearly prevents one from attributing to Augustine himself originality in the recognition of schismatic orders. He did no more than follow up, and justify theologically, an already established tradition. The Roman decision of 313 was itself something of an innovation, but probably more in the pastoral than the theological order for otherwise it would surely have aroused opposition, of which there is no trace.

Though responsibility for the appearance of an 'Augustinian' view of sacramental validity cannot be placed on the shoulders of St Augustine, it is not yet proved that Cyprianic doctrine was not more primitive, and 'Augustinianism' a later growth, due perhaps to motives of Christian expediency, of the third and fourth centuries. This point must now be examined. When Stephen of Rome and Cyprian of Carthage disagreed in the middle of the third century, who could better claim to represent the traditional and primitive position? For Dr Ramsey it is the Cyprianic which is 'the more primitive view',[11] as it is also for Dr Greenslade: 'there is much to be said for the Donatist position', he writes, 'following Cyprian and the still earlier Church generally, that the sacraments have been entrusted to the Church and cannot be administered outside it'.[12] Dom Gregory Dix is most emphatic: 'It is to be noted that down to the fourth century the Church rejected the very *possibility* of valid orders outside the Catholic Church, because outside the

[10] I am quite unable to see how Turner can use this text as proof of the contrary thesis, op. cit. p. 163.
[11] *The Gospel and the Catholic Church*, p. 218.
[12] *Schism in the Early Church*, p. 119.

Catholic Church the Holy Ghost does not operate.'[13] It is my conviction that all this is far too simple a reading of complex evidence, and indeed not only simple but even false. As these writers are in large part following the original study of C. H. Turner, it is his examination of the evidence which it is most profitable to study now.

Firstly, it is clear that in the third century there was no agreed Church attitude on the subject. A growing number of schisms, linked with heresies not touching the essentials of trinitarian belief, placed a practical problem for the Church in widely separate places, and the solution given to it was not everywhere the same. In Africa, already before Cyprian's time, a council held at Carthage under the presidency of Agrippinus had decided against recognition of dissident baptisms. That was *c.* 220. In various councils Cyprian and his brother bishops re-enacted that decision. Yet there is evidence to show that the African Church had not been unanimous on the point,[14] and this is particularly true if the anti-Cyprianic work known as the *De Rebaptismate* was written, as is quite probable, in Africa.

Cyprian was supported in his view by a letter from Firmilian, bishop of Caesarea in Cappadocia; Firmilian gave the opinion of the Church in Asia Minor and a council which had been held at Iconium some years before. He mentioned that there was no memory of a custom contrary to that of rebaptising. Egypt, on the other hand agreed with Stephen of Rome; Eusebius tells us that Denys of Alexandria wrote to Stephen on the subject; he felt less strongly about it than did the pope but he witnessed to the Egyptian tradition of non-baptising;[15] it is a pity that Turner hardly speaks of this Egyptian evidence at all.[16]

The crucial point, however, is Rome. Rome was the apostolic Church *par excellence* and a very conservative one, and in the middle of the third century it came out strongly against re-baptism: did this attitude represent the primitive and con-

---

[13] 'The Idea of "The Church" in the Primitive Liturgies', in *The Parish Communion*, ed. A. G. Hebert, p. 131, n. 2.
[14] Cf. B. Leeming, op. cit. p. 500.   [15] Eusebius, *Hist. Eccl.* VII, 1-6, 9.
[16] Palestine, also, appears from Eusebius's own viewpoint to have agreed with Rome.

tinuous Roman tradition or a third century innovation? If the
evidence existing points to the first answer, it cannot be maintained that *in general* the primitive Christian view rejected all
schismatic sacraments, and that is the point we have at issue.
Pope Stephen claimed to be following tradition: 'Nihil innovetur
nisi quod traditum est',[17] and the author of the *De Rebaptismate*,
whoever he was, spoke equally of the 'vetustissima consuetudine
ac traditione ecclesiastica'.[18] St Cyprian's contrary claim—'Non
est de consuetudine praescribendum, sed ratione vincendum'[19]
—suggests at least that he felt less sure of the primitiveness than
of the reasonableness of his own view, and that he did not
question the foundation of Pope Stephen's position. Perhaps
St Cyprian was being too diffident about this. . . . Perhaps the
author of the *De Rebaptismate* was making obviously wild and
extravagant claims. . . . Perhaps the memory of Pope Stephen
was conveniently of the very shortest length. . . . Perhaps. Professor Turner would obviously have wished it to be so, and it is
at this moment that one begins to suspect an unscholarly anti-
Roman prejudice even in so great a scholar as he was. 'We must',
he tells us, 'give due weight to this evidence: but we must at the
same time remember that Roman churchmen, when writing on
topics of controversy, have been, since controversies began,
somewhat over-ready to claim an immemorial prescription and
apostolic authority for the practice of the Roman Church. And
there are some definite indications that tell in the other direction.'[20] He gives two: the first is that 'Novatian would hardly
have rebaptised converts who joined him, if he had been brought
up in surroundings exclusively dominated by the opposite practice'. That may be so, but Novatian's rebaptisms could equally
well be explained by his natural rigorism: having caused a
schism in defence of the Church's sanctity, it was natural to
follow this up by maintaining that not only Church membership, but also valid sacraments depend on holiness—natural at
least in an age when that view was widely held in the Church
by rigorists.

[17] Denzinger, 46.   [18] Quoted by Turner, op. cit. p. 154, n. 1.
[19] *Ep.* 71. 3; *Pat. Lat.* 4, 423.   [20] Op. cit. p. 154.

The second indication is an exceedingly obscure accusation
made by Hippolytus earlier in the century against Callistus:
'first in this man's time they had the audacity to introduce second
baptism.' On the face of it this accusation would suggest that
Hippolytus, at least, believed the ancient tradition to be against
rebaptism; but we do not know the context of the quarrel, or
consequently the significance of the accusation. Nevertheless
Professor Turner is prepared to speculate.

> Short as Roman memories could be when convenient, it is diffi-
> cult to suppose that even Stephen could have appealed to tradition
> if a pope had taken the opposite line to himself only thirty-five
> years earlier. Yet for myself I half suspect that what Callistus (or
> rather his underlings: Hippolytus only says ἐπὶ τούτου) did was to
> *rebaptise adherents of Hippolytus,* and that this was what Hip-
> polytus resented, because it was to treat him as a bishop who was
> in schism, and so could not validly baptise. If this is correct, both
> Hippolytus and Callistus would have rebaptised converts from
> heresy.[21]

Even though such an interpretation does completely twist Hippolytus's actual words, at first sight it might still seem plausible.
But what does it imply? Professor Turner must indeed have
thought that Roman memories could be quite fantastically short,
and the Church of Rome quite exceptionally un-conservative,
for the conclusion of his hypothesis is that in the time of Hippolytus and Callistus the whole Roman Church was agreed on
the practice of rebaptism; that within thirty-five years the same
practice was questioned and then completely abandoned; while
within the lifetime of many who could remember Hippolytus and
Callistus, and in the face of Roman schismatics who maintained
the original practice, a pope could blandly declare its opposite
to be right for the sole reason that it was traditional. I confess to
finding such an idea not historical interpretation but historical
burlesque rendered plausible by a subtle appeal to the traditional
English distrust of Rome! In fact, there is plenty of evidence of
all sorts to show that the Church of Rome was always most
traditional and conservative, especially in the fields of dogma

[21] Op. cit. p. 155, n. 1.

and liturgy, and therefore most unlikely to break away rapidly from a general and primitive tradition.[22]

No, we can be sure that behind St Stephen there was a long Roman tradition against re-baptism going well back before the third century. Doubtless in Rome as elsewhere there were difficulties and border-line cases between the type of heretic whose baptism must be doubtful and the type of schismatic whose baptism is not, but the point is that both were recognised possibilities in the primitive Church.

The widespread refusal to recognise sacraments administered outside the Church is not difficult to explain without invoking the aid of strictly Cyprianic principles. There were at least three other types of argument militating against recognition: firstly, that of pastoral prudence. The Church's ministers had not administered these sacraments, and consequently she could not *guarantee* their rectitude; but she was here concerned with the actual basis for the Christian life and ministry of her members, and in this field no possible risk could be taken. Secondly, a high standard of sanctity was expected of her ministers, while heretical divisions were felt to involve culpability; if heretical ministers were reconciled to the Church they were rather to be put to penance than publicly appointed to officiate as priests and bishops. But if a further ministry was simply not envisaged, a recognition of orders became quite without point. Thirdly, the types of heresy then in vogue often concerned the form of baptism, as St Basil says of the Montanists: 'Those who have been baptised according to a rite which has not been taught to us have not been baptised.'[23] Apart from actual changes of rite, a heresy over trinitarian doctrine imperilled the sense if not the form of the trinitarian baptismal formula. On this was based the very reasonable Catholic tendency to deny the validity of heretical

[22] Thus Dr Klauser comments on the 'extremely conservative temper' of the Roman Liturgy, p. 39 of *The Western Liturgy and its History*, trans. F. L. Cross, Mowbray, 1952; cf. also G. Dix, 'The Idea of "the Church" in the Primitive Liturgies', in *The Parish Communion*.

[23] *Ep.* 2, 188. *Pat. Graec.* 32, 667. The whole letter is of great interest and importance for the subject, but Basil's views are certainly not entirely clear. For a careful discussion of them, see Dr Florovsky, *Terms of Communion in the Undivided Church*, pp. 54-56.

sacraments, even where the form itself was unchanged, and even when schismatic sacraments were recognised.[24]

All this doubtless demonstrates a confused and difficult situation. There was no obvious scriptural answer to the problem, and no universally known apostolic tradition. The doctrinal question could only really be settled when schisms began to multiply. The Church had its traditions, but they needed clarification, development, an authoritative judgment; and they received it from Rome and from the whole Church. What I have attempted to show, without any complete survey of the evidence which would be out of place here, is that the doctrine which came to be accepted in the fourth and fifth centuries was certainly a clarification and a development, but not a simple rejection, of a primitive doctrine. If it had been the latter, it would indeed be difficult to explain how universally and rapidly the Church judged in the matter.[25] Undoubtedly there were hestitations of many kinds but, in spite of them, Rome, St Augustine, the Greek East, and even the Monophysites all came to recognise the validity of both baptism and orders administered outside the one Church. For the Monophysites we have the testimony of Severus of Antioch,[26] for the Greeks the Second Council of Nicaea, and both were quite free of Augustinian influence. On the general Greek attitude of that time I may quote Dr Florovsky:

The most comprehensive regulation on the whole problem is offered in the 95th canon of the Council in Trullo (692), which at the same time did codify and authenticate all the previous synodical decisions. The Council openly rules that Nestorians and Monophysites should be received into the Church by a renunciation of their errors, Arians and Apollinarians by the sacrament of the Holy Chrism. In neither case was there any question of a new baptism. But this was by no means a new practice: it was, on the contrary, the authorisation of current practice. The canon does not mention the clergy in particular. Yet there is no doubt

[24] Cf. the same letter of St Basil; also Optatus, *De Schismate Donatistarum*, Book I, 9, 10.
[25] Professor Turner had, on his view, to admit that it was a 'wonder' that St Cyprian's theory was 'so largely—and in the end so universally—given up', op. cit. p. 156.
[26] See Turner's *Note on the Letters of Severus*, op. cit. pp. 211-14.

that Nestorian and Monophysite clergy were usually admitted to communion in their orders. This practice was quoted as a precedent at the VIIth Ecumenical Council (787). . . . [27]

Doubtless the East was not always clear or consistent, and recognition was often explained more in terms of Church administration than on strict 'Augustinian' principles (though it would be wrong to read back a consistent application of the modern Greek theory of 'economy' into the practice of the ancient Church) but recognition there was, and recognition based upon the consensus of the whole Church. Rome spoke first, and the whole Church came to accept that decision.

To go back on this view, to refuse validity to schismatical sacraments on the grounds of a Cyprianic approach to Church and sacraments of a rather *simpliste* type, would not show fidelity to the most primitive traditions, in so far as we know them, and it would show a remarkable infidelity to the Church, both East and West, of the period of the great Councils and the Fathers. Little by little they built up a practice and a theology of sacramental validity, which it is for us to use, not to abandon.

2. *Later Eastern Practice*

The Eastern Orthodox have had a considerable influence on modern Anglican sacramental thought, and it will therefore be useful to examine briefly some aspects of Greek and Russian sacramental theology, both as a help for the understanding of Anglican theology, and because it does throw light on general sacramental problems. In general the East is said to be Cyprianic, in contrast with the Augustinianism of the Latin Church, and those who wish to return to some form of Cyprianism find support in what they take to be the traditional witness of the unchanging East. But this, as we shall see, is only partly true. [28]

In the centuries before the Schism, the Greek Church, as represented by the Second Council of Nicaea and the Council in Trullo, had arrived at a largely 'Augustinian' position; this

[27] *Terms of Communion in the Undivided Church*, p. 53.
[28] The best general study of Orthodox theology and practice concerning sacramental validity is to be found in M. Jugie's *Theologia Dogmatica Christianorum Orientalium*, III, p. 89-97 and 103-25.

has already been pointed out in a quotation from Dr Florovsky in the previous section. But greater stress was always laid in the East on the guaranty of the unity of the one faith, and the danger of heresy invalidating the sacraments of dissidents. This same general pattern is discernible in the first centuries after the Schism. The Greeks came to look on the Latins as schismatics and also heretics, and at times they rebaptised their Latin converts: Cardinal Humbert had already accused Michael Caerularius of this in his sentence of excommunication.[29] By and large, however, Latin converts to Orthodoxy in the Middle Ages were not rebaptised, and often not re-confirmed either. It was only in 1484 that a synod of Constantinople standardised practice by laying down that they should in future be anointed with holy oil, but not rebaptised. This ruling continued in force in the Greek churches until 1755.

In Russia in the seventeenth century there was a short-lived period of Cyprianic practice. In 1629 under the Patriarch Nicon of Moscow, a synod laid down that all Western converts should be rebaptised. The Greek Patriarchates remonstrated upon this ruling as being against the Canons, and it was revoked—as regards Catholics in 1667, as regards Protestants in 1718. Since 1757, moreover, the Russian Church has also accepted Latin confirmation and orders. This was largely due to the influence of the *Trebnik* of Peter Mogila, the great metropolitan of Kiev (1632-45), who had himself been much influenced by Latin theology. Since that time the sacramental theology of the Russian Church has been basically 'Augustinian'.

The Greek Church has moved in an opposite direction. In 1755 Cyril V, Patriarch of Constantinople, decreed that Latin and Armenian baptisms were invalid, because administered by heretics and without triple immersion. Cyril V was thereby not only rejecting the normal Orthodox practice hitherto, but also reversing the explicit decision of his immediate predecessor, Paisius II. In spite of opposition, Cyril's views prevailed in the Greek world, and have ever since been normative. The present Greek Orthodox attitude may be summed up in the words of

[29] Jugie, op. cit. p. 91, n. 4.

the delegates to the 1937 Faith and Order Conference in Edinburgh: 'Validity. As regards the validity of the sacraments, the Orthodox delegates would like to confine themselves only to the following statement: According to the Orthodox doctrine valid sacraments are only those which are (1) administered by a canonically ordained and instituted minister, and (2) rightly performed according to the sacramental order of the Church.' A canonically instituted minister is, of course, one instituted by the (Orthodox) Church.

It is not easy, as even the Donatists found, to be really and consistently Cyprianic in sacramental practice; the Greek Orthodox certainly encounter the same difficulty. How to explain the different attitude of the past? Or the present difference of opinion with the Russians? The answer, they say, lies in the principle of *economy*, a principle formulated by St Basil and now much employed by the Greeks. *Economy* means the prudent stewardship in right of which the Church, in Orthodox eyes, has the power to validate for the good of the true Church heretical sacraments which, though invalid, were administered in a correct way. Professor Dyovouniotos even went so far as to hold that the last point was not a necessary condition for the exercise of *economy*, and that 'the Church is able to recognise the Priesthood and Sacraments in general of schismatics and heretics among whom they are not accomplished canonically or the Apostolic Succession has been broken', but the Oecumenical Patriarch has explicitly repudiated such a view.[30] The use of *economy*, then, presupposes, and does not substitute for, the normal Latin conditions for sacramental validity.

Economy appears to be a sort of necessary corollary to an application of Cyprianic sacramental doctrine, the only way left of resolving the 'intolerable uncertainty and inextricable confusion' which, as Father Leeming rightly says,[31] must follow on

---

[30] Cf. *Report of the Joint Doctrinal Commission Appointed by the Oecumenical Patriarch and the Archbishop of Canterbury for consultation on the points of agreement and difference between the Anglican and the Eastern Orthodox Churches*, 1932, quoted by B. Leeming, S.J., *Principles of Sacramental Theology*, pp. 546-7.
[31] *Principles of Sacramental Theology*, p. 502.

that doctrine; yet it might also be that the Orthodox are not really talking about something equivalent to validity in the Latin sense at all, but rather about what we mean by sacramental fruitfulness which is not normally obtainable outside the true Church. It is, for instance, difficult to see how they can claim to apply *economy* to validate a particular sacrament of orders derived from a line invalid and invalidated for hundreds of years; if they do this, it must be because they admit (or logically should admit) that some sort of definite character is passed on through a chain of orders unrecognised in the past by *economy*: in which case application of the latter may be understood as effecting a sort of 'reviviscence' in the hitherto dead, but not wholly null, sacrament—which, for Latins, concerns fruitfulness rather than validity.

With these provisos, I may quote Canon Douglas in a general summary of the Greek view: 'While they do not admit the validity *per se* of any Sacrament whatever outside the One True Church (i.e. their own Communion) and are not prepared to recognise Roman, Armenian, or Anglican Baptism and Orders as principles, they hold themselves able, and are ready, to recognise them by *Economy*.'[32] It is, of course, on an *economy* basis that a number of the Greek Churches have declared themselves able to validate Anglican orders in the same way as Roman ones.[33]

It may be noted here that if, in judging of the orders of others, the Orthodox seem less exacting than Rome in their enquiry into the succession line and the sacramental form, they are, on the point of faith, far stricter than the Latin Church. Whenever the question of recognising Anglican orders has arisen, the first reaction of the Orthodox has always been a request to see the Anglican formularies of belief.[34] This is not only due to the Orthodox concern to judge of the Anglican position *qua* Church, and not only *qua* orders, it is also because heresy can prevent the

---

[32] *Theology*, III, 1921, p. 117.

[33] Constantinople in 1922; Jerusalem and Cyprus 1923; Alexandria 1931; Rumania 1936.

[34] Cf. the examples given in Messenger, *The Reformation, the Mass and the Priesthood*, II, pp. 633-7.

use of *economy* at all: that is to say, it can negate the basic conditions required for its exercise. While schism makes orders invalid, heresy makes them incapable of being rendered valid. Here again it can be suggested that it may rather be a question of the distinction between fruitfulness and validity, and that while schism makes orders unfruitful, it is only heresy which renders them invalid. This is a recognised early view, held by St Optatus and even by St Basil himself. Anyway, this Orthodox preoccupation with right *faith* as a pre-condition for Orders would seem to have influenced Anglican theology, as we shall see.

The modern Greek stress on a Cyprianic view coupled with the use of *economy* has certainly had some influence on Russian theologians, but on the whole the difference between the two remains, and is a deep one. The Russian Church would seem to recognise the validity of Latin and Protestant baptisms, and Catholic orders, not by *economy*, but *per se*. And in this they are faithful to Orthodoxy's traditional position; there is no suggestion in the canon of the Second Council of Nicaea, or in such later official pronouncements as the decree of the synod of Constantinople of 1484 or the letter of the Oecumenical Patriarch Jeremiah II to Peter the Great in 1718, of any doctrine of *economy* or of anything less than full recognition of the validity of Western sacraments.[35] In the line of such documents I may quote the Russian Holy Synod's epistle to the Oecumenical Patriarch in 1903.

> We believe in the sincerity of their (Catholic and Protestant) Faith in the All-Holy and Life-originative Trinity, and on that account we accept the baptism of both one and the other. We respect the Apostolic Succession of the Latin hierarchy, and those of the clergy who join our Church we accept in the orders which they possess, just as we do in the case of Armenians, Copts, Nestorians, and other bodies that have not lost the Apostolic Succession.[36]

This difference between the Greek and Russian Churches is well illustrated by the case of William Palmer of Magdalen

[35] Documents to be found in J. A. Douglas, *Relations of the Anglican Churches with the Eastern-Orthodox*, pp. 159-62.
[36] Quoted in Douglas, op. cit. p. 161.

College who, in the last century, desired to be received into the
Orthodox Church. At first, in 1842, while still a convinced Anglican but ecumenically minded, he asked at Petersburg to be
admitted to communion. This was refused by the Holy Synod,
communion being dependent on full entry into the Orthodox
Church, and the conditions for that were stated to be abjuration
of the heresies contained in the 39 Articles and the recognition
of the Eastern as the Ecumenical Church. At the time Palmer
could not accept such conditions. Nine years later, having meanwhile lost faith in the Church of England, Palmer sought full
admission to the Eastern Church, this time at Constantinople,
only to find a further condition imposed on him: unconditional
baptism. Palmer offered to accept conditional baptism and
stressed that he did not wish to disagree with the Russian Church
which recognised the validity of his Anglican baptism, but on
October 8th, 1851 the Patriarch Anthimus replied in full synod
with a categorical refusal to admit any other than an Orthodox
baptism. This was too much. His friend Khomiakov urged
Palmer to enter the Russian Church, but the latter seemed to
him too much like the Church of England, which he had rejected, in being national and erastian. Eventually, in February
1855, and without—so it would seem—arriving at a fully Catholic ecclesiology, he was received into the Church in Rome, no
new baptism being required.[37]

It is true that since 1888 the Orthodox Church in Greece and
elsewhere has in many cases applied *economy* to validate the
former baptism of western converts, but it is still over-simplify-
ing to say, as W. J. Birkbeck does, that 'both the Patriarchate
of Constantinople and the Church of the modern kingdom of

[37] This William Palmer was born in 1811 and died in Rome in 1879. He has
sometimes been confused with William Palmer of Worcester College (1803-85);
a regrettable recent instance of this confusion is to be found in the note by
J. de Bivort de la Saudée in the *Enciclopedia Cattolica* (IX, 1952, pp. 657-8).
The two Palmers had much the same interests; Palmer of Worcester wrote the
classical statement of the 3 Branch Theory in his two volume *Treatise on the
Church of Christ* (1838). For our Palmer see the correspondence with Khomiakov
edited by W. J. Birkbeck in *Russia and the English Church* (1895); chap. 3 of
S. Bolshakoff's book on *The Doctrine of the Unity of the Church in the works
of Khomiakov and Moehler* (S.P.C.K., 1946); and also the very good study by
S. Tyszkiewicz entitled *La Mission de William Palmer* in *Etudes*, 136, pp. 43-63,
190-210, 329-47.

Greece have now conformed to the practice of the Russian Church, and now no longer rebaptise westerns, whether Roman Catholic, Anglican or Protestant'.[38] Russian theology recognises western baptisms as valid *per se*, while the Greeks—at the very most—are agreed to validate individual ones through *economy*. But some are still doubtful even about this. Evidence for this is the Report of the Delegation of the Oecumenical Patriarch of Constantinople to the Lambeth Conference of 1920. The delegation consisted of Mgr Philaretos, Metropolitan of Demotica, Professor Komnenos of Halki, the Archimandrite Pagonis of London, and the Archpriest Callinicos of Manchester. On the subject of the validity and character of Anglican Orders the delegation stated nothing definite, but Professor Komnenos drew up a private favourable *Report on Anglican Orders*, and in 1922 the Patriarch gave them his 'recognition'. On the question of baptism, however, the view of the delegation was very different.

> First, as to Baptism administered by English priests, we could not accept its validity either *simpliciter* or by *economy* (taking the same position as the Committee from Greece and the other Orthodox Committees), . . . as to the observation made to us regarding the practice of the Russian Church, which does not re-baptise those who come from the Roman Church or the Anglican, it was necessary to develop the arguments by which our Church was brought to the necessity in 1756 of imposing the rebaptism of Roman Catholics, which was yet never strictly observed.[39]

How, if Anglican (or Roman) baptisms are completely invalid and cannot be recognised even by *economy*, there can be any question at all of the validity of their orders, it is difficult to understand.

The general conclusions to this brief survey of the sacramental practice of the separated Eastern Church are three. Firstly, in the first centuries of separation the Orthodox remained largely 'Augustinian': that is to say they followed the Second Council of Nicaea in recognising the validity of dissident sacraments, while there is no sufficient reason to think that this was done

---

[38] *Russia and the English Church*, p. 110.
[39] This report is to be found in Bell, *Documents on Christian Unity*, pp. 52-76; for baptism see pp. 59-60.

according to some theory of *economy*. But there were many exceptions, partly due to simple dislike of the Latins, more profoundly on account of the old fear of the invalidating effects of grievous heresy.

Secondly, after some hesitations which culminated in the seventeenth century, the Russian Church, especially through the influence of Peter Mogila, has continued 'Augustinian' until the present day.

Thirdly, the Greeks fell back into a sort of Cyprianic approach in the eighteenth century; but neither their subsequent practice nor the views of their theologians offer a really coherent or integrated theology; this is due, I feel, to a Christian good sense which forbids them to apply Cyprianic doctrine with rigorous consistency.

3. *Recent Anglican Views*

Traditionally the Church of England has been Augustinian. 'The Church of England is not officially bound to either of these two theories, though in practice she inclines to the Augustinian. Bishop John Wordsworth, of Salisbury, probably the greatest Anglican authority on the subject, was quite clear that the Church of England was Augustinian.'[40] This Augustinianism is at the root of the type of Church doctrine examined in section 6 of the previous chapter, and also of the normal Anglican apologetic in answer to Roman claims; for it is firstly on the basis of Augustinian principles of sacramental validity that the Anglo-Catholic in particular defends the validity of Anglican Orders. He then continues—(in a very un-Augustinian way), 'because we have Orders and orthodox doctrine, we must be part of the true, visible Church'. Really this is a very curious argument. It might indeed be described as the absolute negation of Cyprianic doctrine. In the late O. C. Quick's words 'pushed to its logical extremes, the theory in question would lead us to derive the validity of the Church from the validity of its sacraments, and would come to be the exact opposite of the Cyprianic theory, which derives the validity of the sacraments from the valid and

[40] H. Brandreth, *Episcopi Vagantes and the Anglican Church*, p. 9.

validating authority of the Church'.[41] And again: 'the Anglo-Catholic theologian adheres strictly to the theory that the possession of valid sacraments is in such wise a credential of the "visible" Church, that the validity of sacraments cannot be derived from their authorisation by that Church, but is rather what gives to the Church its visible character.'[42]

At present this view finds very little favour with a large number of Anglican theologians. Dr Quick himself rejects it, together with the whole Augustinian view of which he considers it to be the extreme logical conclusion. Bishop Rawlinson of Derby likewise criticises it as 'ultra-Augustinian',[43] while Archbishop Ramsey writes that

> some of the Tractarians and their successors were led into a view which is Augustinian and "clericalist" rather than Catholic, and which treats validity of orders as in itself the first basis of the Church's life, and even as the sole test of membership in the Church of God. Expositions of the ministry have been common in which the doctrine of the organic body has been ignored. Thus a churchman's manual which was widely used in the early years of this century (*The Catholic Religion*, by Vernon Staley), begins with a treatment of the validity of Anglican orders, and only when this is complete does it pass on to the one Body and its faith.[44]

Now, while it is quite right to criticise this view which turns the whole doctrine of Church and sacraments on its head, it is wrong to label it as Augustinian. Far from Augustine thinking valid orders the sole test of Church membership, they were for him no test at all; his constant contention was that though the Donatists had valid orders, they were not in the Church. To admit the Church status of a communion possessing valid orders but separated from one's own is the most un-Augustinian attitude imaginable; and as Augustine was in this simply typical of all Catholics, it is also most un-Catholic. It is amazing how generally St Augustine and the post-Augustinian Church is misunderstood on this point. The Anglo-Catholic view is really a subtle con-

[41] *The Christian Sacraments*, p. 137.
[42] *Ibid.* p. 138.   [43] *Problems of Reunion*, p. 63.
[44] *The Gospel and the Catholic Church*, pp. 218-19.

fusion of Augustinian and Cyprianic doctrine; Augustinian in
its establishment of the validity of its orders without any prior
Church reference; Cyprianic in its belief that valid orders can
only be found within the visible Church, from which it is deduced
that the Church of England must be within the visible Church.
As a whole the argument is faithful to neither doctor, and indeed
directly contradicts the belief of both in the unity of the Church
as one visible communion.

As we have seen, Anglicans have widely found this Anglo-
Catholic apologetic unsatisfactory. It puts altogether too great
a weight upon orders, and makes of the Church herself a sort
of secondary appendage to a line of tactual episcopal succession.
They are aware that arguments of this kind apply no less well
(and Roman Catholics think better) to some of the *episcopi
vagantes* than they do to the Anglican hierarchy. Moreover they
are influenced by the suggestion that the primitive Catholic
view, still prevailing in the East, was different and Cyprianic,
and they feel that in some way a return to this other view will
produce a more healthy theology and also a stronger defence
for the Church of England.

The Anglican tendency to Cyprianism is first discernible in
the stress on a right 'intention of the Church' as an element
required for a valid sacrament; this is contrasted with the
Catholic idea of the intention of the minister. This intention
of the Church or community, to whom the minister of the
sacrament belongs, is understood to depend upon its orthodoxy
—at least as regards the doctrine of orders itself—and therefore
heresy may become a cause of sacramental invalidity.[45] Yet this
view is not really Cyprianic, because it does not exclude the
possibility of valid schismatical sacraments or even of valid
heretical ones, so long as the heresy does not touch on the nature
of the priesthood. Nevertheless, it suggests a tendency to follow
the modern Greek Orthodox view, and the latter has doubtless
been one of the influences behind the recent Cyprianic movement among Anglican theologians. Other influences have been
the reading of the historical evidence which I have already con-

[45] Cf. F. Clark, *Anglican Orders and Defect of Intention*, pp. 44-46.

sidered, the activities of the *episcopi vagantes,* and the problem of the sacraments in non-episcopal communions. This last problem has been brought to the fore as a result of the ecumenical movement.

Already in *Essays on the Early History of the Church and the Ministry* C. H. Turner admitted that St Augustine's doctrine definitely did not commend itself to his judgment.[46] Dr Ramsey has since appealed for 'a whole-hearted return to the Cyprianic view',[47] while Dr Greenslade has defended 'the healthy Cyprianic apprehension that Church, Ministry and Sacraments are organic to one another and inseparable';[48] many another theologian has written to the same effect.[49]

What really can this 'return to the Cyprianic view' mean? For St Cyprian the Church was one communion, and the sacraments were so much the possession of the Church that it was unthinkable that they should be valid outside that one communion. The whole point of St Cyprian's doctrine was a view of the Church to which the sacraments were rigidly subordinated; now the Church view of theologians like Dr Ramsey is the farthest remove possible from that of St Cyprian. To return to the latter's view of the sacraments, while rejecting the whole foundation for that view, is certainly not to return to St Cyprian.

Yet I can understand why Anglican theologians in particular feel this attraction towards Cyprianic doctrine. The sacraments are most certainly Church things, means of Church entry and of Church life, and the closer one can express their link with the Church, apparently the better. Now on an immediate, if perhaps *simpliste,* view Cyprianic doctrine expresses this better than Augustinian, hence its general attraction. But the practice of the Church and a constant tradition force one to recognise the validity of sacraments in dissident communions of the Donatist type. Hence, with a Catholic view of the Church as one communion, it is necessary to think again and more deeply about

[46] p. xxxii.
[47] *The Gospel and the Catholic Church,* p. 219.
[48] *Schism in the Early Church,* p. 215.
[49] For example, O. C. Quick in *The Christian Sacraments,* chap. 7; Dr Davies in *The Month,* January 1957, p. 61, etc.

the exact relationship of the Church's presence and sacramental validity. If, however, one accepts a theology of a divisible Church, the decisive reason in favour of Augustinianism disappears. Admitting that the Church can subsist in a number of disassociated societies, one can retake St Cyprian's link-up of Church presence and valid sacraments. This is what these Anglicans do, but it must be clearly noted that their Cyprianism is quite a different one from that of St Cyprian himself.

This modern Anglican Cyprianism is of various kinds. There is first of all the type represented by C. H. Turner and Dr Ramsey which does not use Cyprianic doctrine to bypass normal Augustinian requirements for validity of orders, e.g. a proper tactual succession, but considers Church status to be a further, or primary, condition. Secondly, there is the view of Dr Greenslade who is prepared to recognise the validity of at least some non-episcopal sacraments so long as they are performed in the traditional way and within a basically orthodox communion. There is, thirdly, the view of Dr Quick. For him, as for every follower of the Cyprianic view, Church authorisation is an integral condition for sacramental validity, but the authorisation of the whole is not obtainable by anyone in a divided Church, but only the partial authorisation of one's own communion. This limited authorisation must limit the validity of the sacraments authorised, and so instead of having fully valid sacraments, there are at present in the Church only partially valid ones. 'If the authority and the validity of Orders is derived from the unity of the "visible" Church, in a divided Church all orders are more or less defective, and their validity is a matter of degree.'[50] Dr Quick repeats this many times over, but he does not really attempt to explain how a sacrament can be partially valid or more valid than another which is yet itself not wholly invalid. This view has been adopted by writers in the Westcott House Symposium, *The Historic Episcopate* but is firmly rejected by Dr Ramsey,[51] and delightfully derided by Dr Peck as 'Percentage Episcopacy'.[52]

---

[50] *The Christian Sacraments*, p. 150.
[51] *The Gospel and the Catholic Church*, p. 229.
[52] *This Church of Christ*, pp. 67-68.

All those holding Cyprianic views have this in common that they cannot, or at least should not, base their Church status on the possession of valid sacraments or the apostolic succession. The what and where of the Church have first to be established and on different grounds. In this they do, of course, also agree with St Augustine and with modern Catholics. Newman contrasted the Catholic attitude with the pseudo-Augustinianism of Anglo-Catholics when he said, 'Catholics believe their orders are valid, because they are members of the true Church; Anglicans believe they belong to the true Church, because their orders are valid.'[53] Newman did not, of course, mean that Catholics think that if they were not in the true Church they *could* not have valid orders, but that they could only be fully confident of that validity because they were within the Church, while Anglicans (of this particular school) are confident that they are in the Church because they have valid orders.

But nowadays many Anglicans, as we see, have abandoned that position and must defend their Church status on something other than their orders. But on what? Not on Scripture, Antiquity or the Catholic tradition, for all are against them in holding the Church to be of its nature one visible communion. Practically speaking their position consists in drawing various separated elements out of Catholic tradition, such elements as each individual theologian judges of lasting value or of pragmatic utility in the present state of Christendom, and putting them together in a new Church pattern of their own. The resultant modern form of Cyprianic doctrine really arrives at something like this: (1) True sacraments and the visible Church are coterminous; (2) Apparently efficacious sacraments must be accounted true sacraments; (3) We should be making a 'harsh judgement' if we questioned the efficacious character of any sacrament sincerely administered; (4) Therefore we must admit that all bodies who claim to administer Christian sacraments are to be recognised as parts of the Church. This, I think, is the position of Dr Greenslade,[54] and it seems a fairly consistent one, but it is not

[53] *Essays Critical and Historical*, II, p. 87.
[54] *Schism in the Early Church*, chap. XI, 'Some Reflections on Christian Unity'.

a Catholic (or, of course, an Anglo-Catholic) position, and it is
difficult to see what sort of authority it can claim other than
providing an easy pragmatic basis for intercommunion. However, it is almost equally difficult to see any other position
claiming to be Cyprianic, yet admitting a divided Church, which
can be considered consistent at all.

Finally, I must return to the 'ultra-Augustinian', or better,
'pseudo-Augustinian' view, and its most recent exponent Dr
Mascall. It is striking that he has consistently defended Anglican
orders on strictly Augustinian lines. It is strange indeed to find
him, an Anglican theologian, actually attacking some modern
Catholic theologians for veering very mildly in a Cyprianic
direction; just what they say we shall see in detail in the next
section, but in general they consider the possibility of the Church
not simply 'recognising' or not recognising schismatic sacraments, but in some way, and in some circumstances, actually
making them valid or nullifying them. If this is anything, it is
certainly a tendency towards Eastern Orthodox doctrine, and
towards that favoured by so many modern Anglican theologians.
It is due to a fear of an almost 'magical' view of the way the
sacraments work, and a desire to show more clearly their ecclesiological significance. Unfortunately Dr Mascall can only see in it
another instance of Roman self-aggrandisement, and even goes
so far as to suggest that Rome is veering towards a sort of
'sacramental omnipotence'.[55] Dr Peck makes charges even
wilder: 'The Pope claims to be able without reference to fact
or to reason, to add to the deposit of faith which is necessary to
salvation, and arbitrarily to restrict sacramental "validity" even
in Christian communions other than his own.'[56] It would be
interesting to see clear evidence to justify such remarkable statements. The evidence on which Dr Mascall rests his charges
appears to be chiefly that of the attitude of some modern Catholic
theologians towards the recently discovered fifteenth-century
Papal bulls which authorise simple priests to ordain other priests.

---

[55] His remarks will be found on pp. 18-20 of 'Intention and Form in Anglican
Orders', *The Church Quarterly Review*, 1957.
[56] *Anglicanism and Episcopacy*, p. 98.

Rather than admit that a number of popes were mistaken in so grave a practical matter, these theologians are tending 'to admit that a priest can by papal indult confer the sacrament of orders'.[57] Dr Mascall sees in this proof of the Roman tendency 'to submerge the sacramental aspect of the Catholic Church beneath the administrative and juridical'.[58] He concludes that 'in arguing for the validity of the ordinations in the cases just referred to, they (Catholic theologians) are not maintaining the essential validity of ordination by presbyters, but the power of the Pope to overrule by his administrative authority the sacramental structure of the Church: they are arguing not for presbyterianism but for popery'.[59]

This is all very misleading. No Catholic theologian has suggested that the pope can overrule the sacramental structure of the Church. What some do think is that that structure is slightly different from what they had hitherto supposed. Despite what Dr Mascall says, they are—in a way—arguing for presbyterianism, as is quite clear from the following words of Mgr Journet: 'Priests have the physical power of confirming and ordaining'.[60] 'But', Journet goes on, 'the valid exercise of this power is limited (as, analogically, that of absolving is limited); for its valid use a priest requires authorisation.' In this view (and it is no more) the giving of orders becomes an act both sacramental and jurisdictional, and that again is to bring us back to a slightly more Cyprianic view of ordination.

Despite such ripples on the surface, Rome is, and always has been, remarkably conservative in this field. Dr Quick's reading of the Roman mind remains far truer than that of Mascall or Peck; 'it is strange,' he writes, 'that Roman Catholicism should, in reference to the sacraments, seem to belittle unduly the authority of the Church'.[61] If Catholic theologians really are moving at present very slightly and very cautiously in a direction already taken by the East and by so many Anglicans, they hardly deserve Dr Mascall's condemnation.

[57] J. Bligh, S.J., *Ordination to the Priesthood*, p. 9.
[58] *The Recovery of Unity*, p. 212.   [59] Ibid. p. 213.
[60] *The Church and the Word Incarnate*, I, p. 115.
[61] *The Christian Sacraments*, p. 157.

What is more important to notice is the complete insecurity of Mascall's own position and that of traditional Anglo-Catholics. He defends Anglican Orders on strictly Augustinian lines, and then defends the Anglican communion because it possesses valid orders. This involves a complete failure to face up to the Augustinian-Cyprianic issue. Either sacraments are only valid within the visible Church, in which case you can only know who has valid sacraments after deciding the nature and limits of the Church; or it is enough for sacraments to be valid that certain objective conditions of form, minister and intention be fulfilled, in which case the presence of valid sacraments does not sufficiently indicate the presence of the visible Church. The great count against Dr Mascall is that he explains the validity of sacraments in non-ecclesiological terms, and then interprets their presence ecclesiologically.

4. Conclusion

Dr Greenslade thinks, 'We cannot escape the fact that the Church is divided';[62] so, too, Dr Quick's constant premise is, 'the "visible" Church being manifestly divided'.[63] Such sentences express the unproved presupposition behind all this Anglican thought about sacramental validity. Every theology of the sacraments rests on an eccclesiology, and where ecclesiologies differ fundamentally there can be no hope of agreement on the sacramental plane; it has been one aim of this chapter to make this point clear. It is no wonder that Anglican theologians are restless about traditional Catholic views on the sacraments when they have rejected the foundation stone on which those views rested.

Dr Greenslade summed up his own, internally consistent opinion in the preface of his book:

> I express my distrust of some of Augustine's ideas, and still more of the conclusions which have been drawn from them, often quite logically, and which lead to a discontinuity between the doctrine of the Church on the one hand and the doctrine of the Ministry and Sacraments on the other. I do not infer that it would be right to return to Cyprian's position *in toto*. On the contrary, while I

---

[62] Dr Greenslade, *Schism in the Early Church*, p. 218.
[63] Dr Quick, *The Christian Sacraments*, p. 147.

uphold Cyprian's insistence upon the coherence of the Church, Ministry and Sacraments, I suggest that Augustine did not depart sufficiently from the impossible severity and narrowness of Cyprian's outlook. I conclude that little if any modern Western teaching on this subject is consistently patristic, and that those who plead the authority of the Fathers are called to a scrupulous self-examination. For if we allow what the early Church, including both Cyprian and Augustine, would not allow, that various separated communions or denominations are *within* the Catholic Church, our theory of Church, Ministry and Sacraments and their inter-relation must be different as a whole from the theories of the Fathers, even if it draws upon many elements in their teaching.[64]

If we allow what the early Church would not allow, if we begin our theological reasoning with premises quite different from those held by any Catholic in the past, we shall indeed arrive at conclusions as new as our premises. For a new hypothesis we can work out a new doctrine, but it *is* a new doctrine whose origin lies not in revelation but in a particular interpretation of the contemporary situation.

This new doctrine appears not only as fundamentally pragmatic, but also as denying either the centrality of oneness in the work of the Redemption or the effectiveness of God's will in that work. The whole meaning of Redemption is at-one-ment, and if the God-chosen vehicle of at-one-ment is a visible Church, and if also that visible Church has been broken and divided by man's sins, then the sin of man has proved more powerful than the redemption of God. Scandalous as sin is, powerful as the gates of hell are, the Church of the redemption is more powerful still and to speak of 'the scandal that the Church should be divided'[65] is to speak of scandal where it can never be. The sin of man cannot maim the redemptive work of God, and the one, visible Church is of the very essence of the Redemption.

But if the Church is not divided, how, Anglican theologians ask, can we explain, in an adequate and convincing way, the presence of sacraments and of apparent sacramental grace in many separated denominations? How can we possibly avoid that

[64] *Schism in the Early Church*, p. 11.
[65] A. E. J. Rawlinson, *Problems of Reunion*, p. 62.

'discontinuity between the doctrine of the Church on the one hand and the doctrine of the Ministry and Sacraments on the other'?

We must always bear in mind that the sacraments are at one and the same time God's acts, the Church's acts, and the minister's acts; but not in the same way. No valid sacrament can fail to have this triple character, though the three may not always stand out with equal clarity. Given the sacramental order, God requires the instrument of a minister, but the inward effect of the sacrament following upon the performance of the outward sign is an effect proportioned to its principal cause, God, not to man, its subsidiary cause. Without the fulfilment of certain minimum conditions this minister would be no minister at all; the sacrament would simply not have been made. But if these conditions be fulfilled, then the sacrament is valid in spite of the possible unworthiness, lack of faith or grave ecclesiastical irregularity, of the minister. The reason for this is not at all, as some suggest, that Catholics look on the sacraments as mere private acts within the power of any competent minister, but on the contrary because the sacraments are essentially public, ecclesiastical things instituted for the common good which would not be served at all if their validity could be imperilled by the unworthiness or irregularity of the minister.

We recognise valid baptism and valid marriage among Protestants and Anglicans, and also valid orders and valid Eucharist among the Greek Orthodox, and the Old Catholics and others. All these sacraments remain acts of the Church, but they do not give ecclesiastical status to the schismatic bodies in which they are visibly performed, because the very *raison d'être* of those bodies lies in an act of separation from the Body of the visible Church.

Every man baptised becomes *ipso facto* a full member of the visible Church. There is nothing else into which one can be baptised: 'Non est baptismus ille schismaticorum vel haereticorum sed Dei et ecclesiae, ubicumque fuerit inventum et quocumque translatum.'[66] Until there is a definite contrary act of the

---

[66] St Augustine, *De Bapt.* 1. 14 (22).

will (by no means necessarily a sinful act) a baptised person remains a member of the Church's visible communion. He can only be separated from it by an act of his free will, and he does this at the moment of conscious adhesion to a communion or religious sect which is separated from the Church's visible communion.

The Church's baptismal seal remains upon those who have left her, and there remain too—if they are in good faith—the living grace and even the substantial reality of Church membership. Just as those who are never baptised with water, but die in some way wanting it, have a 'baptism of desire' which gives them the effective reality obtained in baptism with water, so, analogously, do those Christians never lose the reality received in baptism or the inner union with the Church which is thus signified. They remain invisibly united with the one visible Church, outside whom there is no salvation, although visibly they are separated from her. If their separation is culpable they cease to share in the Church's life of grace, but even then her baptismal seal remains upon their souls. Similarly, those within the visible communion may be dead to grace through sin. But both one and the other, because they have entered the Church in baptism— whatever may have happened afterwards—can be, in some circumstances, ministers of the Church's other sacraments.

The Church has no desire to prevent the sacramental life of her separated children, at least when they are in good faith. Her authorisation of penance with the Greek Orthodox is a case in point; she has maintained the sacramental jurisdiction of dissident priests when she could have withdrawn it. The question is to what extent the validity of other sacraments possessed by schismatics may also depend on her free authorisation. This authorisation may be given less to the act than to the rite. The Greeks, continuing to use Catholic ordination forms, have valid ordinations: their ordinations remain truly acts of the one Church. Contrariwise, it might be that the fundamental reason for the invalidity of Anglican orders lies rather in the fact that their ordinal was drawn up by heretical schismatics, was never authorised by the Church and was therefore not the 'forma Ecclesiae'

than in a complete incapacity to receive such authorisation and so transmit valid orders.

In the recent past Catholic theologians have tended to neglect the ecclesiastical character of the sacraments and perhaps to minimise the Church's effective power in the sacramental field. It is only theologians such as De La Taille and Masure who have, for instance, rediscovered the full corporate and ecclesiastical significance of the greatest of all the sacraments, the Mass. And only now are theologians coming to examine the extent of the Church's effective authority over the sacraments, one thing which has certainly encouraged this development being the decree *Sacramentum Ordinis* of Pope Pius XII. An example of the new ecclesiological approach to the sacraments may be found in the following words which come from a distinguished Belgian Dominican theologian, Dr Henry Schillebeeckx:

> To what an extent a visible separation from the true Church of Christ exerts an influence on the external rite itself, that is, whether such a rite does or does not continue the ritual profession of the faith of the Church, must be determined by the Catholic Church herself. It belongs to the true Church to determine whether a rite performed in given circumstances is an 'exteriorisation' of her own faith, that is, whether it is *her own act*; or whether it is, on the contrary, an act expressing the faith of another, separated Church, *qua* separated. In this latter case the rite is not valid.[67]

Just what this would mean in practice, if accepted, requires further clarification. All I wish to stress here is that if valid and partly efficacious sacraments do most certainly exist outside the Church's visible communion, they do always remain acts of the Church (whether or not they at times require some sort of formal authorisation) and acts building up the Church, only this effect is to a greater or lesser extent nullified by the free will of those who receive them. And for the possibility of that nullification we have St Paul himself for authority. The effectiveness of the sacraments—both as regards grace and Church membership—is conditional upon human consent. A valid sacrament may be

---

[67] Quoted by F. Clark, S.J., in *Anglican Orders and Defect of Intention*, pp. 9-10; see also Mgr G. D. Smith, 'The Church and her Sacraments', *Clergy Review*, April 1950, pp. 217-31.

received in a state of mortal sin, the latter preventing the spiritual life which should flow from the sacrament; it may likewise be received in a state of schism, and that prevents the visible membership of the Church which would of itself follow upon baptism. In each case a voluntary act of the baptised is impeding part, but not all, of the effects of the sacrament.

Basically we have certainly to remain Augustinian, both because that is the doctrine which came to be universally accepted before the end of antiquity, and because it alone does not lead to an untold state of sacramental confusion, as the history of the East so clearly shows. But the acceptance of true Augustinianism completely cuts away the ground from the traditional Tractarian and Anglo-Catholic apologetic: by recognising the possibility of valid episcopal succession lines outside the visible Church, it makes it impossible to argue from the possession of episcopacy to membership of the Church.[68]

Nor, for a Catholic, does the Augustinan recognition of valid sacraments outside the *una sancta* detract from the equally Augustinian recognition of the Church as a *societas sacramentorum*: the Church is one because of her sacramental unity, but true sacramental unity is not at all the mere common possession of valid sacraments in disassociated sects, but it is the visible fellowship of a unique intercommunion. How this is true will be considered in Chapter VIII.

Once this is clearly understood, it is surely only a matter of rejoicing that the sacraments can still remain partly effective outside the charted boundaries of the visible Church. Thus many people of great good will are helped and strengthened. In them, almost unknowingly, the Church is continuing to work, continuing to bring forth children, form them, nourish them, and prepare them through herself for the kingdom of heaven. At the end of it all, it will be a great wonder and joy to see the Church's mystery fully revealed, and to see how all good men, in one way or another, wherever they were born or lived, were born and

---

[68] True Cyprianism is, of course, equally inimical to the Anglican position, as we have seen. Dr Greenslade is perfectly clear-sighted, from his own viewpoint, when he urges that both Cyprian and Augustine—and indeed the whole of Antiquity—should be dropped overboard.

lived within her, the One, Holy and Apostolic Church, the ark of salvation. The Philistines, Tyre, and the Ethiopians too, all these—the Psalmist sings—were born in Jerusalem. 'All the world, rejoicing, finds its dwelling-place in thee.'[69]

[69] Psalm 86.

Chapter 7

THE APPEAL TO THE BOSPHORUS

The existence of the great Orthodox communities of the East, the Greek and Slav Churches centring upon Constantinople, is without doubt a great source of comfort to many other non-Roman Christians, and particularly to Anglo-Catholics. If the latter knew themselves to be alone in defending a 'primitive' form of non-papal Catholicism, there are perhaps few among them who would really feel confident in denying the claims of Rome and maintaining their own view about the true nature of Catholicism. But, so they feel, they are not alone. There are, of course, the Old Catholics; they are not numerous, but they are clearly Catholic in doctrine, western in culture, and they have orders whose validity even Rome admits; best of all, they are in full communion with the Church of England.

Far more important is the Greek Church. 'Our own defence has always been strengthened by an appeal from the Tiber to the Bosphorus' wrote J. A. Douglas.[1] Orthodoxy is conservative, traditional, unreformed: consequently it is believed to have safely preserved the Catholicism of the early Church, untouched by Protestantism or by Roman centralisation. At least in theory it represents the very ideal for which many Anglicans strive. If we can show that we stand with the East, they feel, then indeed it will be clear that we stand also for the uncontaminated Catholicism of the primitive Church. If we are not now in communion with the East, that is unfortunately due to our flirtations with Protestantism, and the sooner these end the better. Let us, if necessary, even go back to school, and learn from the Greeks in the belief that 'the Anglican Churches ought to approximate more and more to Orthodoxy until at last they could be recognised as actual members of the Orthodox family'.[2] That is the view of

[1] *The Relations of the Anglican Churches with the Eastern Orthodox*, p. 38.
[2] H. A. Hodges, *Anglicanism and Orthodoxy*, p. 9.

Professor Hodges; it is a personal view, but it is in line with much Anglo-Catholic thought. For the most part, however, Anglicans are quite sure that they already possess the necessary essentials of Catholicism, and all that is required is to convince the Greeks of the Church of England's true character. At least on the central points of ecclesiology, it is maintained, Canterbury and Constantinople stand together against Rome. Both deny infallibility or any other type of special divine authority to belong to the see of Rome, both nevertheless believe in episcopacy and in a federal, decentralised system, in a sensible division of the Church universal into national churches. This basic agreement with the East is a great help for an Episcopalian as he stands between pure Protestantism on the one side and Roman Catholicism on the other; it is a guaranty that his own idea of the Church coincides with the primitive one, and that it is Rome, not Canterbury, that is out of step. He feels confident of a consensus of opinion in his own favour: 'The system of the Early Church was a federation of local churches, with an appeal to the General Council of the whole Church. This has never ceased to be the system of the Orthodox Church of the East. It is also the system of the Anglican Church today.[3] The word 'system' is misleading; in so far as it means an outward ordering of government, and it appears to do so here, it is of course something of secondary importance. In quite important ways the system of government of both the Church of Rome and Church of England has changed in the last 200 years, but the decisive issues of ecclesiology go far deeper. Few Anglicans too can really feel very happy about the use of the word 'federation' often as it appears in such contexts. The unity of a federation is derived from the coming together of several independent units, while the unity between local churches is admittedly something which precedes them, within which they exist, not something which they have made to exist.[4]

But, alas, the view of things outlined above is not correct. We already know that on the fundamental ecclesiological issue

[3] Percy Dearmer, D.D., *Everyman's History of the English Church* (Mowbray, 1909, 1919, 1921), p. 70.
[4] On this point I may refer to Dr Lacey's remarks in *Unity and Schism*, Lecture VI.

separating Canterbury from Rome, the Early Church (on the evidence of even the best modern Anglican scholars) stands squarely with Rome. The same must now be said of the chain's middle link: Constantinople, both past and present. Constantinople and Canterbury are agreed in rejecting the papal claims, but their own theologies of the Church are by no means the same, and on the most fundamental questions separating Canterbury from Rome, Constantinople stands well to the Roman side. These questions are the Church's unity and her authority. Is the Church necessarily one visible communion, and has she (on occasion) an infallible teaching authority? Rome and Constantinople are not agreed as to how that visible unity is guaranteed, nor as to the exact organ of the Church's infallible authority, but they are agreed that the Church is one visible communion and has an infallible authority. The twenty-first of the 39 Articles affirming that 'General Councils may err, and sometimes have erred, even in things pertaining unto God' is absolutely unacceptable for the Greek Orthodox. The exact organ of infallible authority in the Church is a relatively secondary matter in comparison with the question whether or not the Church can in some way decide about the faith with the full authority of its founder. Rome and the East give one answer to this question, the Church of England gives another.

With regard to the chief subject of this book, the position is almost equally clear. For primitive Christianity the Church was one visible communion and one only, separation from which entailed division from the Church. This is still, and has always been, the view of Rome; it is exactly contradicted by the Anglican distinction between Church and communion. What does Orthodoxy hold on the point? To that question I shall give first of all the opinion of Fr Congar: 'I, for my part, am convinced that, except for the question of the Roman primacy (which is not always put in an adequate light), the ecclesiology of the Orthodox East and that of the Catholic West are basically the same on the dogmatic plane. . . . Both the one and the other hold that the Church is a single communion.'[5] Fr Congar

---

[5] *Amica Contestatio*, in *Intercommunion*, ed. Baillie and Marsh, p. 147.

has great authority in such matters, and to it may be added that of Dr Greenslade who also places Orthodoxy on the side of Rome and the early Church.[6] Indeed, it would be striking if the Greek Orthodox, conservative as we know them to be, had so departed from a universal conviction of Antiquity. Yet if they have not done so, one of the most valuable supports normally used by Anglicans in defence of their own ecclesiology has disappeared. It is not surprising that this is not easily admitted, and that we can find Dr Mascall, for instance, remarking that 'although, from the strictly canonical point of view, the Eastern Orthodox Church holds that it and it alone is the Catholic Church of Christ, very few of its theologians are today prepared to defend this position without qualification'.[7] This, like everything Dr Mascall writes, is a carefully worded statement; that does not make it less but more misleading, and the suggested divergence of the theological from the canonical viewpoint is not in fact widely verifiable.

It is true that there are Orthodox theologians, mainly, if not wholly, among those who have come under considerable western influence, who have in this country abandoned the traditional claim of their Church. Dr Nicolas Zernov is an example. 'Christians today', he wrote twenty years ago, 'have at last to accept and to bear the reality that the One, Holy, Catholic and Apostolic Church has been divided through the sins of her earthly members, and that as God has allowed sinful man to crucify the Lord of Glory, His Only-Begotten Son, so also has He allowed the members of the Church to divide and torture the living Body of Christ in the world.'[8] There is no doubt that Dr Zernov has here accepted a typically Anglican view of Christian divisions, and his connection with Oxford University may not be without significance in this regard. But in maintaining this view, he has ceased to represent either the Orthodox Church itself, or the most part of Orthodox theologians. For them, undoubtedly, Canon Douglas's judgment still holds good that 'It is perfectly correct to say that as the Papalist Church holds herself to be the

---

[6] *Schism in the Early Church*, p. 147.   [7] *Corpus Christi*, pp. 1-2.
[8] 'The Church and Confessions', in *The Church of God, An Anglo-Russian Symposium*, ed. E. L. Mascall, p. 223. See also his recent book *The Reintegration of the Church*.

One and Only True Church, so also the Eastern-Orthodox Church holds herself to be the One and Only True Church'.[9] Those who have more recently examined the evidence have all come to the same conclusion.[10] The truth is that, in the words of the Delegation of the Patriarchate of Constantinople sent to the Lambeth Conference of 1920, Anglicans and Orthodox have an 'essentially different conception of the idea of the Church and the members who compose it'.[11] The Greeks are not given to clear cut definitions, and they will not always express this 'essentially different conception' with quite the same terms or stress. But the central idea does not change: the Church is a unity of faith shared within one Communion, and that Communion is the Greek Orthodox Church and nothing else.

In the last century Khomiakov, the great Russian theologian, concluded his famous treatise entitled *The Church is One* with the following words: 'By the will of God the Holy Church, after the falling away of many schisms, and of the Roman Patriarchate, was preserved in the Greek Eparchies and Patriarchates, and only those communities can acknowledge one another as fully Christian which preserve their unity with the Eastern Patriarchates, or enter into this unity. For there is one God, and one Church, and within her there is neither dissension nor disagreement.'[12] About this, Khomiakov's Anglican editor, W. J. Birkbeck, felt bound to comment:

> There is much in Mr Khomiakov's writings, both in this correspondence (with Palmer) and in his other works, which no Anglican can unreservedly accept. While we can readily admit that there was much development of western theology after the Great Schism which was one-sided and much that was even altogether erroneous, we can never admit that the West ceased to be part of the Church, or that the whole truth has been committed

[9] *Relations of the Anglican Churches with the Eastern Orthodox* (1921) p. 51.
[10] Cf. A. Dulles, S.J., 'The Orthodox Churches and the Ecumenical Movement', *Downside Review*, January 1957, pp. 38-54; E. R. Hambye, S.J., 'The Nature of the Church—According to the Teaching of the Greek Dissidents', *Clergy Review*, March 1957, pp. 140-51; Clément Lialine, O.S.B., 'Anglicanisme et Orthodoxie. Quelques aperçus sur leurs relations', *Istina*, 1956, pp. 32-98, 183-90, especially the conclusion on p. 77.
[11] Bell, *Documents on Christian Unity*, 1920-4, p. 57.
[12] This essay of Khomiakov's is to be found at the end of W. J. Birkbeck, *Russia and the English Church*; quotation from p. 222.

to the East alone since that unhappy event. . . . The object for
which this book has been published will be very much mistaken,
if it is thought that it is intended to throw doubt upon the claims,
both of the English and the Roman Churches, to be considered
true members of the Catholic Church.[13]

One of the most distinguished of modern 'western' Orthodox
theologians, Dr Georges Florovsky, has recently expressed his
faith in the Church in the following words:

> As a member and priest of the Orthodox Church I believe that
> the Church in which I was baptised and brought up *is* in very
> truth *the Church,* i.e. *the true* Church and the *only* true Church.
> I believe that for many reasons: by personal conviction and by
> the inner testimony of the Spirit which breathes in the sacraments
> of the Church and by all that I could learn from Scripture and
> from the universal tradition of the Church. I am compelled there-
> fore to regard all other Christian Churches as deficient, and in
> many cases I can identify these deficiencies accurately enough.
> Therefore, for me, Christian reunion is just universal conversion to
> Orthodoxy. I have no confessional loyalty; my loyalty belongs
> solely to the *Una Sancta.*[14]

Such testimony could be multiplied almost indefinitely. Nevertheless I think it should be conceded that the Orthodox have a
deep, if unformulated feeling that, while the Church is and can
be only one communion from which other Christians are separated and in schism, all the same the vast East-West schism not
only separated many Christians from the Church, but did also
in some way maim the Church herself in her very structure.
Hence they speak at times somewhat confusedly of the earlier
'undivided Church' or of 'the revival of the one whole Church
through the joining again of those Churches remaining outside
of the one';[15] above all, they feel that until the West is reunited
with the one Church a new oecumenical council cannot be called.
Logically, this position is difficult to explain; the vast Monophysite and Nestorian schisms did not prevent the calling of
general councils in the past, why should the schism of the West

---

[13] *Russia and the English Church,* p. liv.
[14] 'Confessional Loyalty in the Ecumenical Movement', in *Intercommunion,*
ed. Baillie and Marsh, p. 204.
[15] H. Alivisatos in *The Nature of the Church,* edited by R. Newton Flew, p. 52.

do so today? The feeling that it does may be taken as evidence that the Orthodox are not entirely able to conciliate the Catholic doctrine which they have inherited (the Church is one communion) with the Christendom which in fact exists. It is, above all, Rome which presents them with an irresolvable problem; however much they believe in her sins they do not forget that in the past Rome was universally acknowledged to have the primacy among all the Churches, they can still call her 'the sister Church',[16] and they cannot quite reconcile themselves to her exclusion from the Church of the present.

However, the essential Eastern Church doctrine, still most certainly maintained by the majority of Orthodox theologians, remains clear, and it is basically identical with our own: the unity of the Church is that of one visible communion, and of no more. It is true that this doctrine is generally stated in very concrete and *de facto* terms: the Eastern Orthodox communion is the One Church. The theoretical principle behind the statement—that the Church can only be a single visible communion —is rather implied than formulated explicitly; but unless it was in fact believed there could be little justification for the *de facto* affirmation that the Eastern Orthodox alone form the one visible Church. A recent official statement of this doctrine may fittingly conclude this section. It is from an article by Professor Hamilcar Alivisatos, contributed to the *Faith and Order* volume on the nature of the Church. This article was submitted to the Archbishop of Athens and to the Holy Synod of the Church of Greece, and fully approved by them.

Historic developments have resulted in the formation of many Christian Churches.

As to the value and the relationship of these many Churches to the authentic one, there are four possible theories:

(1) This one Church is during the ages lost among the many Churches;

(2) This one Church is divided into fragments, each one forming one of the existing different Churches. Each one of them has

[16] Patriarch Alexis of Moscow in the *Acts of the Pan-Orthodox Conference* held in Moscow, July 1948, vol. 1, p. 90 (Moscow, 1949), quoted by N. Zernov, *The Reintegration of the Church*, p. 97.

kept something essential from the one and their simple union will reconstitute the one broken to pieces;

(3) This one Church is to be identified in several existing Churches, which, though broken apart from each other, may each have retained the essential elements of the one Church;

(4) Out of the many existing Christian Churches there is only one of them which is entitled to be the one as having kept unchanged and uncorrupt the one truth as revealed by the Lord and the Apostles, regardless of later outward developments. The first three theories, with slight modifications, are represented by the theology of the several Protestant Churches, while the fourth is represented by the Roman Catholic Church and the Greek Orthodox Church, each one according to its own conception. . . .

The existence of the One Church, even now and in spite of the many Churches, brings us to the claim of the Greek Orthodox Church that she alone has the right to be this one Church on account of her historically unbroken continuity with the undivided Church. . . . Since the Great Schism, and the events of the sixteenth and seventeenth centuries, the great majority of Christian people, for one reason (Roman Catholicism) or another (Protestantism), have ceased to belong to the one Catholic Church.[17]

The Eastern Orthodox share then with Roman Catholics the central principles of their ecclesiology. Constantinople, like Rome, believes that the Church is essentially a single communion with an infallible teaching authority. The Greeks are separated from us on only small points of doctrine, and they share with us not only the central affirmations of the Catholic faith but also the valid exercise of all seven sacraments. Nevertheless they remain in schism, cut off from the visible unity of the one Church, for no correct understanding of the idea of the Church necessarily involves membership of it in fact (as they themselves would fully agree). Yet their agreement on so many things makes this great rent in the robe of Christendom all the more tragic. The strength and bitterness of schism so often depends on irrelevant

[17] H. Alivisatos, 'The Holy Greek Orthodox Church', in *The Nature of the Church*, ed. R. Newton Flew, pp. 43-44, 47, 50. See also the uncompromising statement of the Orthodox delegation at the 1954 Assembly of the World Council of Churches at Evanston, pp. 92-95 of *The Evanston Report*.

factors, and here above all this is true. The gap between Latin and Greek remains enormous, but it is a gap of culture and political history and the shadow of the personal conflicts of the past, not—to any very large extent—a gap of theology. What is needed most here is human rapprochement, the chance to meet, to love one another, to grow together again. The chief theological theme of this book, so important for separated Christians in the West, is only a confirmation of its accepted views for the Orthodox East, because it already fully agrees.

On the theological level what the East needs is certainly to consider again and in a non-partisan light the traditional role of the Roman See within the structure of an ecclesiological doctrine which is not in question: her pastoral role as the organ of unity within the one flock—a role given her when Jesus, after stressing the shepherd's unifying function in the Church (Jn. 10:16), solemnly invested Peter with the shepherd's work (Jn. 21:15-17)—a role constantly recognised in the earliest centuries of Church history.

The difficulty is to escape, after so many years, from the distorting light of partisanship. It is for us to show with our deeds that Rome is not as she has seemed: to show that she is already, and will always be, as Greek as she is Latin, a mother to all, for she is simply Catholic. When the Church of Rome really appears Catholic to her critics—the Church of the Indians and the Africans and the Germans and the Americans as well as of the Latins—the old narrow rivalry between Tiber and Bosphorus should die of itself, and the Greeks will return because they desire to return, because the heirs of Gregory and Basil and Chrysostom have treasured the Catholic traditions of their past, and will not wish to remain in the servitude of schism when they see all that they love and cherish alive within the ark of a truly world Church holding firm to apostolic tradition yet embracing new things, at home in every nation. It was the narrowness of national rivalry and the clash of two Mediterranean cultures which caused the schism; it is the breadth of Catholic charity which will end it, when the call of Rome is seen again to be the call of liberty and love and truth.

Chapter 8

THE CATHOLIC SYNTHESIS

1. *The Fullness of Communion*

In this chapter I mean to gather the central strands of Catholic Church doctrine together and consider them no more in contrast with various non-Catholic opinions, but rather by themselves and for their own sake. The following discussion consequently provides a sort of anchor against which the examination of particular points elsewhere may be weighed, and in which my own beliefs as to the real nature of Church unity can be seen more easily and as a whole. I hope at the same time it will be noticed how closely akin in many ways is the view of Dr Mascall to true Catholic doctrine, and yet what a great, if subtle, gap remains to divide the one from the other.

In his little book entitled *Bishop Gore and the Catholic Claims* Dom John Chapman devotes a chapter to the unity of the Church, which seems to offer a sound, thoughtful summary of agreed Catholic doctrine, and, though somewhat long, a quotation from it will afford a useful opening for my own discussion.

Theologians demand for the Church a threefold visible unity.

1. The primary unity is UNITY OF FAITH, for the Church is the living witness throughout all ages to the faith once delivered. On this point the Fathers are unanimous and clear. Perhaps the most obvious to refer to is St Irenaeus, who in the second century appealed to the consentient witness of a continuous and universal Church against the heretics of the time. To refer to other Fathers is supererogatory, as I suppose their doctrine on this subject is not denied. This is the 'symbolical bond'. To break it is the sin of heresy.

2. This unity of faith is guarded and demonstrated by UNITY OF INTERCOMMUNION, which is called the 'liturgical bond'. To break it is the sin of schism. Against heretics this unity is pointed out to be a fact, as a means of demonstrating that unity of faith which heresy dares to break. But against schismatics, such as the Novatianists and Donatists, the necessity of communion with

the Church was the point to be proved. It is therefore in the writings of St Cyprian, St Pacian, St Optatus, and St Augustine against these schismatics that we find this doctrine most fully argued and illustrated, though it is indeed taught by all the ancients with one voice. . . .

3. The third kind of unity is UNITY OF GOVERNMENT— the subjection of the faithful to the same pastors. This is called the 'hierarchical bond'. . . . The complete and fully developed hierarchy of the Church has the successor of St Peter at its head, and consequently this third form of unity centres in the Pope. . . .

These three bonds of unity, then, the symbolical, the liturgical, and the hierarchical, are all according to the Fathers, indispensable to the visible Church on earth. One faith, one communion, one spiritual government. The unity of faith is primary and fundamental. It should naturally issue in the union of all believers in one fellowship, without which the unity of faith cannot survive. To guard in its turn the unity of fellowship and communion, the hierarchical bond is needed, on account of the tendency to quarrel which we have derived from original sin. This is a logical theory, and it answers to the facts of history.[1]

Most certainly these three bonds are all essential to the Church's unity, and I cannot materially disagree with anything in the above passage. Nevertheless I do not think that Chapman has quite succeeded in giving us an exact analysis of Church unity, but before criticising him I would like to quote some other passages from Dom Christopher Butler, like Chapman, Abbot of Downside, and in several other ways too his successor.

The Catholic position with regard to the unity of the Church is simple—which is not to say that it is not profound. I am speaking for the moment of unity, not of the reunion of Christendom. It is, that Christ founded a Church which was essentially a society; that he promised indefectibility to this society and that (quite apart from a particular text in St Matthew's Gospel) it is clear from the New Testament that the Christian revelation involves the indefectibility of the Church; and that in consequence unless one (one only) of the extant Christian societies is the society established by Christ, then the claim of Christianity to be a true revelation from God collapses.[2]

A race or a family can exist despite the dissociation of its consistent groups; but a society or fellowship only exists if we can

[1] *Bishop Gore and the Catholic Claims*, pp. 22-24.
[2] 'The Unity of the Church', in *The Spirit of Unity*, p. 13.

point to one, and one only, *association* of members or groups and say '*there*, and not elsewhere, is the society or fellowship of which I am speaking'; a society or fellowship is essentially an associated thing. A dissociated society is a contradiction in terms, though of course a society may have to deplore that some of its members do not pay their subscriptions or obey the rules. If some members of a society set up an organisation on their own account, or secede with the local officers and funds and carry on their local common life without reference to the parent body, then this new organisation or independent group has precisely abandoned the common life of the original fellowship and we are in future faced with the fact of not *one visible society* but two.[3]

Though this approach may seem rather different from that of Chapman's, I believe that Abbot Butler is here coming very close to the most fundamental idea of Church unity: it is the unity of a visible society, association, or fellowship. It is this which the whole of Catholic tradition bears witness to, and it is also this which is radically contradicted by the Anglican location of the Church in a number of disassociated societies or communions. Nevertheless I think that we have still not arrived at quite the most exact possible statement of Church unity, and indeed I can feel almost worried when Abbot Butler, in a further statement, distinguishes this 'unity of association' both from 'sacramental unity' and from 'governmental unity',[4] because the first two types are, I believe, in a Catholic context precisely one and the same. However, Abbot Butler was here replying to criticisms from an Anglican, Mr Warner, and a little examination at once shows that the Abbot is only distinguishing between 'unity of association' and 'sacramental unity' when the latter is understood in Mr Warner's Anglican way.

There are, after all, many kinds of society or association in this world: they associate men together in different ways and for different ends. The question is: what is the special character of the Christian society? What is the decisive principle in the association of the Church? Abbot Butler comes to the right answer at once. 'The Church militant is essentially a society, an associated thing; something essentially incapable of existing as

---

[3] 'The Church in Scripture and History', *The Tablet*, 19 May 1956.
[4] *The Tablet*, correspondence, 2 June 1956.

two or more separate *communions*.'[5] The Church is not several communions; she is a *communion*. This is the deepest statement that one can make about her nature and her unity.

What is a communion but a sacramental society? the Church is not any type of association, it is that association which is made one by sharing in the Eucharist, its sacrament of unity. 'We being many are one body, because we all partake of the one bread' (I Cor. 10: 17). Sacramental unity, rightly understood is (in a Christian context) exactly the same thing as unity of association. The Church is not an association for the sake of being an association: she is an association for the purpose of communicating the Eucharist, and she is associated by this very thing for which she exists. Communion is not, then, an expression of the Church's unity, it is not just one act among others of the Christian association: it *is* that association, it is the Church.

If we now return to Dom John Chapman's analysis of Church unity, we find that this unity of sacramental association has been placed by him in the second place. Is this right, or is it wrong? I think that it is both. 'The unity of faith', he wrote, 'is primary and fundamental.' Again, I agree and disagree. Unity of faith is indeed the foundation of the Church, and the foundation of unity; yet formally it is not equivalent to the unity of the Church. Those who abandon the unity of faith will also cut themselves off, or will be cut off, from Church unity, that is to say from communion. The one communion protects and is built upon the one faith, and communion is the very sacrament of the faith. But the Church, because visible, requires a visible principle of unity, and faith is not a visible principle, while communion is. Again, the principle of Church unity must be strictly a principle of association, of society; communion means just this, faith does not, and it can indeed exist outside the visible society, which by definition communion cannot.

Again, as Chapman says, to break the bond of faith is 'the sin of heresy', but to break the bond of communion is 'the sin of schism'. Now it is schism, not heresy, which is opposed *per se* to the unity of the Church ('Peccatum schismatis dicitur quod

[5] *The Tablet*, correspondence 2 June, 1956.

directe et per se opponitur unitati' S. Thomas, *Summa Theologica* II-II, q. 39, a. l.). Consequently *per se* the unity of the Church must be identified with the bond of communion, not of faith. The unity of the Church does not 'issue' in intercommunion, it is not manifested or demonstrated by it. It is it. Paradoxically enough, among modern theologians it seems to be an Anglican who has best expressed this most fundamental of ecclesiological truths. In the words of Dom Gregory Dix:

> The communicants receive 'that they may be made one' (with one another). The unity of the Mystical Body derives from the unity of the Sacramental Body. The Eucharist is *not*—as has been so unscripturally said by a succession of Lambeth Conferences— the 'expression' of the Church's unity. (That is to make the Church a mere human association). It is the *cause*, Because (ὅτι) the Bread is one, we being many are one Body. For we all partake of the one Bread (I Cor. 10:16). Breach of communion, excommunication, does not register a breach already made in the Church's unity; it *is* that breach, though not the reason for it. The unity of the Glorified Body of Christ constitutes the unity of his Sacramental Body and it is by the unity of communion in that one Sacramental Body that the Church is one.[6]

As a visible society, the Church-communion requires, and has always possessed, human ministers, a human authority. From the very beginning of Christianity the Church has had a unity of government. This, too, is essential to it: it is not the inner principle of unity, but it flows immediately from that inner principle, and is its most easily recognisable external form. 'Let that be held a valid Eucharist which is under the Bishop or to whom he shall have committed it', wrote St Ignatius of Antioch to the Church of Smyrna. And as all the Eucharists in the Church are one, so are all the bishops one: there is unity of government.[7]

---

[6] 'The Idea of "The Church" in the Primitive Liturgies', in *The Parish Communion*, p. 122. 'By the unity of communion . . . the Church is one.' Presumably Dom Gregory Dix did not really understand what he was saying here, or he could not have continued to believe that the Church consisted of more than one communion.

[7] Cf. Dom Sebastian Moore: 'What formally constitutes Catholic unity is communion in one single Church . . . obedience to the Pope is the necessary consequence, not the formal cause of Catholic unity.' 'The Logic of Unity', *The Tablet*, May 24th, 1958, p. 480.

The Church is one communion, the sacrament of one faith, ruled over by one hierarchy.

Chapman wrote that 'this third form of unity centres in the Pope'. It does indeed, but equally so do the other two. Church government is centred in the Pope, but so is the acceptance of the one faith entrusted to the apostles and passed on to the Church of all the ages, and so is the unity of communion. All Catholics are in communion with one another, but the chair and centre of this unity is the chair of Peter. Truly cut off from the communion of Rome, one is cut off from the communion of the one Church. In the words of Mgr Duchesne, speaking of the Church of Rome in the pre-Constantinian period, 'She knows herself to be, and is considered by all, the centre and the organ of unity'.[8] The Pope, in Karl Adam's words, is 'the visible embodiment of the unity of the Church'.[9]

The One, Holy, Catholic and Apostolic Church is the one communion of the sacraments, the ark of salvation, the teacher of truth. The whole Church possesses the fullness of revealed truth, of sacramental life, of the jurisdictional power to bring souls to salvation by the forgiveness of sins. But each member does not possess that fullness equally. There are many members with many gifts, but one body. The fullness is focused in a central organ, which itself possesses no more than the whole body, but also no less. The see of Rome is the Petrine chair of the Church's unity. The see of Rome possesses the Petrine keys of binding and loosing. The see of Rome is the Petrine rock of the Church's infallible authority.

What authority is there for this view of the Church as essentially a visible communion? First, I Cor. 10: 16-17 and the New Testament witness in general; secondly, continuous Catholic tradition; thirdly, theological reasoning.

St Paul to the Corinthians I have already quoted. The New Testament as a whole shows the Church to be a visible fellowship, not restricted to any one place, entered into by baptism, centred on the Eucharist, ruled hierarchically. 'The word

[8] Quoted by Fr St John, *Blackfriars*, November 1955, p. 414.
[9] *The Spirit of Catholicism*, p. 38.

"Church"—ekklesia—' says H. Burn-Murdoch, 'occurs a hundred and ten times in the New Testament; it carries the meaning of an invisible Church only once, and there the reference is to the heavenly Church, the New Jerusalem. Elsewhere, the Ekklesia is a visible fellowship or society, a community that *continued steadfastly in the apostles' fellowship*'.[10]

The Fathers have precisely the same teaching to give us, as we have already seen many times in the course of this study. C. H. Turner sums up this patristic period as follows: 'There was complete agreement as to the doctrine of the Catholic Church, the visible fellowship of the disciples, the Body of Christ. The separatist communities, at least from the middle of the third century onwards had with the idea of the Church no quarrel; for the most part the *rationale* of their separate organisation was that each set of them claimed in turn for itself to be the true embodiment of this unique society'.[11] For a detailed confirmation of this, as regards the third century, I may refer to Abbot Butler's very careful study entitled 'St Cyprian on the Church'.[12]

> The Universal Church [Abbot Butler says] as represented to us by Cyprian and in his writings, is made up, then, of baptised persons constituting the communicating membership of local churches, these local churches being in communion with each other. Each local church is a concrete association of actual living human beings, baptised and 'in communion' with their bishop; it is a historical entity, a 'flesh and blood' reality. And the universal Church, comprising these local communities, and only such as are in the world-wide communion, is itself also necessarily a historical entity, an actual world-wide association. . . . The unity of the universal Church, like that of a local church, is a unity of actual association by intercommunion.[13]

The Church is one Communion, schism is an act of separation from communion and consequently also from the visible Church. St Optatus defined the Church better than anyone else when he called her the 'Una communionis societas',[14] and St Augustine

---

[10] *Church, Continuity and Unity*, p. 29.
[11] *Essays on the Early History of the Church and the Ministry*, p. 194.
[12] *Downside Review*, 1953, pp. 1-13, 119-34, 258-72.
[13] Ibid. pp. 9 and 129.
[14] *De Schismate Donatistarum*, lib. 2, c. 3 (*Pat. Lat.* 11, 949 A).

said the same thing when he called it the 'Societas sacramentorum',[15] or the 'Communio sacramentorum'.[16] Without the understanding of what this means, all the documents of the Church lose their meaning: take St Ambrose's letter *Provisum* written to Gratian from the Council of Aquileia in 381, and its reference to the 'iura communionis',[17] or the Formula of Hormisdas and its insistence on the 'Communio Ecclesiae Catholicae'.[18] Outside the one communion one is outside the Church, and that one communion is necessarily centred upon the see of Peter from whence the rights of communion flow.

It was the common doctrine of antiquity that the unity of the Church was the proper, adequate effect of the sacrament of the Eucharist, it was its *res*. The unity of the Church was held inexplicable in other than sacramental and eucharistic terms. Let me quote Fr de Lubac.

> In the thought of the whole of Christian antiquity, Eucharist and Church are bound together. With St Augustine, under the influence of the Donatist controversy, this bond was stressed with a quite particular force, and the same is true of the Latin writers of the seventh, eighth and ninth centuries. For them as for Augustine, on whom they all depend either directly or indirectly, and whose formulas they incessantly reproduce, the Eucharist is related to the Church as cause to effect, as means to end, and at the same time as sign to reality.[19]

Still speaking of these seventh to ninth century writers, Fr de Lubac says again: 'The *sacramentum panis* leads them straight to the *unitas corporis*. In their eyes, the Eucharist is essentially, as it already was for St Paul and for the Fathers, the *mysterium unitatis*, it is the *sacramentum conjunctionis, federationis, adunationis*.'[20]

On the eve of the First Vatican Council when Pius IX appealed to all Protestants and non-Catholics, it was to those cut off from

---

[15] *In Psalmum* 67, n. 39 (*Pat. Lat.* 36, 837).
[16] *De Civ. Dei*, I, 35.
[17] Cf. Batiffol, *Cathedra Petri*, p. 55.
[18] Denzinger, 172; quoted by the Vatican Council, Denzinger, 1833.
[19] *Corpus Mysticum*, p. 23. For the Patristic doctrine see Gasque, *L'Eucharistie et le Corps Mystique*, Paris, 1925.
[20] *Corpus Mysticum*, p. 27. Evidence for this will be found especially in chaps. I, IV and VIII of the same work.

the 'Communion of the Catholic Church' that he addressed himself;[21] the First Vatican Council itself describes the Church's fundamental unity as a 'unity of faith and communion', again as a 'unity at once of communion and of the profession of the same faith'.[22]

In Question 39 of the II-II of the *Summa Theologica* St Thomas Aquinas treated of schism as the sin *per se* opposed to the unity of the Church. He went on to explain in what this unity itself consists. 'The unity of the Church has two aspects, one is the connection of Church members with one another, or communion; the other is the relationship of all the members of the Church to one head.'[23] Unfortunately in this article St Thomas did not go beyond this simple statement of these two essential elements in Church unity; unity of communion and unity of government; but it is noticeable that he did not speak of unity of faith, to which, of course, he opposed heresy and not schism. In another place St Thomas explained how the Eucharist has a triple significance—for past, present and future—he went on to speak of its second—present—context. 'In regard to its present consequence it further signifies the unity of the Church, to which men are gathered through this sacrament. And for this reason it is called communion or synaxis (assembly)'; for as Damascene says 'it is called communion because through it we communicate with Christ; we participate in his flesh and divinity; and through it again we communicate and are united with one another'.[24] Here St Thomas simply gives us traditional Catholic doctrine: it is through the Eucharist that men are united, not only with Christ, but also with the Church and with one another.

[21] 13 September 1868; complete text in J. K. Stone, *The Invitation Heeded: Reasons for a Return to Catholic Unity*, New York.

[22] 'Fidei et communionis unitas', 'tam communionis quam eiusdem fidei professionis unitas', Denzinger 1821 and 1827.

[23] 'Ecclesiae autem unitas in duobus attenditur, scilicet connexione membrorum Ecclesiae ad invicem, seu communicatione; et iterum in ordine omnium membrorum Ecclesiae ad unum caput', *Summa Theologica* II-II, 39, 1.

[24] 'Aliam autem significationem habet respectu rei praesentis, scilicet ecclesiae unitatis, cui homines aggregantur per hoc sacramentum. Et secundum hoc nominatur communio vel synaxis; dicit enim Damascenus, IV libro, quod 'dicitur communio, quia communicamus per ipsam Christo; et quia participamus eius carne et deitate; et quia communicamus et unimur ad invicem per ipsam' *Summa Theologica* III, 73, 4. The reference to Damascene is to *De Fide Orthodoxa*, iv, 13.

I turn next to what St Thomas's greatest commentator, Cajetan, has to say about schism. His commentary on question 39 of the II-II is a true mine of ecclesiological wisdom. Cajetan begins by asking in what the unity of the Church, to which schism is opposed, formally consists. He decides first that it cannot consist in the simple common possession of the theological virtues and the sacraments. This would merely make all the faithful like one another, it would not make them truly *one*: 'All the faithful believe one thing, hope in one thing, love one thing, that is to say God three and one, etc., and they possess the same sacraments. But if the faithful had no other unity than this, the Church would not be, properly speaking, one; but the faithful would be similar on these points.'[25]

With these words, we may say, Cajetan rejected the characteristic Anglican view of Church unity, that is to say as consisting in common possessions. Next Cajetan went on to find inadequate another view of Church unity, this time the governmental one: the idea that a common head is sufficient to make the body truly one. No, he decides, a common rule makes all 'under one', it does not as such make them, strictly speaking *one*.[26]

A third type of unity and the only adequate one, Cajetan continues, is a social unity by which each of the faithful is a part of a whole, related to the other parts: each lives and acts as a member of the ecclesiastical body.

> We find, thirdly, the unity of the gathering of all the faithful. From this unity each of the faithful obtains a new relationship, that is to say to be part of numerically one people, city and home.

[25] 'Singuli namque fideles credunt unum, sperant unum, amant unum, scilicet. Deum trinum et unum, etc., tenent eadem sacramenta. Et si fideles non haberent aliam unitatem, Ecclesia non esset, proprie loquendo, una; sed fideles essent similes in praedictis.'

[26] 'Invenimus ergo, secundo, unitatem capitis, non solum in caelo, Christi: sed in terra, sui Vicarii. Ex qua unitate apponitur in ipsis fidelibus esses relativum ordinis, scilicet ad caput unum; et actionis et passionis, secundum praecipere et obedire. Moventur siquidem singuli fideles a Spiritu Sancto non solum ad credendum, sperandum, etc., sed etiam ad obediendum uni et eidem capiti, Christi Vicario. Et si apud fideles nulla alia esset unitas, Ecclesia non diceretur una, sed sub uno: essent enim fideles sicut multa regna sub uno rege.' Cf. also de Lubac: 'Recognition of authority in the Church is the first and indispensable condition without which we cannot have any part in her vitalising work; but it is only a condition. A unity realised at that level alone could be nothing more than an external bond such as exists in human societies', *The Splendour of the Church*, p. 103.

Through this each becomes dependent on the whole, for a part does depend on its whole. . . . Each of the faithful believes himself to be a member of the Church, and it is as a member of the Church that he believes, hopes, administers or receives the sacraments, teaches, learns, etc.; . . . hence it comes about that between churches which seem to be altogether separated, such as those of Scotland and Spain, there is not only agreement in faith, hope, charity, the sacraments and obedience to one head; there is also a binding of part to part in what is numerically a single congregation, which primarily and principally is ruled by the Holy Ghost.[27]

Similarity in faith and the sacraments, subjection to the same hierarchical head, these though necessary, are not sufficient to make the Church one. In the words of Dom Polycarp Sherwood, 'it is only the being and acting as part of one whole that formally imparts unity',[28] that is to say fellowship, association in Christian living. It must be admitted that Cajetan does not appear to have seen the fundamental Eucharistic character of that fellowship; that failure may be explained by reference to the age in which he lived. He referred at once to the ultimate principle of the Church—the Holy Ghost; but the Holy Ghost is the 'external' principle of the Church's unity and is no substitute for the formal internal principle of unity within the Church's visible constitution: the very consequence, on the essential associational level, of the Holy Spirit's continuous influence.

There is, in fact, no strict principle of association possible for the Church other than that of the sacraments, and as the sacraments themselves are ordered to one among them—the Eucharist —I am convinced that the only type of unity within the Church which is adequate as a principle and explanation of all the others

---

[27] 'Invenimus igitur, tertio, unitatem collectionis universorum fidelium. Ex qua unitate apponitur singulis fidelium esse relativum: scilicet esse partem unius numero populi, civitatis, domus. Ac per hoc dependentia apponitur unicuique a toto; pars enim quaelibet a suo toto pendet . . . Quilibet enim fidelis credit se membrum Ecclesiae, et ut membrum Ecclesiae credit, sperat, ministrat sacramenta, suscipit, docet, discit, etc.: et propter Ecclesiam haec facit ut agit propter totum, *cuius est quidquid est*; et secundum Ecclesiae fidem et traditionem haec operatur. Et hinc fit ut inter ecclesias quae videntur omnino separatae, puta Scotiae et Hispaniae, non solum sit convenientia in fide, spe, caritate, sacramentis et obedientia ad unum caput; sed etiam colligatio partis ad partem in una numero congregatione, quae primo et principaliter regitur a Spiritu Sancto.'

[28] 'The Sense of Rite', *Eastern Churches Quarterly*, winter 1957-58, p. 123.

to be found there is that of Eucharistic communion. In one of his writings while still an Anglican, Newman put his finger on the very heart of the difference between a Catholic ecclesiology and his own Anglican one. For an Anglican, he wrote, the essential note of the Church is 'the possession of the Apostolic Succession', but for a Catholic it is quite simply 'intercommunion'.[29]

It would, of course, be quite wrong to understand the unity of the Church, as a communion unity, in a bare, narrow way. When I distinguish it from unity of faith or unity of government, it is not so as to separate them, or to exclude these other elements. On the contrary, unity of communion can only be fully understood when baptism, faith, charity and the hierarchy are also all brought well into the picture. But it alone is the *formal* principle of unity, that is to say that it causes the unity of the Church and every other type of unity to be found in the Church, and it is the only one in terms of which all the others can be organically explained.

The Eucharist is certainly no isolated sacrament; on the contrary it is one of seven. Together they form one organic whole centred on, and explained by the Eucharist, which is, St Thomas says, the 'end of all the sacraments'.[30] In one way or another all the others prepare us for the Eucharist and have the nature of means: 'The sanctifying work of all the sacraments is a preparation for receiving or consecrating the Eucharist.'[31] The Eucharist alone has the nature not of means but of end, because it alone gives not only the grace of God but God himself, not only some ministry of the Church but her effective symbol. The Eucharist is Christ: body and blood, soul and divinity. It also is in some way the 'mystical body', the Church, whose effective symbol and sacrament it is. In the words of the Council of Trent, it is the 'symbol of the one body, of which Christ is the head'.[32] The real effect of this sacrament, say St Thomas, is the Church's unity: 'Res huius sacramenti est unitas corporis mystici.'[33]

[29] *Essays Critical and Historical*, II, p. 39.
[30] 'Finis omnium sacramentorum', *Summa Theologica* III, 73, 3.
[31] 'Per sanctificationes omnium sacramentorum fit praeparatio ad suscipiendam vel consecrandam Eucharistiam', ibid.
[32] 'Symbolum unius corporis, cuius ipse (Christus) caput exsistit', Denzinger 875. [33] *Summa Theologica* III, 73, 3.

It is certainly at the moment of baptism that one actually enters the unity of the Church and even if one dies without receiving the Eucharist one dies within that unity. How can this be? Because baptism is precisely entry into communion, and without the Eucharist baptism would itself be meaningless. Salvation is possible without actually receiving the Eucharist, but not without desiring it. 'By baptism man is put on the road for the Eucharist. Consequently by the very fact of their baptism, children are put by the Church on the road for the Eucharist. And thus, as it is on account of the Church's faith that they believe, so it is on account of the Church's intention that they desire the Eucharist and in consequence receive its proper effect.'[34] Baptism is incapable of imparting grace unless it is linked with an (at least implicit) desire to be truly a member of the Church, i.e. to receive that sacrament which constitutes the Church and its unity: 'The fact is that this sacrament (the Eucharist) has the power of itself to confer grace and no one receives grace before receiving this sacrament unless it be through desire for it, his own, if he is an adult, the Church's, if a child.'[35]

It is clear from this that to be a member of the communion does not simply mean to communicate. No one can communicate all day long, but the members of the Communion remain so all day long. Just as the physical separation of Eucharists does not divide the Eucharistic fellowship, so physical separation from any Eucharist does not of itself divide from the fellowship. The Catholic isolated on a desert island remains a member of the Church. Only by a voluntary act can a man be separated from this fellowship, and celebration of the Eucharist after such an act cannot maintain the unity of communion. The sacrament of unity maintains in unity all those who by baptism have been consecrated for the reception of that sacrament and, though

[34] 'Per baptismum ordinatur homo ad Eucharistam. Et ideo ex hoc ipso quod pueri baptizantur, ordinantur per Ecclesiam ad Eucharistiam. Et sic, sicut ex fide Ecclesiae credunt, sic ex intentione Ecclesiae desiderant Eucharistiam, et per consequens recipiunt rem ipsius', III, 73, 3.

[35] 'Dicendum quod hoc sacramentum ex seipso virtutem habet gratiam conferendi; nec aliquis habet gratiam ante susceptionem huius sacramenti vel nisi ex aliquo voto ipsius, vel per seipsum, sicut adulti, vel voto Ecclesiae, sicut parvuli', III, 79, 1, ad. 1.

physically separated, are not morally separated. The essence of schism (regardless of subjective guilt) lies in the moral act of communion breaking, and everyone adhering to the new 'communion' thereby re-wills the original act of separation, at least as regards its essential effect. Subsequent to the moral act of schism the unity of communion cannot be maintained by the mere valid possession of the Eucharist on the part of the schismatics. This is the crucial point dividing Catholic, orthodox and traditional theology from that of the type of Dr Mascall.

The act of excommunication again causes much confusion. Strictly speaking the Church and Church authority does not, I think, separate anyone from the Church. There could be no possible reason for her to do so. What the Church can and must do is to state the conditions of communion, for instance to define the faith. To refuse to accept the orthodoxy of the Church is to exclude oneself from the Church and from communion, and the Church will declare that this has taken place. But excommunication normally means a much lesser thing than this: prohibition to receive communion on account of such and such an offence. The person excommunicated is then excluded from actual 'communicatio' but not from communion. The same is true of any man living in mortal sin; he cannot communicate but he has not thereby ceased to be a member of the visible Church's communion.

Authority is required in every society, and visible authority in a visible society, and the Church's communion *is* a visible society. The whole jurisdiction of the Church derives from this source: authority to explain what the Eucharist is, authority to ordain priests to perform the Eucharist, authority to decide who can be admitted to the Eucharistic table, authority to forgive the sins of those wishing to communicate. It is in such terms, as St Thomas has explicitly said,[36] that the hierarchy of the Church, both in orders and in jurisdiction, is to be explained. In fact, authority in the Church—it is an obvious truism—is not for its own sake, but a means for the furtherance of man's union with

[36] For instance *Contra Gentiles*, IV, 74; Congar, *Esquisses du Mystère de l'Eglise*, p. 86.

God; as the earthly consummation of that union, and the bridge
to heaven, is the Eucharist, it is to the Eucharist that Church
authority is ordered, and the unity of the Eucharist and the
Eucharistic society is necessarily shared by the authority which
rules it. The unity of the Mystical Body, which is the *res* of the
Eucharist, necessarily includes and manifests itself in the unity
of one visible head.

Though the unity of the Church is a visible unity, it is not
entirely visible. A sacrament is an outward sign of inward grace,
and the Church's nature too is both outward and inward. In
commenting on the Apostles' Creed St Thomas described the
Church's unity as consisting of three things: faith, hope and
charity.[37] Here we have the invisible reality of Church unity to
which all that is visible is, in the last resort, simply ancillary.
The point of the use of visible things in the Christian dispensation is to carry men into this invisible union with God through
faith, hope and charity. It is of the nature of the sacraments to
be in both fields, visible and invisible; they are the effective
means of the spiritual life, while the Eucharist is furthermore
not only a means but the spiritual life of divine union itself. It is
the sacrament of these virtues and their efficient cause. When
we say that the *res* of this sacrament is the unity of the Church,
and that this unity (so far as it is invisible) is precisely a unity
of faith, hope and charity, we are saying that these virtues and
the unity they effect is the real consequence of the Eucharist,
and that they cannot be possessed except by those who are or
wish to be within the one Eucharistic communion. The unity
of these virtues is not a substitute for, but a consequence of, the
unity of communion. They can only come through that sacrament which is truly the 'mysterium fidei'.

The Eucharist is also, and most especially, the mystery of love.
Love and love alone can bring about true unity. God became
man and died upon the cross out of love for men. The Eucharist
is the one sacrifice of Calvary continually present among men,

---

[37] 'Causatur autem unitas Ecclesiae ex tribus, Primo ex unitate fidei . . .
secundo ex unitate spei . . . tertio ex unitate charitatis', *Expos. in Symbolum*,
in art. 9.

and communion signifies the consequent and mutual loving union of God and man. God loved us that we should love him. The Church is the fellowship established by this love, and the Eucharist is the sacrament of this fellowship. To both Church and Eucharist have been given the simple name of *Agapē*.[38] This is the union of love, of God with man, and man with his brother, accomplished upon Calvary, renewed upon the Christian altar, and—as we firmly hope—to be continued in all eternity.

All this was simply taken for granted until the fourteenth century, but thereafter a certain degeneration in ecclesiology set in during the period immediately preceding the Reformation. It started in the early fourteenth century with such treatises as that of James of Viterbo's *De Regimine Christiano*, which has been rather highly praised as 'the most ancient treatise on the Church'. The tendency continued in the following centuries as a reaction to the Conciliar movement and to Protestantism. More and more the deeper theological, sacramental and mystical sides of the Church were neglected in favour of a rather juridical and jurisdictional approach limited to the idea of a visible society. The modern reaction to this has received official approbation with the encyclical *Mystici Corporis Christi*. Nevertheless the reaction has had its own weaknesses which it has been necessary for Church authority to point out. Ideas about some vague transcendental 'mystical reality' may be even more removed from the best traditional ecclesiology than the rather juridical conceptions of the recent past, and Pope Pius XII had to insist firmly that the Mystical Body must be identified with the visible Church in communion with Rome. 'That the Mystical Body of Christ and the Catholic Church in communion with Rome are one and the same thing, is a doctrine based on revealed truth and as such was set forth by us in an encyclical a few years back.'[39] One mistake has been to seek for an understanding of these problems in some special 'mystical' sphere, when the real

---

[38] Cf. the fine study by Fr Plé O.P., 'The Church and Charity', *The Life of the Spirit*, January 1953, pp. 283-90.
[39] *Humani Generis*, August 12th, 1950.

and traditional *locus* was the sacramental field. Up to the four-teenth century the Church was consistently thought of in con-nection with the Eucharist; but after the fourteenth century this connection has been greatly neglected. St Robert Bellar-mine, most influential ecclesiologist of the Counter-Reformation, has nothing at all to say about the relation of Church and Eucharist.

We shall gain nothing, however, if when remembering this relationship, we forget the equally traditional doctrine, which has been so greatly stressed since the fourteenth century, that the Church of God is a visible society. As we know, that doctrine was no invention of the fourteenth century jurists; it is integral to the whole of Catholic tradition and in this book I have always tried to work *through* this idea, not away from it. But the point is : what does a visible society mean in Christian terms? It means, we have discovered, a sacramental society, a communion. It is the fellowship of men made one by the Eucharist. Once we realise this, it is impossible to make any irresolvable contrast between pre-medieval and post-medieval ecclesiology. One was concerned more with the sacramental cause, the other with the jurisdictional superstructure, but both teach the same thing that the Church is one visible fellowship.

If the Church is one because she is joined together and fed by the one Eucharistic body of Christ, this is also the funda-mental reason why she is herself the very body of Christ. Per-haps the most constant theme to be found in modern ecclesio-logical writing is this one of the relationship between the Church as a mystical reality and the Church as a visible society. We have seen that the Pope has condemned any separation of the two. That is most right and traditional. Nevertheless these 'two aspects' remain to worry theologians. What exactly is the relation between them, one asks? It may surprise many to know that it is a relation of perfect identity. Not only are they identical in actual extension, but also in idea. Far from being two ideas at opposite poles from one another, as is generally supposed, they have, in fact, on the contrary, the same explanation, the same cause, existence and extension.

We have seen that when we speak of the Church as one visible society, we are speaking of the direct and formal consequence of the Eucharist. But when we speak of the Church as the one mystical body of Christ, we are speaking of precisely the same thing—it is again the direct and formal consequence of the Eucharist.[40] Why is this so? It is because this statement provides the precise reason why the Church is the body of Christ. In a general way, of course, she might be called a body like any other society, a corporate group of men: she might be called Christ's body because Christ is her founder and ruler; but in much the same way all mankind might be called God's body. No, the Church's claim to be the Body of Christ rests upon a far more exact and specifically Christian foundation. She is the body of Christ because she is formed of his body, fed upon his body, united by his body. Those who feed upon this body, become it. In St Augustine's words, Christ can say to us: 'You will not change me into yourself, as you do with the food of your flesh, but you will be changed into me';[41] or again, as St Leo remarks, 'the participation of the body and blood of Christ effects nothing short of this, that we pass over into that which we receive'.[42] Communion in the Eucharistic body *makes* the mystical body. The Church is, then, the body of Christ for the very same reason that she is one and that she is a visible society. Hence it is obvious that it is absolutely necessary to make a complete and formal identification of the Church as visible society and the Church as mystical body.

One may state the truth very simply by means of a triple formal affirmation:

The Church is one because she is the communion of the one Eucharistic body of Christ.

[40] See especially H. de Lubac, *The Splendour of the Church*, chap. IV, 'The Heart of the Church'; the same author's *Corpus Mysticum*; Gasque L'Eucharistie et le Corps Mystique; R. Velarde, 'Eucharistic Union', *Life of the Spirit*, May 1952, pp. 458-60.

[41] 'Non me in te mutabis, sicut cibum carnis tuae, sed tu mutaberis in me', *Confessions*, book 7, chap. 10; quoted by St Thomas, *Summa Theologica* III, 73, 3, ad 2.

[42] Quoted by de Lubac, *The Splendour of the Church*, p. 112, where many other similar references are also given.

The Church is a visible society because she is the communion of the one Eucharistic body of Christ.

The Church is the mystical body of Christ because she is the communion of the one Eucharistic body of Christ.

Let me put it another way. The Eucharist is the cause of the Church's unity: unity of men with Christ as his body; unity of men among themselves in a sacramental communion. But these two are only one, unity among men being found only in Christ, while unity with Christ brings at once union with one's fellow men. That is the message of the Church, and of its effective sign, the sacrament of the Eucharist.

'THE CUP OF BLESSING WHICH WE BLESS, IS IT NOT FELLOWSHIP IN THE BLOOD OF CHRIST? THE BREAD WHICH WE BREAK, IS IT NOT FELLOWSHIP IN THE BODY OF CHRIST? BECAUSE THERE IS ONE BREAD, WE, THAT ARE MANY, ARE ONE BODY, FOR WE ALL PARTAKE OF THE ONE BODY.'

2. *Membership of the Church by desire*[43]

It would seem to follow from all this that all non-Roman Christians are excluded from the Church. She is one visible society, a communion, of which it is only logical to say that one is either a member or one is not. Speaking strictly, it is not possible to have degrees of membership. I know well that in writing this I am going against a good deal of rather vaguely expressed modern opinion, though it is possible that this disagreement is more with the phraseology than with the substance of what has been written. It is of course true that the Church has not only good members and bad, but also members so weak that it may be difficult to know whether they continue within the one society at all. But the principle remains clear: Church membership is not the aggregate possession of a number of

[43] For the relevant texts, bibliography, and a much fuller treatment of this matter, I refer to the very important article of G. Vodopivec, 'Membri in re et appartenenza in voto alla Chiesa di Cristo', *Euntes Docete*, 1957, 1, pp. 65-104. See also the very useful correspondence on the subject, chiefly between Fathers Ripley and St John, in the pages of *The Tablet* between July 1st and September 16th, 1961.

points, something admitting of degrees, it is life in a visible and determinate society—the Roman Catholic Church.

One enters this society by baptism, and baptism is the sacrament of faith; but the gifts of baptism and faith do not guarantee indefectible membership of the Church. Baptism is entry into the fellowship, but after entering a man must continue within it, and the most evident outward mark of that continuance is recognition of the authority directing the society. To be a member of the communion of the Catholic Church, we may, therefore, say: one must be baptised, profess the true faith, and submit to the authority of the Church centred in the papacy. In the words of Pope Pius XII: 'Only those are to be accounted really members of the Church who have been regenerated in the waters of Baptism and profess the true faith, and have not cut themselves off from the structure of the Body by their own unhappy act or been severed therefrom, for very grave crimes, by the legitimate authority.'[44]

Those for whom one of these conditions is lacking are not two-thirds members of the Church or partly members, but—quite simply—they are not members. The Church is one visible society, and they are clearly not members of it. That is an evident and necessary conclusion of this whole study.

What then are we to say about the status of those cut off from our communion? Before trying to answer that question, let me state the essential principles.

1. God wishes all men to be saved and Christ died for all. If anyone is not saved it is his own fault, not God's. Everyone is given the true possibility of salvation, but it is an obvious fact that many people outside the Catholic Church, both Christians and non-Christians, have had no possibility at all of joining the Catholic communion. Very many more, we can well believe, even though they have been in fairly close contact with the Catholic Church, have never received the grace to join her. Either their inherited prejudices have been too great or for some other reason they have, in good faith, always remained outside the one visible Church. Such people—and how many millions there are

[44] *Mystici Corporis*, C.T.S. translation, p. 16.

of them, no man can say—may be saved. That is to say, people living and dying outside the visible Church can be saved.

2. The name of Jesus 'alone of all the names under heaven has been appointed to men as the one by which we must needs be saved' (Acts 4:12). Every man who is saved, is saved through our Lord Jesus Christ. Those saved through him, and thus united with him, are *ipso facto* members of his body, and his body is the Catholic Church. It is a true principle, and one we must maintain, that outside the Church there is no salvation, and by 'the Church' in this context we cannot mean anything different from what we mean in other contexts—that is to say, the Roman Catholic Church; moreover, the alternative to 'outside' is 'inside', and to be 'inside' the Church is to be a member. I cannot find the view of some, like Fr Ripley,[45] that *Extra Ecclesiam nulla salus* should really be translated 'apart from the Church there is no salvation' very satisfactory or even meaningful; and in the end it seems to militate more against the unique claims of the Church and of Church membership than does the position these theologians would like to put out of court: that to share in the Church's gift of salvation one must be in some way truly within her and one of her members. Equally, Monsignor Fenton's attempt to distinguish between being 'within' the Church and being 'a member' is unmeaningful.[46] The Church always means a visible society, as Mgr Fenton himself is ever ready to insist, and someone who is within a visible society is of necessity a member of that society.

Hence it is certainly true that:

1. Non-Roman Catholics can be saved.

2. Only members of the Church can be saved.

3. By the Church we mean the Roman Catholic communion. How are these principles reconcilable?

To speak of partial membership of the Church, or imperfect membership, degrees of membership, or even membership of the 'soul' of the Church as opposed to her body, all these ways of

---

[45] *The Tablet*, September 16th, 1961, p. 887.

[46] 'Questions about Membership in the Church', *The American Ecclesiastical Review*, July 1961.

expression seem rather to confuse than clarify the question, because none of them seems to fit in with the essential way that we have to conceive of Church membership. If a man is baptised and has faith, but has not fellowship with the one society, he does indeed fulfil two out of the three 'conditions' for membership, and yet quite clearly he is not a member. He is outside the society, and to speak of his being an incomplete member is not meaningful. There is no easy way into the Church. Her nature remains for ever the same, and for all the same: no one can be a member unless in some way he fulfils all the conditions for membership. These are not just juridical conditions, they derive from the very nature of the Church. If just one person was a member of the Church on any other conditions, the Church herself would at once cease to be what she is.

The problem of Church membership can be greatly clarified, I believe, by the close analogy of baptism. Baptism is the sacrament of entry into the Church, and is as essential for salvation as the Church herself. If there is no salvation outside the Church, it is equally true that 'unless a man be born again of water and the Holy Ghost, he cannot enter into the Kingdom of Heaven' (John 3:5). Baptism, like the Church and for the same reason, is the *only* road to salvation. Nevertheless it is fully agreed, and affirmed by the very Council of Trent (Denzinger 796), that the *desire* for baptism may substitute for its actual reception. A man not visibly baptised may yet receive the substance of baptism through desire for it: in St Thomas's words, God reckons the will for the deed, *voluntas apud Deum reputatur pro facto.*[47]

It is important at this point to stress that there are not two types of baptism—baptism of water and baptism of desire—but only one baptism (that of water), yet those who do not actually receive it may still be saved through desire for it. A catechumen who dies unbaptised is the first and obvious example. But it is further agreed that this desire for baptism may be implicit as well as explicit. That is to say, a good pagan who, responding to the grace of God, does God's will in all things known to him has an implicit and effective desire for baptism.

[47] *Summa Theologica* III, q. 68, 2, ad 3.

I have already pointed out in the first part of this chapter, on St Thomas's authority, how the salvific effect of baptism is dependent upon desire (again, at least implicit) for the Eucharist, the sacrament of the Church's unity. That is to say, baptism does not have an effect apart from whole membership of the Church, to which it is the means of entry. Baptism of desire must mean as a consequence Church membership of desire. Like desire for baptism, so the effective desire for Church membership may be implicit or explicit, and it may take various forms.

The good pagan away in the woods has an implicit desire for every part of Christian Church life; but the catechumen at an Anglican mission in Africa has an explicit desire for baptism and the faith, while perhaps only an implicit one for the true Church fellowship. The separated Christian may possess baptism and faith, but as he is cut off from our communion, he does not possess Church membership, but if implicitly he desires the third element of fellowship and submission, he too is a Church member by desire (*in voto*). There are, then, different degrees of possession of the conditions for Church membership, different degrees, one may say, of proximity to the Church, but there are not degrees of membership. However near someone may be, if he is not visibly within the fellowship, he is still at best only a member by desire: desire for something not formally possessed. From this viewpoint there are only three states: that of members, that of those who desire to be members, and that of those who do not.

Two men, both baptised and granted the gift of faith, may be in quite different states. One may knowingly have set his face against the true Church and have no desire implicit or explicit for submission to Rome. Lacking an essential condition for membership, he is no member at all. The other may have a full implicit desire for membership (which will be included in his supernatural life of grace and charity) and is then in desire a full member of the Church.

All people who are saved without being members of the Roman Communion are saved through this desire for such membership.

As we read in the letter—*Suprema haec Sacra*—of the Holy Office to the Archbishop of Boston dated August 8th, 1949:

> That one may obtain eternal salvation, it is not always required that he be incorporated into the Church *actually* as a member, but it is necessary that at least he be united to her by desire and longing (*voto et desiderio*). However, this desire need not always be explicit, as it is in catechumens; but when a person is involved in invincible ignorance, God accepts also an *implicit desire,* so-called because it is included in that good disposition of soul (whereby a person wishes his will to be conformed to the will of God).[48]

Is a member of the Church by desire a member or not? He is and he is not. In a similar way one might ask whether baptism of desire is or is not baptism. Desire is necessarily for something which we do not possess. We cannot both be baptised and desire it, both be members of the Church and want to be. Both baptism and Church membership are clearly definable realities and are not possessed by those who, we say, have them by desire.

On the other hand, desire for baptism or for Church member-ship, in our sense, is quite different from an ordinary human desire. If you want a piece of cake, you neither possess it nor enjoy the consequences that its possession brings. Desire and possession are with natural material things entirely exclusive. Now this dichotomy between desire and possession does not appear in the same way in spiritual things. Once the will wants them, in a way it enters into immediate possession. This is a crucial point and it is one that many theologians do not seem to have grasped. Fr Ripley, for instance, has written that 'the desire to be in the Church does not give even a partial membership of it. The desire to be a member of Parliament does not give one even half a seat in the House of Commons.'[49] Fr St John's attempted reply to this argument was equally mistaken: 'I should have thought that apart from a desire for it no one has ever become a Member of Parliament.'[50] But this is no answer: if you don't

[48] The complete translation, from which this is taken, can be found in the *Life of the Spirit*, March 1958, pp. 419-20.
[49] *The Tablet*, August 19th, 1961, p. 798.
[50] Ibid., August 26th, 1961, p. 816.

want a piece of cake, you won't indeed get it; but wanting it is equally not the same as getting it. You can always want it, but never have it. You can always want to be a Member of Parliament, but may never become one. In such a case *voluntas non reputatur pro facto*. But to bring up such an analogy at all shows a failure to appreciate the true significance of theological desire. Desire for membership of Parliament does not bring with it any effect of membership, but desire for baptism does bring with it enormous consequences: here the will is actually reckoned for the deed, so that if someone dies with the baptism of desire alone and you were to ask the absolutely simple question: 'Was he baptised or not?' the answer 'Yes, he was' would undoubtedly be truer than 'No, he was not'; that is so because of the principle *voluntas apud Deum reputatur pro facto*. In spiritual things, then, once the will wants them, in a way it enters into immediate possession. With God desire for Church membership is reckoned for the deed, and of someone who dies with such a desire it is consequently truer to say 'Yes, he was a member', than 'No, he was not'. In fact, both statements are true. Membership of the Church in desire includes the full substance of membership without being an alternative to it, and those who are thus invisibly united with the Church and brought into the Church by desire may equally well be called members (*in voto*) or not members (*in re*).

3. *Historical Difficulties*

'I was not convinced of the Catholic belief of the Church's indivisibility; I thought that history disproved the claim.'[51] Many non-Catholics would agree with these words of the late E. C. Rich. History, after all, is the acid test for theology, especially for the theology of the Church. The Church is an historical phenomenon, not only a present reality. It is the whole of our contention that its nature cannot change, and hence it is absolutely fair to test the Catholic view not only against the opinions of past Christians, but also against the facts of past history. Now

---

[51] E. C. Rich, *Seeking the City*, Burns and Oates, 1959, p. 108.

there are two periods in history which may seem to provide justification for maintaining that the Catholic belief in the Church's indivisibility is unhistorical. One is the fourth century; the other the fifteenth. It is clearly necessary to examine these cases individually, and that is the purpose of the following pages.

A. The Meletian Schism of Antioch

The Fourth century Schism of Antioch has often been regarded, and notably by the late F. W. Puller, as providing the unanswerable historical objection to the Catholic view of the Church as a single communion centred upon the see of Rome.

The first thing is to state the clear facts of the case, in so far as we know them.

In 330 or 331 St Eustathius of Antioch was deposed by a group of Arianising bishops. He was replaced by Euphronius, who was himself succeeded by a series of more or less Arian bishops, Flacillus, Stephen, Leontius and Eudoxius. The greater part of the Christian community of Antioch, not only the Arians, accepted these bishops, if reluctantly, and they were also recognised, by and large, as the true bishops of Antioch. However, a small group of Catholics refused to acknowledge these Arian intruders and established themselves as a separate community; these we will call the Eustathians. They were led by a priest named Paulinus. In this way from about the year 330 the Church of Antioch was split into two parties out of communion with one another. But there is no reason to believe that either of these groups was at first out of communion with the Church in general; consequently, theologically speaking, it must be held that they were also in communion with one another (the state of being in communion is not incompatible with that of a violent quarrel).

In 343, however, Bishop Stephen, an Arian ringleader, was declared deposed and excommunicated together with seven others by the orthodox Western council of Sardica. This sentence, of course, had no practical effect in the East. Stephen was in fact deposed by the bishops of his province a few months later for other reasons, but it is probable—though hardly certain—

that the Council of Sardica's personal sentence on bishop
Stephen was subsequently enlarged to cover the whole East in
so far as it was under Arian control. Hence it may be presumed
that from about 343 the majority group at Antioch, together
with most of the churches around, was really outside Rome's
communion.

Rather strangely, and this is an interesting example of his
tendency to multiply breaks of communion beyond the evidence,
Puller held that the Eustathians also were out of communion
with Rome and the whole Church in those years. 'The small
body of the Eustathians, which had seceded in 331 from the communion of the Antiochene bishops, and so from the communion
of the rest of Christendom including Rome, remained out of
fellowship with the Pope until 375.' And again, 'Between the
years 343 and 375 neither of the two rival communities of Antioch
was recognised by the Roman Church'.[52] There is no reason to
agree with this. The Eustathians withdrew themselves from the
bishops of Antioch precisely because the latter were Arian; this
did not involve a break of communion with the orthodox
Catholic world. It was simply a local anticipation of the decision
of Sardica, and was justified by the troubled state of the Church
at that time. What happened in 375 was not the restoration of
communion between Rome and the Eustathians but a formal
recognition of Paulinus as bishop of Antioch. Equally it is untrue
to say, as Puller does, that the Eustathians were admitted to communion with the Church of Alexandria by Athanasius on his
passage through Antioch in 346. He communicated with them
on that occasion because they were orthodox and already in communion with him: they were all within a communion from
which they had never been separated. In the Alexandrian *Tomus
ad Antiochenses* of 362 the Eustathians are described as 'they
who have *ever* remained in communion with us'.

It is probable, then, that from 343 to 361 the majority group
at Antioch was out of communion with the Catholic Church, the
minority group in communion. In 361 St Meletius was elected
bishop of the majority group. He was a man with something of

[52] F. W. Puller, *The Primitive Saints and the See of Rome*, p. 232.

an Arian past, but shortly after election delivered a sermon of such unimpeachable orthodoxy that he was at once banished by the emperor Constantius. A full-blooded Arian named Euzoius was put in his place, but this time the great majority of Antiochenes remained faithful to their exiled bishop. Later that same year Constantius died, Julian succeeded him, and for a time the Arian persecution came to an end. Meletius returned to Antioch, as did Athanasius to Alexandria.

In the summer of the following year, 362, Athanasius held a synod at Alexandria of quite exceptional importance. Its aim was to draw up terms on which those in schism who were, however, substantially orthodox could be reconciled to the Church. The application of their decisions at Antioch presented a special problem. Nowhere else had two quite separate Christian communities taken shape. By now, one led by Meletius the other by Paulinus, both were orthodox, yet the suspicions and prejudices of the past continued to divide them. An effort on Athanasius's part to be reconciled with Meletius failed to take effect, and as a consequence he continued to communicate only with the Antiochene minority group ruled over by Paulinus who had now been consecrated bishop.

Most of the East, however, and above all St Basil of Caesarea, was firmly in communion with Meletius and not with Paulinus. For long Rome appeared to hesitate as to which to recognise, but by 375 Pope Damasus had come out clearly for Paulinus. Meanwhile in the 370's there was another long persecution and Meletius was again in exile. This only ended with the death of the Emperor Valens in the summer of 378. Meletius returned from exile, but his great friend and supporter, St Basil, died only a few months later on January 1st, 379. Meletius at once set about trying to restore peace to Antioch and to the Eastern Church as a whole. Two years later, in 381, a great council—subsequently recognised as oecumenical—met at Constantinople, and Meletius appears to have presided over it. In the course of its deliberations he died, and is recognised as a saint in both East and West. It was only years later that the Antiochene schism was entirely ended, but for our purpose its subsequent history is of little importance.

The question which concerns us is whether St Meletius, as also St Basil, died while out of communion with Rome.

If the schism of Antioch is to constitute an argument against the Catholic theory of the Church as a single communion, it is evidently not sufficient for non-Catholics to show that one or another saint was mistaken in his ideas about the Church, or that he was at some time outside the communion of Rome. Both these things are quite compatible with our own ecclesiological principles and do not therefore constitute arguments against them.

To produce a convincing argument it must be shown:

(a) that the Church has only recognised as saints people who have died within her visible membership;

(b) that such and such a saint died outside Rome's communion.

From such premises it could legitimately be concluded that the Church's visible membership does not coincide with the one communion of Rome, and that is the essential presupposition of Anglican ecclesiology.

F. W. Puller endeavoured with immense learning to demonstrate that St Meletius was still out of communion with Rome at the time of his death.[53] Very recently, Dr Amand de Mendieta has further maintained that St Basil of Caesarea lived and died out of communion with Rome.[54] Evidently if these facts are correct the Church has either canonised non-members, or her membership can be more extensive than a single communion. I do not know that it is impossible for the Church to recognise officially the sanctity of her children separated from her by a state of schism, nevertheless I feel reluctant to admit such an explanation for such saints as these—one a doctor of the Church, the other president of an oecumenical Council.[55]

It is best to take the case of St Basil first. Dr de Mendieta holds very simply that as St Basil was quite clearly in communion with

[53] Almost the whole second part of *The Primitive Saints and the See of Rome* is written to this end.

[54] 'Damase, Athanase, Pierre, Mélèce et Basile', in *L'Eglise et les Eglises*, Chevetogne, 1954, I, pp. 261-77.

[55] Strictly speaking most saints of that time, such as Meletius, have not been 'canonised' in the exact sense of the word. (That process started in the Middle Ages.) But personally I would not wish to lay stress on this point.

Meletius and not with Paulinus, and as—at least at the close of his life—the bishops of Rome and Alexandria were equally clearly in communion with Paulinus, and apparently not with Meletius, so Basil himself could not have been in communion with Rome and Alexandria. In this he disagrees with the view held hitherto by both Catholics and Anglicans, according to which, while trying persistently to bring Meletius and Rome together, Basil was in communion with both sides and was trying to resolve a schism in which he was not himself involved. Puller, for instance, held that St Basil entered into communion with Athanasius in 363 and into direct communion with Pope Damasus in 372. De Mendieta, on the contrary, holds that he was out of communion with the churches of Rome and Alexandria right up to his death in 379. Yet, if there is no absolutely clear statement in his correspondence to show that he was in communion, there is equally none to the contrary. It is incredible how little evidence de Mendieta offers us for his novel interpretation of the facts. After all, the reasons why St Athanasius did not enter into communion with Meletius were entirely special to Antioch. There is no reason to believe that the wholly exceptional conditions prevailing there prevented the Synod of Alexandria from achieving anything in the East; moreover all the subsequent correspondence refers precisely to Antioch. For these reasons I agree with Dr Greenslade's conclusion on the factual situation, that 'mediate communion was possible. Basil seems to have been in communion with both Athanasius and Meletius, though Athanasius was in communion with Paulinus'.[56]

As regards Rome, Basil most probably entered into her communion mediately, through Alexandria, in 363. Further, he was in communion with her directly either from 365, following the Roman mission of Eustathius of Sebaste, Theophilus of Castabala and Silvanus of Tarsus, or at least (as Puller held) from 372 when the deacons Sabinus and Dorotheus carried to Asia the Roman synodical letter addressed to the Catholic bishops of the East.

The mission of Evagrius of Antioch from Rome to the East in 373 seems to me to present extremely strong evidence to show

[56] *Schism in the Early Church*, p. 165.

that at that time Basil and Pope Damasus were in communion. Evagrius, who had lived long in Rome and was a faithful emissary of Damasus, visited Basil on his way to Antioch. While at Caesarea he apparently indicated to Basil that he would communicate with the partisans of Meletius at Antioch. But when he arrived at Antioch for one reason or another he failed to do this; instead he held aloof from both parties, much to St Basil's dismay. Now it seems to me to be clear that this situation never could have arisen if at Caesarea Evagrius had not communicated with Basil. Clearly, then, if Rome did not recognise Meletius, this did not affect her communion with St Basil and the East generally, and indeed scholars—with the solitary exception of Amand de Mendieta—have always recognised this.

The case of St Meletius himself is more difficult, but a chief reason for this difficulty is certainly the obscurity of the evidence we possess. Many of the most important documents are lost; others, which we do possess, we cannot date with certainty, while their meaning is often far from clear. The one thing which it is rarely safe to do is to dogmatise upon one or another piece of the historical detail.

It seems to me to be not impossible that Meletius, whose dogmatic position was the same as that of Basil and the Catholic East generally, was personally in communion with Alexandria, Rome and the whole Catholic Church (whether he or they knew it or not) from 363 onwards. If not, he may well have benefited from the reconciliation of 365 or that of 371-2. Because the West did not recognise him as bishop it does not necessarily follow that he was cut off from its communion.

However, let us admit that he was still in a state of schism in 378 when he returned from his second exile. Was he united with Rome's communion before he died in 381? Now there can be no possible doubt that he wished to be. Conclusive evidence for that is to be found in the work of the synod of 153 bishops which met under his presidency at Antioch in September of 379. This synod went out of its way to put itself right with Rome by drawing up, not merely a thoroughly orthodox profession of faith, but one drawn verbally from Rome's own letters to the

East. This statement of faith, signed by all the bishops, but by Meletius first of all, was at once dispatched to Rome. Rome had always made the unequivocal profession of the orthodox faith the primary condition for her communion, but she had also explicitly granted it to those who made such a profession. It is difficult to see how the bishops at Antioch (if not already within Rome's communion) were not by means of this profession of faith stepping into it, and it is interesting to note that Dr Amand de Mendieta, so sure that Basil remained outside Rome's communion to the day of his death, does not doubt that this synod re-established ecclesiastical communion between Rome and Antioch.[57]

The chief reason why Puller held that, in spite of this, Meletius still continued outside Rome's communion was his interpretation of the document beginning *Post Concilium Nicaenum* and often called the *Tomus Damasi*.[58] This document is addressed to Paulinus of Antioch and its ninth paragraph runs thus : 'Those who have migrated from church to church we hold to be alien from our communion, until they return to those cities in which they were first appointed. If while any is travelling about, another is ordained in his place, then he who forsook the city is deprived of the priestly office until his successor rest in peace.'[59] Now Meletius, before being elected at Antioch, had been consecrated for Sebaste; as the *Tomus* is addressed to Paulinus, this paragraph seems clearly to refer to Meletius. The important point is its date. Puller held that it was written at the Roman synod of 380, after the reception of the Antiochene profession of faith; in which case it would seem to signify a clear Roman refusal to communicate with Meletius as long as he remained at Antioch. But the same cannot be said if its date was earlier; yet it is this which is now coming to be accepted. Certainly the anathemas of the whole document seem singularly pointless and out of place after the East had made such a clear profession of faith as that of September 379. It is not surprising then that Schwartz holds the date of the *Tomus Damasi* to be 378, and that he is followed

[57] Op. cit., p. 277.   [58] *Patrologia Latina*, 13, 360-1.
[59] Translation taken from E. Giles, *Documents Illustrating Papal Authority*, p. 138.

by others, such as Mgr Amann and Dr Jalland.[60] If the 378 date is correct, this document ceases to provide support for the view that Meletius remained outside Rome's communion after the Antiochene synod of 379.

Furthermore, on the strictly jurisdictional plane, some sort of agreement had also been reached at Antioch between Meletius and Paulinus. In Puller's words: 'Whatever Paulinus' motives may have been, it is certain that before St Meletius started on his journey to Constantinople, a compact of some sort was agreed upon between the two bishops.'[61] Strangely enough Puller continued: 'It is to my mind out of the question to suppose that the two bodies at Antioch were brought into communion with each other by the mere fact that the two bishops had agreed to a compact, which, until it was ratified, remained in a purely inchoate condition.'[62] As we cannot be sure of the terms of the 'compact' and have not any positive reason for believing that it needed ratification, this seems a little strong. Rome had long ago empowered Paulinus to receive others into her communion (Damasus's third letter), and the question of faith now quite definitely no longer existed. Furthermore, it is clear from the account of the historian Theodoret (Giles, pp. 136-7) that at this time Sapor, representative of the orthodox emperor Gratian, believed Meletius to be in communion with Pope Damasus. Altogether there is absolutely no clear evidence to show that at the close of his life St Meletius was separated from the communion of Rome, while there is considerable circumstantial evidence to the contrary.

There are various general remarks which should be made in conclusion. The first is that it is highly dangerous to build a Church theory on a very obscure situation about which we know far too little. It is one thing to show that such a situation does not contradict a norm already established; it is another to try and draw from it some otherwise unsuspected general conclusion.

Secondly, in this matter of communion as in other fields of dogma, while the essential doctrine has not changed between

---

[60] It is a pity that Giles accepts the 380 date unquestioningly, op. cit. 138.
[61] Op. cit. p. 339.   [62] Ibid. p. 341.

then and now, there has been an advance in clarity. It is evident
from a study of fourth century history that while all held the
Church to be one visible communion, from which heretics should
be rightly separated, there was a good deal of confusion about
how to apply this principle in practice.

Thirdly, it is not exactly the same thing to be in communion
with someone and to recognise him as the lawful bishop of a
certain town. One is a question of Church membership, the other
of jurisdiction. But these two were not clearly distinguished at
that time. Thus it is perfectly possible that in the 360's and 370's
both groups at Antioch were within the Church's communion
(and both clearly claimed to be in communion with Rome: cf.
Jerome's sixteenth letter, to Damasus), but that out of caution,
and lacking sufficient information, Rome had simply not committed itself to the recognition of either bishop.

Finally, let the obvious fact be stated that far more people
are within Rome's communion than Rome can know by name.
Because we hold that the Church is one communion centred
upon Rome it does not mean that in practice it is sufficient to
ask Rome if one wants to know whether Mr X or even bishop Y
is in the Church. This was even truer in the past than it is at
present. Nowadays Rome does at least know the names of all the
bishops within her communion. In the fourth century she did
not. There were certainly bishops in her communion of whom
she was unaware, and presented with a particular case, with no
gift of omniscience, with persecution and widespread heresy
throughout the Church, and very poor communications, she
could only temporise. But the pope's contemporary ignorance of
whether such and such a person, subsequently canonised, was
within his communion, is no necessary indication that he was
not. In conclusion I may safely say that while much about the
Meletian Schism remains extremely obscure, nothing we know
with certainty about it presents us with any good objective reason
for questioning the traditional Catholic doctrine that the Church
is a single visible communion.

B. The Great Schism and the Conciliar Movement

There is no episode in Church History which might seem better suited to support an Anglican view of the nature of the Church than that of the great schism of the West (1378-1417) and the consequent Conciliar Movement. Here, it might appear, we have a schism *within* the Church of considerable duration, a clear parallel to that between Rome and Canterbury. Furthermore, the Church theory developed as a consequence by the Conciliarists is claimed as very similar to the Anglican and shows that the latter has, after all, a Pre-Reformation ancestry. Here, then, are two questions to be tackled separately; the first concerns a certain situation through which the Church passed, the second a certain theological movement.

In April 1378 Urban VI was elected by the Cardinals at Rome. A few months later the same cardinals declared that the election had been made under duress and elected Clement VII instead. The consequence was thirty-nine years of divided rule. Urban remaining at Rome, Clement returning to Avignon where the popes preceding Urban had for long resided. In due course Urban died but his line was continued with Boniface IX, Innocent VII and Gregory XII, while Clement for his part was succeeded by Benedict XIII. Catholic Christendom was divided in half between these two allegiances, some countries recognising one pope, some the other. There is now little doubt that Urban was true pope, and so also his successors; at the time, however, most people in Christendom were hardly in a position to decide securely one way or the other. As time went on, the position became still more complicated with three struggling popes instead of two. Everywhere Christians realised the gravity of the situation, but how to deal with it when the popes themselves would generally not co-operate was not easy to see. In the end, owing to the united pressure of Christendom, the schism was terminated in a quite legal way at the Council of Constance with the election of Pope Martin V in 1417.

What concerns us is simply the theological significance of these events. Can it be rightly held that the great schism rules out of court the traditional Catholic view of Church unity? Many Anglicans think so. Thus, as we have already seen, R. P. C. Hanson claims that the great schism 'was surely, even by Roman Catholic standards, the division of the indivisible'.[63] In a recent book Dr Mascall has taken up the point at some length:

> If communion with the Pope is the test of visible membership of the Church of God, half of Europe throughout this period did not enjoy it. It is irrelevant to point to the fact that most of the members of the schismatic body—whichever it was—were in good faith and so were blameless; that if they had known which was the true Church they would have adhered to it, and that their schism was not formal but purely material. This would only impart to them that invisible membership of the visible Church which modern Roman Catholic theologians are ready to extend to sincere members of the Eastern Orthodox obedience and even to Anglicans and Protestants. The alternatives are plain. It must either be held that during the Great Schism half of Western Christendom was deprived of visible membership of the Catholic Church or else it must be admitted that visible membership of the Church does not depend upon visible communion with the Pope. That even Rome has been unable to hold out consistently against the latter alternative seems to be shown by the fact that she has canonised saints on both sides: Catherine of Siena on the Urbanist, Vincent Ferrer on the Clementine. If this can be taken seriously, the theological consequences will be remarkable.[64]

Are such views justifiable? Few people would maintain that half of Western Christendom was outside the visible Church during the schism, and hence it seems we must admit that the schism was a division within the Church, not a separation from the Church. It was not, then, (in our strict sense of the term) a schism at all. Consequently the question we have to face is on what theological grounds this long and terrible division can be admitted to have taken place within the Church, when at the same time we hold that the division between Rome and Canterbury separates not *in* but *from* the Church.

[63] 'A Modern Defense of Infallibility', *Theology*, 1954, p. 380.
[64] *The Recovery of Unity*, p. 219. The argument from the canonisation of the 'clementine' Vincent Ferrer has no validity, as he died in 1419 after the schism was over. His support for a mistaken pope can have no ecclesiological significance. He died in communion with a certainly true pope.

In fact the difference between the two is very great. The crucial point is not, of course, that most people on both sides were in good faith and blameless, nor is it that there was doctrinal unity, for both these can co-exist with a complete schism. The essential point is that there was no true rupture of communion at all. At the beginning of the schism all were in communion with the see of Rome: throughout the schism all those in good faith continued, and intended to continue, in that communion. They were not separated from that communion either in desire or in act. A mistake on the part of some as to who was pope may involve the appearance of rupture but it cannot separate those mistaken from the Church. Nor, by itself, does a *sentence* of excommunication have that effect; it deprives one of the privileges of Ecclesiastical Communion, not of the Communion itself; and such a sentence, like other Canonical punishments, is anyway without force in the case of someone innocent of grave sin (cf. canon 2218, 2). There is no reason to think that the majority of those on either side were committing grave sin by adhering to the pope of their choice.

Furthermore, although in some places there was an outward break in communion between the two parties, this was far from universal, and at least the wisest heads on both sides recognised the continued Church status of the other party.[65]

Just as, when the Holy See is vacant, Catholics are united in communion with the see of Rome but not with the person of any pope, so during the schism there was the same practical situation: *Papa dubius, papa nullus.*[66] The obligation of communion with the See remained and no one questioned it or left it but there could be no absolute obligation of obedience or submission to a particular man who was not certainly pope.

The Great Schism of the West truly illustrates how grievous divisions within the Church can be; it illustrates the disastrous consequences of the sinful and irresponsible use of ecclesiastical authority, and it also shows—a most important point—that the divinely constituted structure of the Church is not in itself a

---

[65] Cf. Jean Leclercq, 'Points de vue sur le Grand Schisme d'Occident', in *L'Eglise et les Eglises,* Chevetogne, II, pp. 223-40.
[66] Cf. Journet, *The Church of the Word Incarnate,* I, p. 482.

'fool proof' system, such as could dispense with the continuous guidance of the Holy Spirit. Equally, however, it does *not* show that in difficult circumstances the Holy Spirit will dispense with the normal structure of the Church, nor does it show that the type of unity which Catholics claim to be of the essence of the Church at any time ceased to exist.

Out of the schism developed the Conciliar Movement. That is a somewhat vague term covering many people and many ideas. Roughly speaking there were two aims: to end the scandal of a double pope and at the same time to reform the system of Church government. In part this reform was intended to be simply a practical one, in part it went deeper, involving a revolution in the principles of Church Government. Some conciliarists held a general council superior even to an undoubtedly true pope, others went less far. It is not my aim to survey the whole body of Conciliar doctrine here, but I must refer to it because Anglicans have claimed that their own ecclesiology, which has been examined in the course of this book, lies fully in the tradition of the Conciliar movement. The chief exponent of this view was the great scholar Dr Figgis, who was not only very learned but also an extremely clear-minded person. The following are two passages from his book *Churches in the Modern State* in which he outlines this position.

In order to justify the English Church now and since the Reformation, you have to establish two things: (1) that the parts, in this case a nation, or if you will the two provinces, have such inherent powers of life and self-development, that the breach with the Papacy did not affect them vitally; (2) that what they did or suffered was not of such a nature as to cut these parts off from that stream of universal communal life we call the Catholic Church. For that purpose it is needful to reassert the principles set out in the fifteenth century at Constance and at Basel (p. 156).

The interest of this period (1378-1450) does not lie in the practical success of the movement, which was little or none, but in the ideas which animated it. Broadly speaking, it may be said that those ideas, and those ideas alone form the *raison d'être* of the Church of England, as against Ultramontanism on the one hand and individualistic Protestant sectarianism on the other. The claim of Rome that we are but a sect among many other sects would be justified if the Conciliar movement was based on a fundamental

falsehood. Roughly speaking, the ideals of Gersen and his con-
geners were those of a reformed Episcopal communion, with
nationalism recognised in the Church as a real thing, with a
constitution limiting the dangers of centralised bureacracy (the
real evil of Rome far more than mere monarchical government)—
in a word with federalism in the Church preserving the unity of
the whole while securing the independence of the parts (pp. 235-6).

What basis is there for this view? Certainly, on the level of
government there is a considerable affinity between the views of
some of the Conciliarists and of Anglicans. For instance:

1. The Conciliarists continually appealed for help to the
   kings of Europe. This is paralleled by the role given in
   early Anglican theology to 'the Godly Prince'.

2. A strong belief in the importance of general councils is
   common to both.

3. So is stress on the authority of diocesan bishops, who
   ought not to become mere local agents of the pope.

4. There is the same desire for decentralisation in the
   Church.

All this is true, but the important point is that it does not in
any way touch on what we have seen to be the fundamental
principle of the Anglican position and the fundamental difference
between a Roman and an Anglican ecclesiology. Is the Church,
or is she not, essentially one communion? What is necessary
is to distinguish clearly between the nature of Church unity
and systems of Church government. Even at their most revolu-
tionary the Conciliarists were maintaining views about the latter
and not about the former, which they simply did not seriously
consider. It is striking that, in spite of the discredit into which
the papacy had fallen on account of the schism, they never
suggested that communion with the pope had ceased to matter,
or that each national church would do better to get on by itself
and put its own affairs in order. The whole urgency of Conciliar
activity is only explicable on the supposition that for these men
the really important thing was to be in communion with one
true and certain pope. Even the extremist rump of the Conciliar-

ists at Basel after 1440 did not believe that a council could dispense with papal communion. In conflict with the true and certain pope they still found it necessary to elect a new one of their own.

Consequently it cannot be maintained that the Conciliar movement provides any authority for Dr Figgis's principle, formulated in the first quotation given above, that parts of the Church 'have such inherent powers of life and self-development, that the breach with the Papacy did not affect them vitally'.

Neither the Great Schism of the West nor the theology of the Conciliar Movement, I conclude, offer any real support for the essential presupposition of Anglican ecclesiology.

Chapter 9

ONE, HOLY, CATHOLIC AND APOSTOLIC

I believe in One, Holy, Catholic and Apostolic Church.

The Church is one. She is the vehicle of the Atonement. Sin caused division—between God and man, between man and his brother. Christ came to bring back unity—of God with man, of man with his brother. He came, as he said to his Father, 'that they should all be one, as we are one; that while thou art in me, I may be in them, and so they may be perfectly made one' (John 17:23). This unity extends from end to end of the Christian economy, from God to man, from the invisible to the visible: 'One body and one Spirit, as you are called in one hope of your calling. One Lord, one faith, one baptism. One God and Father of all, who is above all, and through all, and in us all, who is blessed for ever and ever' (Eph. 4:4-6).

Through one baptism man enters the unique fellowship, visible and invisible, of the redeemed, and he is prepared to meet his God and perfect his oneness with both God and his brethren at the one table of the Eucharist: this is the bread from heaven which establishes the Church, making of the many one, of men the body of Christ.

The Church is holy. She is the vehicle of the sanctification of man. His will was twisted by sin; Christ came to bear on his shoulders the weight of our sins, to give us back the holiness of God. In Christ the grace of sanctification has flowed out into men, and it has flowed through his body, which is the Church. Her sacraments, her bible, all that she is and has, are directed to this one end of human sanctification. The fruit of her work shines out in the faces of the martyrs and the virgins, the widows and the confessors, the fathers and mothers of families, the legions of the blessed. She opens her arms to sinners, and the Church is full of them, in high places and low, but she receives that she may heal: her mission, like her master's, is to bring sinners to repentance. Her sanctity is not static but dynamic, it does not consider the tares in the field, but it looks to the reaping of the harvest. She is holy, for her master and bridegroom is holy: but she is never far from sinners, and at times one can hardly see her for sinners, because her master too was their friend.

The Church is Catholic. 'Go and teach all nations': the command in her origin is the promise of her character. She is the *Catholica*, the universal thing, the one body in the world which is not one-sided or partisan, or sectarian or nationalist, which does not possess in her essence any of the limitations of place or race or ism. All truth, all men, all human values find in her their mother and their home. To be separated from her is to be in a party and in a schism, to be joined to her is to be joined to the restorer of all the good things of nature and the source of all the better things of grace. She is not the Church of the Latins or of the white man; not the Church of the West or the Church of the Middle Ages—she is the world Church of every age, the bride of the new Adam, the restorer of the *orbis terrarum*.

The Church is Apostolic. 'Apostles and prophets are the foundation on which you were built, and the chief cornerstone is Jesus Christ himself' (Eph. 2:20). To the apostles Jesus entrusted the establishment of his Church, and all that we have received we have received through them. They taught, they ruled, they administered the sacraments, and the rectitude of their work was guaranteed by the assistance of the Spirit: 'It has seemed good to the Spirit and to us.' Their character did not die with their persons: as St Irenaeus tells us, they appointed bishops to succeed them in their work, to carry on the Dominical tradition. The Church not only was apostolic, she is apostolic; she speaks in every age with the voice of the apostles and her teaching is no other than the authentic interpretation of that revelation once and for all committed to the Twelve.

At the centre of the apostles stood Peter possessing in himself the fullness of their office, as his successors possess in themselves the fullness of the episcopal office: the rock, the shepherd, the support of his brethren. His see is the apostolic see *par excellence*, to its teaching and succession line alone it is sufficient for Irenaeus and for each one of us to point. Rome presides in charity, in her voice Peter speaks, hers is the chair of unity. Here the fullness of apostolicity is preserved: the voice of truth, the ark of a single communion. Here is the Church founded on rock, certain to prevail against all the gates of Hell: the One, the Catholic, the Apostolic, it is all here and it is here alone.

BIBLIOGRAPHY

(* denotes Anglican writers: † denotes Eastern Orthodox writers.)

ADAM, K. *The Spirit of Catholicism*, Sheed and Ward, 1929; U.S.A.: Macmillan.

†ALIVISATOS, H. 'The Holy Greek Orthodox Church', in *The Nature of the Church*, ed. R. Newton Flew, London, 1952.

*ANNUNCIATION GROUP. *Dr Mascall and South India—A Reply*. 1955.

AQUINAS, ST THOMAS. *Summa Theologica*.

BARDY, G. *La Théologie de l'Eglise de saint Clément de Rome à saint Irenée*. Cerf, 1945.

BATIFFOL. *Le Siège Apostolique*. Paris, 1924.

—— *Le Catholicisme de saint Augustin*. Paris, 1929.

*BELL, G. K. A. *Documents on Christian Unity*, I, 1920-4. Oxford, 1924. Also O.U.P. 1955.

BEVENOT, M., S.J. 'Church Relations in England,' *The Month*, March 1951, pp. 175-8.

—— *St Cyprian. The Lapsed. The Unity of the Catholic Church*, translated and annotated. Longmans, 1957.

—— 'Tradition, Church and Dogma,' *The Heythrop Journal*, January, 1960, pp. 34-47.

*BIRKBECK, W. J. *Russia and the English Church*, vol. I, containing a correspondence between Mr W. Palmer and M. Khomiakov, Rivington, 1895.

BIVORT DE LA SAUDEE, J. *Anglicans et Catholiques*. Paris, 1948.

*BRANDRETH, H. *Unity and Reunion, A Bibliography*. London, 1945.

—— *Episcopi Vagantes and the Anglican Church*. S.P.C.K., 1947.

*BURN-MURDOCH, H. *Church, Continuity and Unity*. Cambridge, 1945.

BUTLER, C., O.S.B. *The Church and Infallibility*. Sheed and Ward, 1954.

—— 'The Unity of the Church,' in *The Spirit of Unity*, pp. 4-19. Published by Blackfriars, 1950.

—— 'The Lost Leader,' *Downside Review*, 1951, pp. 62-73.

—— 'St Augustine's Teaching on Schism,' *Downside Review*, 1951, pp. 137-54.

—— 'St Cyprian on the Church,' *Downside Review*, 1953, pp. 1-13, 119-34, 258-72.

—— 'Schism and Unity,' *Downside Review*, 1953, pp. 353-71.

—— 'The Church in Scripture and History,' *The Tablet*, May 19th, 1956 (together with subsequent correspondence).

—— 'St Peter: History and Theology,' *Clergy Review*, August and September 1958, pp. 449-61, 513-29.

*CAREY, K. M., ed. *The Historic Episcopate*, especially chapter VI by H. W. Montefiore. Dacre Press, 1954.

*CATHOLICITY. A study in the conflict of Christian traditions in the West, being a Report presented to His Grace the Archbishop of Canterbury by a group of Anglo-Catholic theologians. Dacre, 1947.

CERFAUX, L. *La Théologie de l'Eglise suivant saint Paul*. Cerf, 1948. English trans.: *The Church in the Theology of Saint Paul*. Herder, 1959.

*CHADWICK, O. *From Bossuet to Newman. The Idea of Doctrinal Development*. Cambridge, 1957.

CHAILLET, P., ed. *L'Eglise est Une. Hommage à Moehler*. Bloud et Gay, 1939.

CHAPMAN, J., O.S.B. *Bishop Gore and the Catholic Claims*. Longmans, 1905.

CLARKE, F., S.J. *Anglican Orders and Defect of Intention*. Longmans, 1956.

CONGAR, Y., O.P., *Chrétiens désunis*. Paris, 1937; English trans., *Divided Christendom*. Bles, 1939.

—— 'Schisme,' in *Dictionnaire de Théologie Catholique* XIV 1, cc. 1286-1312.

—— *Esquisses du Mystère de l'Eglise*, revised edition. Cerf, 1952.

—— *The Mystery of the Church*, Helicon, 1960.

—— *Vraie et Fausse Réforme dans l'Eglise*. Cerf, 1950.

—— *Le Christ, Marie et l'Eglise*. Desclée de Brouwer, 1952. English trans., *Christ, Our Lady and the Church*. Longmans, 1957.

—— 'Amica Contestatio' in *Intercommunion*, pp. 141-51. ed. D. Baillie and J. Marsh. S.C.M. 1952.

—— *Jalons pour une Théologie du Laïcat*. Cerf, 1954. English trans., *Lay People in the Church*. Bloomsbury, 1957.

—— 'Dogme Christologique et Ecclésiologique, Vérité et Limites d'un parallèle,' in *Das Konzil von Chalkedon*. ed. A. Grillmeier and H. Bacht, III, pp. 239-68. Wurzburg, 1954.

—— 'Neuf Cents ans après: Notes sur le "Schisme oriental" in *L'Eglise et les Eglises*. Etudes et Travaux offerts à Dom Lambert Beaudouin, I, pp. 3-95. Chevetogne, 1954.

—— *After Nine Hundred Years: An Analysis of the Oriental Schism*. Fordham University Press, 1959.

DE LUBAC, H. *Catholicism*. Burns Oates, 1950. Translation of *Catholicisme*. Cerf, 1938. U.S.A.: Sheed and Ward, 1958.

—— *Corpus Mysticum, L'Eucharistie et l'Eglise au Moyen Age*, 2nd edition, Aubier, 1949.

—— *The Splendour of the Church*. Sheed and Ward, 1956. Translation of *Méditation sur l'Eglise*. Editions Montaigne.

DENZINGER, H. *Enchiridion Symbolorum*, 28th edition. Herder, 1952.

*DIX, G. 'The Idea of "The Church" in the primitive Liturgies,' in *The Parish Communion*, pp. 95-144. Ed. A. G. Hebert, S.P.C.K., 1937.

*DIX, G. *The Question of Anglican Orders*. Dacre Press, 1944.

*DOCTRINE IN THE CHURCH OF ENGLAND. The Report of the Commission on Christian Doctrine appointed by the Archbishops of Canterbury and York in 1922. S.P.C.K., 1938.

*DOUGLAS, J. A. *The Relations of the Anglican Churches with the Eastern-Orthodox*. London, 1921.

DUPONT, J., O.S.B. 'Le Schisme d'après saint Paul,' in *L'Eglise et Les Eglises*, I, pp. 111-27. Chevetogne, 1954.

EVANSTON REPORT, S.C.M., 1954.

*FAIRWEATHER, E. R. and HETTLINGER, R. F. *Episcopacy and Reunion*. Mowbray, 1953.

*FARRER, A. 'Eucharist and Church in the New Testament,' in *The Parish Communion*, pp. 73-94. Ed. A. G. Hebert. S.P.C.K., 1937.

FENTON, J. C. 'Contemporary Questions about Membership in the True Church,' *The American Ecclesiastical Review*, July 1961, pp. 39-57.

*FIGGIS, J. N. *Churches in the Modern State*, Longmans, 1913.

†FLOROVSKY, G. 'Terms of Communion in the Undivided Church,' in *Intercommunion*, pp. 47-57. Ed. D. Baillie and J. Marsh. London, 1952.

—— *Confessional Loyalty in the Ecumenical Movement*, pp. 196-205 of the same work.

GASQUE, G. *L'Eucharistie et le Corps Mystique*. Paris, 1925.

GILL, J., S.J. *La Chiesa Anglicana*. Milan, 1948.

*GORE, C. *Roman Catholic Claims*, 9th edition. Longmans, 1905.

—— *The Church and the Ministry*. Edition of 1919 revised by C. H. Turner. Longmans. U.S.A.: Allenson, 1949.

*GREENSLADE, S. L. *Schism in the Early Church*. S.C.M., 1953.

*HANSON. R. P. C. 'A Modern Defence of Infallibility,' *Theology*, pp. 378-83. 1954.

*HEBERT, A. G. *The Form of the Church*. Faber and Faber, 1944. U.S.A.: Allenson, 1954.

*HETTLINGER, R. F. See FAIRWEATHER, E. R.

*HICKINBOTHAN, J. P. 'The Church of England and Intercommunion,' *Church Quarterly Review*, CXLIX, pp. 1-14. 1949-50.

*HODGES, H. A. *Anglicanism and Orthodoxy*. S.C.M., 1955.

JAKI, S., O.S.B. *Les Tendences Nouvelles de l'Ecclesiologie*. Rome, 1957.

*JALLAND. *The Church and the Papacy*. S.P.C.K., 1942.

JOHNSON, V. *One Lord—One Faith*. Sheed and Ward, 1929.

JOURNET, C. *L'Eglise du Verbe Incarné*. Paris, 2 volumes so far published of which the first is translated into English as *The Church of the Word Incarnate*. Sheed and Ward, 1955.

JUGIE, M. 'Theologia Dogmatica Christianorum Orientalium,' vol. III, *De Sacramentis*. Paris, 1930.

*KIRK, K. E., ed. *The Apostolic Ministry*. Hodder & Stoughton, 1946. U.S.A.: Morehouse, 1946.

KNOX, R. *The Belief of Catholics*. 4th edition. Sheed & Ward, 1953.

*KNOX, W. 'Anglo-Catholicism and Episcopal Authority,' *Theology*, 1921, I, pp. 339-344.

—— 'The Nature of Catholic Authority,' *Theology*, 1929, XVIII, pp. 86-94.

—— *One God and Father of All*, written in collaboration with E. MILNER-WHITE. Mowbray, 1929.

*LACEY, T. A. *Unity and Schism*, Mowbray, 1917.

—— *The One Body and the One Spirit*. London, no date.

LEEMING, B., S.J. *Principles of Sacramental Theology*. Longmans, 1956. U.S.A.: Newman, 1956.

LIALINE, C., O.S.B. 'Anglicanisme et Orthodoxie,' *Istina*, 1956, pp. 32-98, 183-190.

MACGILLIVRAY, G. J. *Father Vernon and his Critics*. Burns Oates, 1930.

*MANNING, H. E. *The Unity of the Church*. London, 1842.

*MASCALL, E. L. *Christ, the Christian and the Church*. Longmans, 1946.

—— *Corpus Christi, Essays on the Church and the Eucharist*. Longmans, 1953.

—— *The Convocations and South India*. Mowbray, 1955.

—— 'Intention and Form in Anglican Orders', *The Church Quarterly Review*, 1957, pp. 4-20.

—— *The Recovery of Unity*. Longmans, 1958.

MESSENGER, E. C. *The Reformation, the Mass and the Priesthood*, 2 vols. Longmans, 1937.

MOORE, S., O.S.B. 'The Logic of Unity,' *The Tablet*, May 24th, 1958.

*MOORMAN, J. 'Charles Gore and the Doctrine of the Church,' *Church Quarterly Review*, 1957, pp. 128-40.

NEWMAN, J. H. *An Essay on the Development of Christian Doctrine*.

—— 'The Catholicity of the Anglican Church,' in *Essays Critical and Historical*, II, pp. 1-111.

—— *Lectures on the Prophetical Office of the Church viewed relatively to Romanism and Popular Protestantism*.

NOEL, R. A. *The Church of England, is 'Reunion' possible?* C.T.S., 1955.

PARENTE, P. *Theologia Fundamentalis.* 4th edition. Marietti, 1955.

*PASS, H. L. 'The Credentials of our communion,' *Theology,* 1920, I, pp. 1-9, 59-66, 187-195.

*PECK, A. L. *This Church of Christ.* Mowbray, 1955.

—— *Anglicanism and Episcopacy.* Faith Press, 1958.

PIOLANTI, A. *De Sacramentis.* Marietti, 2nd edition, 1947.

—— *Il Mistero Eucharistico,* Libreria Editrice Fiorentina, 1955.

PIUS XII. *Mystici Corporis Christi.* English translation, *The Mystical Body of Christ,* C.T.S., 1943.

PLÉ, A., O.P. 'The Church and Charity,' *Life of the Spirit,* January 1953, pp. 283-290.

*PULLER, F. W. *The Primitive Saints and the See of Rome.*

*QUICK, O. C. *The Christian Sacraments,* Nisbet, 1927.

*RAE, D. *The Church of South India and the Church.* Confraternity of Unity, 1956.

*RAMSEY, A. M. *The Gospel and the Catholic Church.* Longmans, 1956.

*RAWLINSON, A. E. J. 'Corpus Christi', in *Mysterium Christi,* pp. 225-44. Ed. G. K. A. Bell and D. A. Deissmann. Longmans, 1930.

—— *Problems of Reunion.* Eyre and Spottiswood, 1950.

*RELATIONS BETWEEN ANGLICAN AND PRESBYTERIAN CHURCHES. A Joint Report. S.P.C.K., 1957.

*RICH, E. C. *Spiritual Authority in the Church of England.* Longmans, 1953.

*ROBERTS, V. *In Terra Aliena.* No date.

*ROBINSON, J. A. *The Vision of Unity.* Longmans, 1908.

—— *St Paul's Epistle to the Ephesians, An Exposition.* Macmillan, 1909.

*ROUSE, R. and NEILL, S. C. *A History of the Ecumenical Movement, 1517-1948.* S.P.C.K., 1954.

SMITH, G. D. 'The Church and her Sacraments,' *Clergy Review,* April 1950, pp. 217-31.

STEVENSON, A., S.J. *Anglican Orders.* Burns Oates, 1956.

ST JOHN, H., O.P. 'Essays in Christian Unity,' *Blackfriars.* 1955.

—— 'Fallible Infelicities,' *Blackfriars,* December 1953, pp. 522-7.

—— 'The Authority of Doctrinal Development,' *Blackfriars,* October-December, 1955, pp. 372-81, 412-24, 483-93.

—— 'Authority and the Ecumenical Dialogue,' *Blackfriars,* May 1956, pp. 196-205.

*STONE, D. *The Christian Church.* Rivingtons, 1905.

*SYKES, N. *Old Priest and New Presbyter.* Cambridge, 1956.

TAVARD, G. H. *Holy Writ or Holy Church*. Burns Oates, 1959. U.S.A.: Harper, 1960.

*THORNTON, L. S. *The Common Life in the Body of Christ*. Dacre, 1942. U.S.A.: Allenson, 1950.

—— *Christ and the Church*. Dacre, 1956.

*TURNER, C. H. 'Apostolic Succession: A. The original conception: B. The Problem of non-catholic Orders,' in *Essays on the Early History of the Church and the Ministry*, ed. H. B. Swete, 2nd edition, 1921, pp. 93-214.

*TURNER, H. W. E. *The Pattern of Christian Truth*. Mowbray, 1954. U.S.A.: Allenson, 1954.

*TURNER, H. W. 'The Assumption of the Blessed Virgin Mary,' *Theology*, 1951, pp. 64-70.

—— 'Infallibility,' *Church Quarterly Review*, CLV, pp. 302-5.

VODOPIVEC, G. 'Membri in re ed appartenanza in voto alla Chiesa di Cristo', *Euntes Docete*, pp. 65-104. 1957.

WHITE, V., O.P. *God the Unknown* (part III), Harvill, 1956. U.S.A.: Harper, 1956.

*WILLIAMS, N. P. 'The Theology of the Catholic Revival,' in *Northern Catholicism*, ed. N. P. Williams and C. Harris, pp. 130-234. S.P.C.K., 1933.

†ZERNOV, N. 'The Church and the Confessions,' in *The Church of God*, ed. E. L. Mascall, pp. 209-27. S.P.C.K., 1934.

—— *The Reintegration of the Church*, S.C.M., 1952.